Black Yankees

Black Yankees

The Development of an Afro-American Subculture

in Eighteenth-Century New England

WILLIAM D. PIERSEN

The University of Massachusetts Press

Amherst

Publication of this book was assisted by the American
Council of Learned Societies under a grant from the
Andrew W. Mellon Foundation.

Printed in the United States of America
Set in Linoterm Janson
Printed by Cushing-Malloy and bound by John Dekker & Sons

Library of Congress Cataloging-in-Publication Data

Piersen, William Dillon, 1942–
    Black Yankees.

    Bibliography: p.
    Includes index.
      1. Afro-Americans—New England—History—18th
century. 2. New England—History—Colonial period,
ca. 1600–1775. I. Title.
E185.917.P54   1988   974'.00496073   87–13862
ISBN 0–87023–586–9 (alk. paper)
ISBN 0–87023–587–7 (pbk.: alk. paper)

British Library Cataloguing in Publication data are available.

Dedicated to those who have shown me the way:

George E. Brooks, Jr., Richard M. Dorson,
Melville J. Herskovits, Peter H. Wood,
and the students of Fisk University

Contents

Introduction   ix

Part 1   African Immigrants and Black Yankees

1   New Slaves in a New World   3

2   A Clustered Minority   14

Part 2   The Forces of Enculturation

3   Family Slavery   25

4   The Training of Servants   37

5   A Christianity for Slaves   49

Part 3   The Blending of Traditions

6   The Great Awakening: What Might Have Been   65

7   An Afro-American Folk Religion   74

8   To Build a Family   87

9   Aspects of Black Folklife   96

Part 4   In Celebration of Afro-American Culture

10   Black Kings and Governors   117

11   The Functions and Character of Black Government   129

Part 5   On Resistance: A Summary Conclusion

12   A Resistant Accommodation   143

Appendix   161

Notes   177

Index   225

Introduction

This book examines the development of an Afro-American subculture in eighteenth-century New England. It is not so much a history of slavery in the Northeast as it is a historical study of the building of American culture, in this case from an Afro-American and interdisciplinary perspective. I am not primarily concerned with the machinery of slave control or the political and social disabilities of bondage since these topics remain well covered in Lorenzo J. Greene's classic study *The Negro in Colonial New England*.[1] Instead, I examine the processes of cultural change and creation from the black bondsman's point of view. What was it like to be an African immigrant in colonial New England? What attitudes and assumptions underlay the Afro-American response to Yankee culture? What does the development within the confines of predominately white and ethnocentric New England of an Afro-American folk culture in religion, public rituals, folk arts and crafts, social mores, and daily behavior say about the creation of American culture?

On the face of it, the master class called the tunes and slaves danced the beat. Blacks who were taken into New England's bondage were clearly engulfed in a pervasive, narrow-minded Euro-American society that had no interest in fostering Afro-American autonomy. The New England experience was often cruel, and the numbers alone suggest it was among the most unequal of black/white cultural contacts in the New World. Nonetheless, despite the strictures of bondage, the black Yankees of eighteenth-century New England created a sustaining folk culture of their own.

Far more than we might have imagined, during the eighteenth century the region's black population maintained African values and approaches to life—especially in the free hours they shared together. In their religious beliefs and styles of worship, their work habits, folk arts and crafts, in their food preparation, their styles of dress and playing music, in their dancing and physical postures, their folk medicine, their ways of speaking and gambling, in their styles of resistance to oppression and in their holiday celebrations, the black Yankees were truly Afro-American. The Afro-American subculture they created was not the product of isolation but, instead, a body of shared traditions and values that black New Englanders purposefully maintained to give themselves a double identity, a positive sense of themselves within the larger Yankee community.

As both folklorist and historian I have searched widely for the materials that will illuminate this folk culture and thereby the lives and spirit of the black Yankees. For too long the black men and women of history have been encased in the passive voice of what was done to them, while their own vision of their lives remained hidden.

Clearly, there are special problems inherent in the historical reconstruction of a folk culture like that developed by the Afro-Americans of eighteenth-century New England. Compared to white New Englanders (who, although renowned as taciturn, left libraries bulging with the loquacious records of their civil, personal, and religious lives), black slaves and free Negroes were truly laconic, leaving few historical materials of the kinds normally scrutinized by scholars. No matter what sources we use, our knowledge of black life in the eighteenth century too often derives from white observers unfamiliar with, and indeed uninterested in, the African heritage and personal lives of the region's Afro-American population.

Because evidence that illuminates New England's black folk culture is sparse and (at least as I collected it) wildly eclectic, conclusions about the details of black life cannot be finely drawn. The reconstruction of black attitudes rests all too commonly on generalizations drawn from impressionistic glimpses assumed to be typical, but which can never be "proved" to be so.

Fortunately, such generalizations about black life in New England can usually be bolstered by comparative evidence taken from similar cultural developments among black populations elsewhere. Some readers, spoiled by the more detailed histories of white New England life, may be put off by so much cross-cultural reference. But if the strategy of fleshing out the black

New England experience by using comparative materials from different Afro-American populations spanning a wider period of years is often adopted as much from necessity as by choice, it will also become apparent in the course of this study that the Afro-American culture of early New England can no more be understood outside the context of Africa and Afro-America than the early history of white New England can be understood without reference to Europe and the remaining colonial New World.

The geographical scope of this study is nominally "New England," but areas encompassing the present states of Vermont, Maine, and New Hampshire (excluding Rockingham County) receive scant attention because in the 1700s these areas lacked significant black populations. Even in the areas of greatest attention—Rhode Island, Connecticut, and Massachusetts—little distinction is made between the culture of coastal or urban blacks and that of those residing in the relative isolation of the rural, agricultural interior. Although it is likely, given the greater density of the coastal/urban Negro populations, that Afro-American culture may have been stronger in the cities and along the coast, the record does not prove the point.

Similarly, intermarriage between blacks and Indians (usually Negro males with Indian females) must have fostered some blending of cultures like that which has been noted elsewhere in the Americas; but either the integrity of New England tribal cultures had been sufficiently destroyed by the eighteenth century to render them inconsequential in this regard, or most of the evidence of Indian cultural influence on northern blacks has been lost.

Just as the limited nature of the evidence precludes asking and/or answering certain basic questions, so too it precludes precision regarding the contributions of particular African cultures to the generalized Afro-American culture of New England. But if the African heritage discussed here is a generalized one, it is, nonetheless, appropriate to the nature of the immigration and the evidence available.

There never seem enough sources for any historian to feel certain about the past, and in early Afro-American history there is rarely enough evidence to even offer security. It is an occupational hazard of eighteenth-century Afro-Americanists to have to fry whatever fish they catch, while their colleagues studying white cultural elites may disdain all but trophy-sized lunkers. Folk peoples have their own forms of fishing and their own forms of evidence; and, as I have argued in the *Handbook of American Folklore*, what is needed now in our studies of the common people of the colonial era is "an imaginative consummation of the long-promised union of colonial folklore and history."[2]

Removing the bundling board of discipline permits a warmer courtship between the more formal traditional printed sources and the looser but livelier anecdotal materials from nineteenth-century town histories. To spice their sometimes bland subject matter, the region's white historians seasoned their work with anecdotes about black life collected from local folk humor and folk traditions (both black and white). As they intended, these homey remembrances out of the oral tradition make zesty primary sources, and they are unparalleled in capturing the earthy humor of colonial black folk life.

Such folk traditions have rarely been used by contemporary historians; this is in part because some of the anecdotes, like other creations of their era, reflect a crudely patronizing if not racist tone. Moreover, folk sources lack a "primary" historical parentage; often they have no legitimate print forebears at all. Nonetheless, we shall see here that the essential truths of the folk anecdotes directly parallel, but better illuminate, the evidence on the same subjects developed from more traditionally used forms of documentation.

I have tried to use such folk-based narratives with some circumspection. Perhaps my folkloristic training has made me relish "local color" items too much; then again, perhaps my historical interests have made me draw too much particular significance from their rather universal themes. I hope not. Whatever the case, I am certain these sources animate the lives and attitudes of the early black Yankees in a way other forms of evidence cannot. The study of folk peoples requires the insights of folk sources. When we use them, the belief of the first Afro-Americans of New England who lived in faith that they would be reborn in a better time and place is at least partially realized.

Part 1

African Immigrants
and Black Yankees

Chapter 1

New Slaves in a New World

ATURE as much as Christianity carved a puritanical character on the New England way of life. The region's rigid climate and parsimonious soil far more than its morals banned the prodigal excesses of plantation slavery from the Yankee colonies. While slave labor could be used in New England, it would never reap immense profits. Thus, from the start, the region's black population remained peripheral to the economy. This made the Afro-American experience in New England quite different from the plantation stereotype so often used to define the setting for the development of Afro-American culture.

Since few Yankee masters held more than one or two bondsmen, it was common for white owners and black servants to work side by side during the day, and it was common for them to retire to the same house at night. In such intimacy the common humanity of Yankee bondsmen could not be easily denied. That made New England's bondage no less frustrating for those who were forced to serve, but it did lessen the brutality of the system.

Northern merchants had little need to gamble cruelly on purchasing large cargoes of African slaves with their high mortality rates; it was more convenient and economical to purchase from the West Indies and the continental colonies small retail lots of mixed slaves better suited to northern markets. This northern trade in slaves was noted as early as 1679 by Connecticut's Governor William Leete, who explained, "As for blacks, there comes sometimes three or four in a year from Barbados." Except for an increase in the size of cargoes, conditions changed little during the next century.[1]

According to Governor Samuel Cranston's report to the board of trade in 1708, Rhode Island received its blacks solely from Barbados, "from whence yearly they have between twenty and thirty Negroes." The governor and council of Connecticut reported to the board of trade in 1709 that there were few Negroes in the colony, with new slaves generally being "supplied from their neighbors, and sometimes with six in a year from the West Indies."[2]

As the northern slave trade expanded, the West Indian connection continued in importance. During the course of the eighteenth century, for example, small retail lots from the islands accounted for at least half the slaves imported into Massachusetts; the others were said to have been brought on ships directly involved in the African trade.[3]

Slavers followed current, wind, weather, and the vagaries of market from Africa to the tropical West Indies and upward to the southern and middle colonies. Slaves in poor condition or those who could not be sold for reasonable profits in plantation markets were carried on to New England, where Yankee slavers found an excellent market of last resort. As James Brown of Providence suggested to his brother Obadiah, who was selling a cargo of African slaves in southern waters in 1717, "If you cannot sell all your slaves to your mind, bring some of them home; I believe they will sell well."[4] Slaves were also preordered by local merchants and purchased out of the general cargo by Yankee crew members. Ezra Stiles of Newport, Rhode Island, reserved a slave boy for himself by the simple expedient of sending a keg of rum aboard an African-bound ship; while fellow Newport townsman William Ellery directed the captain of his sloop *Antis* to save eight likely boys for his return home in 1745.[5]

Southern and island slave merchants often sold their undesirable "refuse" slaves northward, just as in the nineteenth-century United States troublesome slaves were sold south. Buyers complained that refuse slaves from the West Indies were "refractory" and "very bad"; indeed, in 1708 Governor Joseph Dudley of Massachusetts argued that they were usually "the worst servants they have." In that same year the general assembly of Rhode Island acted to restrict such imports as uneconomical and troublesome, arguing that the newcomers were "the worst sort of Negroes: some sent for murder, some for theft, some were runaways, and most were impudent, lame and distempered." As Governor Samuel Cranston explained to the board of trade, few such slaves were imported from the islands because of "the dislike our planters have for them, by reason of their turbulent and unruly tempers."[6]

Nonetheless, despite their drawbacks, slaves who had been in the Americas for a year or so and learned some basic English could still be more desirable than new Africans, especially since Africans who had not survived a period of New World "seasoning" were vulnerable to the new diseases and liable to die soon after arrival. In the tropical climate of the Caribbean, seasoning generally lasted from two to three years, during which from one-fourth to one-third of the African immigrants perished from shock, suicide, maltreatment, dysentery, or a host of other ailments.[7]

In New England, though conditions were better, the longer voyage and cold climate continued to take a toll. For example, four of the five new slaves William Pepperell of Kittery Point, Maine, purchased from Antigua in 1719 died at sea; the one exception—a black woman branded with a Y on her breast from the African coastal trade—died after three weeks ashore. The high mortality of New England seasoning is suggested in the mortality statistics from Newport, where in 1763 one-quarter of the blacks who died in that city were "new Negroes." In light of such dangers, Massachusetts allowed drawbacks on the import duties charged to newly imported slaves if they died in the first six weeks to a year after arrival in the Bay Colony.[8] Since smallpox immunity, often a part of seasoning, increased the likelihood that a new slave would survive, Peter Fanueil of Boston demonstrated good sense in requesting in 1738 that his West Indian agent send him a tractable Negro boy of twelve to fifteen years who had already had the smallpox.[9]

Young slaves were often welcome in northern markets for the very reasons they were sometimes avoided in plantation areas. Plantation masters wanted slaves of at least middle teenage years who could be put to work immediately in the fields under the direction of experienced hands. New England masters, on the other hand, expected to personally train their servants for specialized business or family roles; thus, they were often willing to buy juvenile slaves who might not be immediately productive, but who could be more effectively assimilated. As John Watts of New York noted, for the local northern markets imports "must be young, the younger the better if not quite children. Males are best."[10] Typical sale notices, such as the ones in the *Boston Gazette* in 1761 and the *Connecticut Courant* in 1766, offered for sale parcels of "likely Negroes, both male and female, from ten years of age to twenty, imported the last week from Africa," and "one boy 17, two girls 10 or 11, have been in country 3 months."[11] Slaves imported into northern markets seem to have averaged between fourteen and twenty years of age, perhaps a year or so younger than the general New World trend.[12]

New England masters assumed that in training their servants they would simply replace African patterns of behavior and belief with Yankee ones; therefore, there was little reason for northern owners to demonstrate the concern of their Jamaican, Brazilian, or South Carolina counterparts in choosing slaves on the basis of a set of stereotyped "national" characteristics: the supposed industry, tractability, faithfulness, honesty, and physical strength of certain African peoples.[13] In New England most new slaves were advertised simply as "lately imported" or "just arrived." Where precisely they came from was not as important to buyers as their availability for purchase.

A study of New England newspaper advertisements for new slaves undertaken by the historian Lorenzo Greene indicates that almost two-thirds of the notices did not specify the origin of the slaves. In the other cases, Africa was mentioned more commonly than the West Indies by a ratio of four to three. But new slaves of African origin were only vaguely noted as "from Guinea" or "from the Gold Coast."[14] Slaves from the "Windward Coast" and from the island of Goree off Senegal were also specifically mentioned in New England's advertisements, perhaps because, as a New Jersey sale notice of May 1762 suggested, with seller's overstatement, it was "generally allowed that the Gambia slaves are much more robust and tractable than any other slaves from the coast of Guinea, and are more capable of undergoing the severity of the winter seasons in the North-American colonies, which occasions their being vastly more esteemed and coveted in this province and those to the northward than any other slaves."[15]

Slaves from the West Indies commonly came from the English islands, primarily Barbados, but also from Jamaica, St. Kitts, and Monserrat.[16] But for New Englanders the West Indies were not so much a source of origin for new slaves as a way station on the transatlantic trade. Many of the slaves brought from the islands were simply surplus in transshipment, as a Massachusetts advertisement noted in 1728: "A parcel of likely Negro boys and one Negro girl, arrived from Nevis, and were brought from Guinea."[17] The majority of the slaves shipped from the West Indies to New England were native-born Africans, however long they may have resided in the islands. Thus, of the eighty Barbados slaves sold by Hugh Hall of Boston in 1729, roughly two-thirds held African names, one-tenth possessed the classical cognomens commonly given to new slaves, and only one-quarter owned Christian or English names that might imply American birth or, at least, that the slaves were converted, acculturated Afro-Americans.[18]

It is probable that more than three-quarters of New England's black immigrants were African by birth.[19] Extrapolation from what is known of the English and American slave trades suggests that Africans shipped from the Gold Coast area were common among the new slaves, as were, in descending order, blacks from the Bights of Benin and Biafra, and from Senegambia, Sierra Leone, the Grain and Windward Coasts, and Central Africa.[20] The continued use in New England of Gold Coast day names (names given to record the day of birth) reinforces the probability of important ties to the Fanti-Ashanti cultures of West Africa. Childrens' day names like Quashi for Sunday or Quamino for Saturday were used by New England masters who appear to have recognized them because of their commonness—a recognition more general among slaves than masters elsewhere in the New World.[21] But while the derivation of specific tribal connections between Africa and the Afro-American population of New England remains vague, the cultures of the African peoples along the coast from Senegal to Angola were similar enough to give a certain unity to the cultural heritage of New England's African immigrants, a unity that was reinforced by the general experience of northern slavery and a common bond from the Atlantic crossing.

For most African emigrants, slavery had begun many weeks and miles from the barracoons of the African coast. The majority entered bondage as displaced people—captives from the losing side of a battle or war. Others were taken as kidnap victims by raiding parties of local slave dealers. A sizable minority entered the Atlantic slave trade through traditional African legal processes (often corrupted by the international market) which punished adultery, witchcraft, and other crimes or satisfied personal and family debts. And while such debt pawns, like domestic servants of more than one generation's standing, were rarely sold directly to coastal slave traders, the circuitous route of human barter nonetheless brought many such nominally protected Africans to American shores.[22]

The blacks who came to America had first experienced African slavery at its worst. As new slaves—kidnap victims, debt pawns, criminals, or prisoners-of-war—they had few of the traditional slaves' rights, and little attachment to the African societies that had taken them into bondage or would sell them away from the coast. Indeed, in many areas of the Americas the tribal animosities fostered during these last bitter days in Africa continued to sour later attempts at slave unity.[23] The trauma of entry into slavery was horrible enough, but it was only the beginning of the sufferings of bondage. Often from far inland in Africa individual slaves were moved inexorably toward the coast in a merchant's slave coffle or by a slow exchange from owner to owner and from one village to another. Most new slaves soon lost all hope of returning home alive. The harshness of this passage left the slaves in poor and weakened conditions, as one observer said, "by reason of the barbarous usage they have had in travelling so far, being continually beaten, and almost famished."[24]

Yet, in one sense, these survivors could count themselves as lucky. At the point of kidnap or capture, victims who were too old or too recalcitrant were often executed on the spot. The sickly, weak, or elderly fared little better on the coast, where they were reported by slavers to have made "the most piteous entreaties" to be sold and so not left behind. This has a certain ring of truth since on the Gold Coast such refuse slaves were sacrificed in grand funeral displays, while in Old Calibar they were often worked to death on local plantations.[25] While waiting disposition, barracoon slaves found disease, boredom, and depression their constant companions. Successful escape was impossible for people from inland; and their anguish for a lost homeland and family was made the more searing by the knowledge that the sea voyage would be inevitably one way.

New slaves often refused nourishment and medication in an attempt to end their misery, and on leaving the coast would sometimes leap into the shark-infested waters. For bad as leaving Africa was, many slaves believed their ultimate fate was much worse—to be served as dinner in the cooking pots of hideously ugly, white cannibals in the New World. Those who could not endure the hardships, separation, and fears succumbed to disease or self-destruction, perishing on the coast, during the middle passage, or in the first months of slavery in the Americas. Most went willingly to their deaths as martyrs, convinced that they would be resurrected in the spiritual afterlife of their native homelands.[26]

A stronger group survived. Battered by the tempests of ill fate, the survivors had bent before the gale. Like folk peoples everywhere, they knew the wisdom of waiting out a storm. A new land would bring new possibilities. Olaudah Equiano, taken from Africa as a child by men he believed to be cannibals, left in his autobiography a rare description of the moment when the psychological darkness of the midpassage was lightened by the first grey traces of an American dawn. His countrymen aboard the slaver, he recalls, "gave me to understand we were to be carried to these white people's country to work for them. I was then a little relieved, and thought if it were no worse than working, my situation was not so desperate."[27] Weary and sick from a difficult and brutally uncomfortable sea voyage, new slaves were understandably eager to go ashore, especially when they were told that they would be met by fellow countrymen and that they would be working in tillage much as they had in Africa.[28] But even the strongest had been changed by the crossing. They had experienced the power of their new owners, and most understood that their own futures, and perhaps freedom, were linked to the new culture and would be dependent upon their own control over it.

The trappings of this new society had already been felt on the African coast, where the whites' mastery of literacy and ocean navigation especially impressed local traders. King Holiday of Bonny, who had a head for business, pointed this out as he flattered a visiting ship captain, Hugh Crow, in 1807. A tear of self-pity (or salesmanship) forming in his eye, King Holiday told his guest, "God make you sabby book and make big ship. . . . But God make we black and we no sabby book, and we no head for make ship."[29] Flattery or not, no coastal trader could fail to see the advantages of literacy and naval technology.

Nor could the captives of the Atlantic trade overlook the slavers' power. In Boston an African-born slave diplomatically eased Benjamin Colman's amazement that Africans had developed a prevention for smallpox before the Europeans by saying he supposed that God had taught Africans rather than whites the practice of variolation because the whites already possessed so much more knowledge and skill. Similarly, Jamaican slaves told the early nineteenth-century historian J. Stewart, "They require no greater proof that the almighty chose the whites as his favored people, than that he has communicated to them every useful and curious invention."[30]

Since such evidence comes from white observers, it should be taken with a grain of salt; nonetheless, blacks had little reason not to acknowledge the superiority of the alien European technology. The African coastal societies appear to have rationalized this imbalance between African and European cultures by ascribing it to the greed which followed from their own favored position in the world. The explanation was recorded by a white traveler, William Bosman, in 1698:

> The Africans tell us that in the beginning God created black as well as white men; thereby not only hinting but endeavoring to prove that their race was as soon in the world as ours; and to bestow a yet greater horror on themselves, they tell us that God, having created these two sorts of men, offered two sorts of gifts, to wit, gold and the knowledge of arts and reading and writing, giving blacks the first election, who chose gold and left the knowledge of letters to the white. God granted their request, but being incensed at their avarice resolved that the whites should for ever be their masters and they be obliged to wait on them as their slaves.[31]

The essence of this creation myth was even clearer when Thomas E. Bowdich recorded Ashanti and Fantee versions in 1819:

> The white men opening the paper it told them everything. God left the blacks in the bush, but conducted the whites to the water side. . . . communicated with them every night, and taught them to build a small ship which carried them to another country, whence they have returned after a long period, with various merchandise to barter with blacks, who might have been the superior people.[32]

Most of the new African arrivals to the Americas must have been impressed by the technological and material culture of the New World. Olaudah Equiano, for example, recounted his awe of the great sailing ships and navigational aids of the Atlantic trade and his amazement on coming ashore to horse-drawn wagons, multistoried houses, representational paintings, clocks, and other exotic products of Euro-American technology.[33]

Perceptive masters used this awe of American material culture to try to convince new slaves that bondage would be a happy state. Theodore Canot reported that Africans arriving in nineteenth-century Cuba were immediately provided with fresh fruits and other provisions to raise their spirits. Soon they were also given new clothes and blankets, items that, he contended, seemed especially valuable to new slaves. Highlighting the arrival was the display of a Cuban postilion dressed in a sky-blue coat, silver-laced hat, white breeches, polished jackboots, and ringing spurs, who jumped from his prancing horse to welcome the arrivals in their native tongue. Every newly arriving slave rushed to snap fingers in African greeting with this equestrian brother who, following orders, forthwith preached a propagandistic sermon on the happiness of being a white man's servant.[34]

The new slaves soon learned that they were not to expect a fair share of the New World's material grandeur. This was burdensome, for while they might question white justice, they never discounted the materialistic and ideological attractions of American culture. Indeed, for the slaves the American dream of prosperity and personal freedom soon became a bitter and taunting mirage. In return for their hard work even the poorest of the new slaves hungered to win some small gain from the new society; however, the rewards were more often a set of cast-off clothes than any longed-for consummation with the American goddess of success.

Ironically, the new slaves probably saw the secondhand clothes they received as a first taste of the wealth of America. Such garments had been worn only by the elite in Africa, where European clothes had long been treated as prestige items. Thus, Senegambia, an African-born slave in North Kingston, Rhode Island, was known to brag that his own father, who he claimed was a Gambian king, was beautifully dressed in white man's clothes, given as some of the innumerable presents handed out to him by British slaving captains.[35]

Ottabah Cugoano, who was taken into slavery in the mid-eighteenth century, reported that, at their factories on the Fantee Coast, the Europeans kept black servants "with gaudy clothes and a gay manner, as decoy ducks" to deceive new arrivals as to the attractiveness of slavery.[36] Throughout West and Central Africa, as Captain Hugh Crow so condescendingly noted, the coastal elite was "extremely fond of any thing gaudy or uncommon amongst them in dress," and if they obtained a showy article of imported clothing, such as a coat or vest, they would "strut about in it with all imaginable consequence."[37] Proud of their expensive and imported European finery, Africans wore the new garments with their own eye for style and flair. But what looked colorful and dashing to the local gentry usually looked vulgar and bizarre to European observers, who found the effect of African leaders in mismatched European hats, perukes, shirts, breeches, and coats grotesque and humorous.[38]

Thus, the African-born slaves of New England, however motley they may have looked to their masters, probably remained pleased with their own ability to dress as well as the elites did back home. Moreover, besides European-style clothing with metal buttons and buckles, New England slaves had available to them other items that either were shipped to Africa as luxuries or were unavailable in the homeland: rum (which was "so estimable an article [in West Africa] that none but chiefs could pay for a jar"), horses, carriages, wagons, carts, mirrors, Western furnishings, European musical instruments, and all manner of useful tools.[39]

Perhaps none of the material wealth of New England would have induced a single African to emigrate to the New World had blacks been given the freedom to arrive in the normal immigration channels, but slaves were given no such choice. Once in America, Africans could either make the best of their new, if limited, opportunities, or they could reject them. In New England, most newly arrived Africans were willing to make certain accommodations.

The majority of the new slaves in the northern colonies were young people who had spent long months in slavery far from their villages and homelands. Most were ready to assimilate themselves enough to be comfortable in their new lives, and some were clearly ready to master what they considered valuable in the new culture. Olaudah Equiano recalled in his autobiography a reaction that was probably typical of many of the younger slaves after their first days of adjustment:

> I could now speak English tolerably well and I perfectly understood everything that was said. I now not only felt myself quite easy with these new country-men, but relished their society and manners. I no longer looked upon them as spirits, but as men superior to us, and therefore I had the stronger desire to resemble them, to imbibe their spirit and imitate their manners; I therefore embraced every occasion of improvement, and every new thing that I observed I treasured up in my memory. I had long wished to be able to read and write, and for this purpose I took every opportunity to gain instruction.[40]

The new slaves did not reject their African heritage, but they learned that if they were to function comfortably in New England, they would often have to be willing to change. Thus it was that the blacks of New England began to become Americans. Unlike European immigrants they had never desired to leave their home continent; neither had they come seeking freedom or fortune. Instead, for the slaves the American dream had begun as a nightmare. Still, the bondsmen were not impervious to the possibilities of the new land. The siren song of the Americas must have shaped their dreams, too, as they tossed on hard pallets during cold New England nights. Indeed, their lives must have been especially frustrating since, unlike the fieldhands of plantation America, the Yankee bondsmen could not escape the pervasiveness of the surrounding Euro-American culture. In New England the slaves had to live, work, eat, and sometimes even sleep, alongside their masters in an environment that remained predominately white.

Chapter 2

A Clustered Minority

DESPITE the arrival of thousands of African and Afro-American immigrants in eighteenth-century New England, the vast preponderance of the region's population remained Anglo-Saxon. At least three of every four citizens were of English heritage, and among the community leaders this percentage was even higher. Inhabitants of Scottish or Irish ancestry were also important numerically, comprising at least 8 percent of the population by the end of the eighteenth century.[1] Africans and Afro-Americans were the fourth most populous ethnic group in New England but constituted from only 2 percent of the population at the beginning and end of the eighteenth century, to around 3 percent in midcentury. Prior to 1700 the black population was even smaller, amounting to less than 1,000 Negroes, or less than 1 percent of the total population.[2]

Although the Afro-American population of New England was a distinct minority, the picture the numbers seem to suggest is misleading. The black population was not evenly or sparsely divided throughout New England but was, instead, concentrated in areas of much heavier black residence. In the second half of the eighteenth century, for example, as the Negro population grew from over 11,000 to 16,000 people, the blacks were not scattered randomly throughout New England but were, instead, primarily concentrated in and around the coastal urban centers, along the river systems, and in the Narragansett region of Rhode Island. This clustering of the Afro-American population was important because it permitted the development of a black subculture in New England which a more scattered settlement might have precluded.

The concentration of the black population can be illustrated in New Hampshire, where there were few slaves. Blacks were only about 1 percent of the population in 1767; but nearly one-third, or 187, of the colony's blacks lived in Portsmouth, where they doubtless knew each other well— even if they comprised only 4 percent of the town's population. Along with other Negroes residing in surrounding Rockingham County, these Afro-Americans lived in close proximity to one-half of the colony's total black population of 633 people.[3] Clearly, the Afro-Americans of New Hampshire did not live as isolated from their fellows as the bald statistics might seem to imply.

The same situation can be seen even more explicitly in the other colonies. For example, in Massachusetts the black population clustered around the colony's largest city, Boston, where approximately 1,500 blacks resided in 1742. In 1754, one-half of Massachusetts's nearly 2,700 adult Negroes continued to live in the Bay City and surrounding Suffolk County; indeed, over three-quarters of Massachusetts blacks lived in the maritime and commercial counties of Suffolk, Essex, and Plymouth, clustering along the coast and in town centers. The concentration of 989 adult blacks in Boston in 1754 constituted over one-third of Massachusetts's entire adult Negro population in a city which had been roughly 10 percent black for over a decade. Suffolk County as a whole was around 4 percent black, while the four maritime-commercial counties were roughly 3 percent black.[4]

The situation was similar in midcentury Rhode Island, where blacks constituted 17 percent of the total population of Newport County, 15 percent of Kings County, and 11, 7, and 5 percent of Bristol, Kent, and Providence counties respectively. Moreover, Newport and Kings counties, with their high percentages of black population, were the home of three-quarters of Rhode Island's Negroes. In 1755 one of every four Rhode Island blacks resided in Newport alone, where they comprised nearly 20 percent of the total city population. Other Rhode Island townships also had significant populations: South Kingston was nearly 30 percent black and Charlestown nearly 40 percent.[5]

In Connecticut nearly one-half of the colony's black population in 1774 resided in the coastal commercial counties of New London and Fairfield.

Figure 1. *Negro Population by Town in the Colonies of Connecticut,*
Massachusetts, and Rhode Island circa 1755

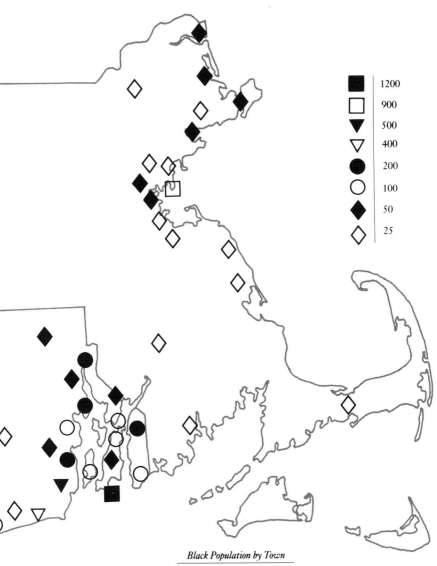

	1200
■	
□	900
▼	500
▽	400
●	200
○	100
◆	50
◇	25

Black Population by Town

	Massachusetts	Connecticut	Rhode Island	Total
1–24	91	15	4	110
25–49	12	8	2	22
50–99	6	7	5	18
100+	1	13	14	28

These counties had Negro populations of about 4 percent each. The cities of New London and Fairfield contained one of every eight Connecticut blacks, and had black populations of 9 and 7 percent respectively.[6]

Thus, while blacks were a tiny fraction of New England's total population, the majority of Yankee Negroes lived in areas where the percentage of black population was much higher. The clustering of black population around major towns, along the rivers and coasts, and in certain agricultural areas meant that most Yankee blacks were not particularly isolated from their fellows, and surely not as isolated as the general colony or regional statistics might imply. Such black population clustering accounts for the development of an Afro-American folk culture in a society otherwise so dominated by its white population.

During the first half of the eighteenth century, the black population of New England was increasing at an average of nearly 50 percent a decade, compared to about 30 percent a decade for the white population in the same period.[7] Such growth conservatively suggests an average importation into New England of at least 1,200 black immigrants a decade from 1700 to 1750, or an increase of at least 30 percent a decade from immigration alone.[8] Importation seems to have decreased after 1750 and was brought to a stop by the American Revolution. Overall, in the second half of the eighteenth century black population increased at an average of only about 11 percent a decade during a period when the white population growth averaged a rate of over 25 percent.[9]

Between 1700 and 1750 the foreign-born portion of the black population declined from at least 70 percent at the beginning of the century to roughly one-half that in 1750. In general, one-half of the black population of New England was foreign-born during the first fifty years of the eighteenth century. After the midcentury mark the majority of the black population was native-born, until by 1800 only a few African immigrants remained. Nonetheless, since the adult population always contained a much higher percentage of foreign-born blacks than the total population, it can be conservatively estimated that at least one-third of the adult Negro population was still foreign-born at the time of the American Revolution.[10] This large reservoir of foreign-born and largely African population continued to remember the African heritage, a fact which decisively shaped the development of northern Afro-American culture.

The eighteenth century saw a low rate of natural increase among New

England's Negroes.[11] Many masters did not prize fertility in their female slaves, who were sometimes sold, as was one sixteen-year-old Connecticut girl in 1733, "for no fault but because she is like to be a good breeder." Slave owners did not attempt to increase their capital by pushing marriage onto bondswomen for breeding purposes; on the contrary, many masters saw marriage duties as potentially costly to them in the attention and labor of servants preoccupied with their own families. This meant some slave women probably tried to avoid having children so that neither they nor their babies would be sold.[12]

Since slave spouses often lived in separate residences of different masters, the opportunities for conception were limited, a condition probably pleasing to the masters. Rhode Island figures from the 1755 census suggest a 15 percent lower ratio of children to women among blacks than among whites, and Connecticut statistics from 1774 based on children under twenty to women over twenty seem to confirm the general trend by suggesting over a 30 percent lower ratio of children to women among blacks than among whites.[13] Nonetheless, newspaper advertisements for slaves suggest that black women who became mothers bore their first children somewhere between eighteen and twenty-one years of age, perhaps slightly before white women in the surrounding society.[14]

The rate of increase of black population was also adversely affected by an unbalanced sex ratio caused by a preponderance of men within the serving society. Male slaves were predominant in the African trade by a margin of as much as two to one over women, in part because they could fill a greater variety of job roles than could their female counterparts. Therefore, it is not surprising that during the eighteenth century there were more black men than black women in New England. This imbalance was slowly corrected by natural increase as the heavy importation of slaves declined, but censuses from Massachusetts, Connecticut, and New Hampshire still suggest a black sex ratio of about 1.3 males per female in 1770 when the sex ratio for whites was about 1.00.[15]

Some black males married local Indian women, for northern Indians were also suffering the effects of a badly skewed sex ratio—seventy-six males to 100 females among Massachusetts Indians in 1764, and sixty-five males per 100 females among adult Indians in Connecticut in 1774.[16] William Brown offered additional insight into such marriages by explaining from his family's history that in Rhode Island "Indian women observing the colored men working for their wives, and living after the manner of white people, in comfortable houses, felt anxious to change their position in life." They achieved this by purchasing black husbands, who treated their wives with greater consideration than did Indian males, a situation leading to both an increase in Negro-Indian marriages and a strong animosity between Indian and Negro men.[17] For many black males there were no women; these men remained single, a factor which contributed importantly to the low rate of black population growth.

Sexual imbalance was exacerbated in the cities, where employment opportunities for males in industry, shipping, and common labor meant sex ratios even higher than the general averages. In Boston, for example, the black sex ratio was 1.89 males per female in 1754, while for the rest of Suffolk County the ratio was 1.79, and for Massachusetts as a whole it was 1.64. By 1765 Boston's black sex ratio had dropped to 1.68 at a time when Boston's white ratio was .95; comparatively, Massachusetts's sex ratio was 1.36 among blacks and .97 among whites in 1765.[18] In Portsmouth, New Hampshire, the black sex ratios were 1.97 and 1.67 for 1767 and 1773 respectively, while the colony's general sex ratios among Negroes were 1.54 and 1.29, and the ratios for whites were 1.02 and 1.03.[19] By contrast, Newport, Rhode Island, in 1755 had a sex ratio among blacks of 1.11, only slightly higher than the black average of 1.03 for the colony as a whole and only slightly different from corresponding white ratios of 1.00 and .96 respectively.[20]

The low birth rate among blacks meant that the percentage of the Negro population under adult years was lower than was typical in the surrounding white society. The older black population was also caused by higher infant mortality among blacks and by the effects of importation of new slaves. By 1755, 46 percent of Rhode Island's blacks were children under sixteen, compared with 49 percent of the whites, while in Connecticut the situation was more pronounced: as late as 1774, 49 percent of the blacks were under twenty, as compared with 57 percent of the whites.[21] The high sex ratio among black youth in the Connecticut census of 1774 should also be noted; since a normal sex ratio among children is 1.03 males per female, Connecticut's 1.51 ratio seems to indicate continued strong evidence of slave importation.[22]

The mortality rate for blacks appears to have been much higher than that for whites, but the evidence may be skewed since it comes from urban areas, and principally from the relatively unhealthy city of Boston. Between 1730 and 1760 the black mortality rate of Boston fell steadily from 145 deaths per 1,000 population in the smallpox year of 1730 to fifty-two in 1760.[23] The general rate for the first three-quarters of the eighteenth century ranged from around forty-five to thirty-two deaths per 1,000 population.[24] Between 1704 and 1749 blacks accounted for about 16 percent of the burials in Boston, nearly twice what might be expected considering they constituted only about 8 percent of the Boston population. As the years progressed, the black burial rate continued at about double the percentage of the city's black population.[25]

Evidence from the smallpox years of 1752 and 1764 helps confirm the disparity between black and white mortality rates. In 1752 fewer blacks became ill with smallpox either naturally (9 percent of those afflicted were Negro) or from inoculation (7 percent of the afflicted) than their 10 percent total of the population would warrant, presumably because of earlier African knowledge of variolation and because many blacks were purchased as seasoned slaves, thereby having immunity before their arrival. Nonetheless, blacks contracting smallpox died from the disease at rates much higher than white averages. Twelve percent of those who died from natural contact were black, as were 20 percent of those who died after inoculation. By 1764, with more American-born blacks in the population, Negroes both came down with smallpox, naturally (8 percent) and by inoculation (6 percent), and died of it (18 percent from natural contact and 7 percent from inoculation), at rates higher than their 5 percent of the city's population should have dictated.[26]

In contrast, the black burial rates of Newport, Rhode Island, were not significantly different from corresponding white rates; about 19 percent of the total Newport burials were black, only slightly higher than the black percentage of Newport's total population. The black mortality rate of Newport might be estimated at about thirty-two per 1,000 population in the 1760s.[27] More detailed information is also available for Newport since, scattered in the burial data for 1763, were recorded the deaths of eleven new Negroes and eleven children, together accounting for over one-half of the year's forty-three burials. In 1761, two of the thirty-four buried were "new Negroes" (that is, recently imported), while in 1764 twelve of the thirty-seven buried were children. The high percentage of new Negroes (about 17 percent) among those who died in 1761 and 1763 suggests that seasoning was as harsh in New England as it was elsewhere. The death rate for children for the years 1763 and 1764 of eleven to twelve a year (29 percent of those who died) suggests a mortality rate among black youth of roughly twenty-three per 1,000 population. Interestingly, in 1762 two-thirds of the thirty-two burials were males in a city that had an almost even sex ratio.[28]

Unfortunately, the Boston and Newport mortality rates do not distinguish between freedmen and slaves; but in Boston, where the mortality was higher, there appears to have been a much higher percentage of free blacks, since some 40 percent of blacks in Massachusetts may have been free in 1764, compared to probably less than 10 percent a decade later in Rhode Island.[29] Thus, these mortality statistics could suggest that, in material comforts and health care, slaves fared better than freed blacks, a hypothesis that seems well supported by the more descriptive forms of historical evidence.[30] As Jeremy Belknap explained, Boston's free blacks "often suffer by damp unwholesome lodgings, because they are unable to pay the rent for better; and they are subject to many infirmities and diseases, especially in the winter."[31] But the difference in mortality rates between Boston and Newport may also be correlated to the significant differences in sex ratios also found between the two cities, since old black men were more liable to live alone and suffer from improper care.

The demographic evidence clearly suggests that since Afro-Americans were only a small percentage of New England's population, the cultural contact between the African and Euro-American heritage was strongly weighted toward a rapid assimilation of the black immigrants. Nonetheless, room for the development of an Afro-American folk culture within predominantly Yankee New England was made possible by the clustering of blacks within areas of significant minority population, and by the constant reinfusion of African culture produced by a continuing importation of African and Afro-American slaves until the American Revolution. An Afro-American consciousness was probably additionally fostered in the black community by the low birth rate. As an older society with many single men, Afro-American New England surely placed greater emphasis on conserving the old traditions than would have a more youth-centered culture. Nonetheless, by 1800, when the black population of New England was almost entirely native-born, the Afro-American years were, culturally speaking, effectively disappearing.

Part 2
The Forces of Enculturation

Chapter 3

Family Slavery

UNLIKE elsewhere in the Americas, where black populations considerably Africanized their surrounding societies, the black community of New England had relatively little influence on the development of mainstream Yankee culture. New England's blacks were too small a minority to retain much autonomy or greatly alter white folkways. Since Yankee slaves spent the greater part of their daily routine as subordinate members of white households, separated from the society of fellow blacks, they could not maintain a viable African culture; neither were they, as supposed inferiors, permitted to develop into fully assimilated "Americans." Instead, a combination of choice, circumstance, oppression, and exploitation led the African immigrants to become black Yankees—a very special breed of Afro-American New Englanders.

In New England, bondage meant a form of family slavery. Because of the restricted economic opportunities for gang labor, the majority of Yankee bondsmen found themselves in service to masters who could afford no more than one or two slaves to help them with household, farm, or business chores. Since northern slave owners rarely held enough bondsmen to permit the expense of separate living quarters for the races, common residence during the more domestic hours reinforced the proximity of workday relationships. Even in the exceptional cases where gang labor was used on the large farms of eastern Connecticut and Narragansett, bondsmen were treated more as family domestics than as plantation field slaves.

The precedents for Yankee slaveholders to bring black servants into their own households residentially, socially, and religiously go back to the early years of the seventeenth century, when Puritan precepts of patriarchal control led Massachusetts leaders to organize groups of unattached white male servants into artificial family units and to place stray bachelors and maids under the family discipline of local households.[1] Slavery in eighteenth-century New England continued to follow this biblical model of the patriarchal family. These religious and social precedents were reinforced by the intimacy of sharing work and home life, leading the Reverend Cotton Mather to conclude that Yankee slaves were "of our own household" and "more clearly related to us than many others are." Indeed, proximity intensified the requirement that masters recognize their responsibility under the "familial" nature of slavery because, as the Reverend Elihu Coleman warned in 1733, otherwise the sins of the servants would show their masters' families "to be unclean and adulterous."[2] The same connection was underscored when black slaves were baptized into the Christian covenant as members of their masters' families—a policy that followed earlier precedents instituted with white servants in seventeenth-century New England.

"Familial" relationships between slaves and masters were most common when new slaves were purchased as children. Since it was believed that the best domestic slaves were purchased near birth and raised within the family unit, some masters, like George Reed of South Woburn, Massachusetts, made a specialty of getting their servants very young.[3] Other masters, normally too poor to afford the luxury of buying a slave's child, who would remain unproductive for a number of years, occasionally undertook the expense of purchasing newborn slaves after their own wives lost infants.[4] Such young slaves were usually native-born because few infants were transported in the Atlantic slave trade.

New England slave owners bought young slaves in order to train the children entirely within their own families so that the children would grow up anticipating their masters' wants and needs, likes and dislikes. If young slaves in New England were rarely presented to young masters as they were elsewhere in the New World, so the master and slave could grow up together, nonetheless, where slaves did grow up alongside their masters' children, close relationships usually developed. Thus, between the slave Boston and his master, Mr. Potter of Concord, a reciprocal good will was said to have subsisted; "the servant was all obedience and the master's will was exactly Boston's pace and Boston's habits and knowledge."[5] Elsewhere in the New World, children were recommended, as the *Practical Rules* for planters suggested with self-serving overstatement, because "their juvenile minds entertain no regrets for the loss of their connections. They acquire the English language with great ease, and improve daily in size, understanding and capacity for labor."[6] There was probably some truth in this, at least in the long run, for the Yankee poet Phillis Wheatley claimed to have no other memory of the native shores she left at the age of seven other than her mother pouring out water before the sun at its rising—a custom which Lucumi Yoruba slaves continued to practice in nineteenth-century Cuba.[7]

In New England the initial cost of purchasing a native-born slave child was low because masters who already had slaves usually could afford no more and regarded black babies as an unproductive expense. Such masters were willing to sell or give away their slaves' children for other masters to raise. Isaac Fellows of Woodstock, Connecticut, for example, had to pay but a pistareen for his slave Cuff, bought while yet a "rickety babe." Other slave children were given away, it was reported, "like puppies," or even with a cash bonus.[8] The selling of newborn children away from their natural parents may have been instigated in many cases by the death of the natural mothers in childbirth or soon after; other sales of young slave children may have resulted from cases of bastardy. Nonetheless, many legitimate black children seem to have been sold away from their mothers by callous masters who wished to avoid the costs of their upbringing.

Since the practice of separating white children from their natural parents to follow training and domestic work in other households had been relatively common in seventeenth-century New England, the developing practice of separating black families probably did not seem especially cruel to northern slave owners. The binding out of both white and black children as apprentices remained a normal practice of poor relief and guardianship throughout the colonial era; Solomon Townsend of Malden, Massachusetts, for example, received something over thirteen pounds for the bringing up of a mulatto child given over to him by the town as a slave in 1761.[9]

Even after the ending of slavery, the tradition of separating black children from their parents so that they could be reared in household service continued. Black youngsters spent early childhood at home, but on reaching adolescence they were sent to live as servants with white families. Nancy Freeman left her parents at the age of nine to live with, and to serve, the Truman Coes, who gave her a cow and feather bed as compensation when she reached her nineteenth birthday. Generally, boys remained in service until twenty-one, and girls to their eighteenth birthday.[10]

Raising young slaves within their masters' families away from their natural parents could be an effective (albeit cruel) assimilating process. Consider Phillis Wheatley again. She was taken into the Wheatley family of Boston in 1761 at the age of seven. She was soon taught to read and write by Mrs. Wheatley's daughter; at the same time, her clear intelligence and amiable disposition led her mistress to treat her almost as a daughter. Since she was not devoted to menial slave occupations and was kept constantly at the side of her mistress, the young Phillis became better versed in the cultural manner of upper-class Boston than most of the white working class. Unfortunately, she was also not allowed to associate with the other black domestics of the family, and soon her rare combination of black skin and white education alienated her from the majority of both races.[11]

Rose, a slave child taken from Africa at about two years of age in 1737, was a more typical example of a black child raised in her master's family. Rose was purchased by Lieutenant Stephen Putnam of Danvers, Massachusetts, and grew up among his ten children. As soon as she was old enough, she was put to work taking care of the children and assisting her mistress in the household chores. She probably never attended school, but as part of the family of a conscientious master "she learned her letters, and was able to read a little in her Bible, and was constant in her attendance at church."[12] For a slave, hers was a comfortable existence and she was soon assimilated as part of the Putnam family.

Not all black children brought up in white families were so effectively separated from their true parents. Hagar Merriman's autobiography movingly records the problems of the slave child who had, in effect, two mothers and two mistresses. When Hagar was nine months old her mother's owner, Mrs. Brown, failed in business and was obliged to sell her servant.

> Mrs. Lovejoy of Stratford, bought her. Mrs. Brown was not willing to sell me too, but my mother said she would spill her last drop of blood, but that I should go with her. Mrs. Brown kept my mother several weeks, before she would let her go, as she insisted upon taking me also. Mrs. Lovejoy came over, and as she had no children, she promised to treat me well, and so we both went. My

mother having a great deal to do, the lady took and weaned me herself; she took all the charge and care of me. I used to sleep in a little crib that she had made for me, in her room, until I was five years old. . . .

Every other day, I was allowed to take my little chair, and go in to see my mother; I was so afraid of my mother that I used to go into the kitchen trembling, and hardly dared to look up to her. My lady had three persons visiting her, and I was requested to dance and sing to these ladies, who promised me nine coppers, when they had been down street shopping. I watched eagerly for their return, and when they came, I went to the parlor to claim the coppers; they were given, but my mother gave me a beating, because I was so ill-mannered as to ask for them; I shall never forget it.[13]

Black children separated from their parents and placed into white families became as assimilated as their masters permitted. That few achieved the cultural attainments of the white middle class bespeaks the stunted expectations of Yankee slave owners. While generally treated well for slaves, young Negroes in New England were rarely treated as Caucasian children would have been. Since whites were educating blacks for a special role in service, and under the weight of prejudiced expectations about Negro character and ability, many masters retarded their slaves' assimilation. This miseducation continued even after the abolition of slavery, as J. P. Brissot de Warville noted with regard to the handling of a black child in Rhode Island in 1788:

I saw in Newport a twenty-month-old Negro who repeated everything that was said to him, understood clearly what he heard, obeyed instructions, mimicked others, danced, etc. He showed signs of extraordinary intelligence. People amused themselves by getting him to make funny faces. This seemed to me a cruel and thoughtless sort of diversion. It was an indication of the contempt in which Negroes are still held.[14]

A reciprocal, if unequal, relationship between slave and master was at the heart of the paternalism of northern slavery. Owners might expect loyal service from their slaves, but in return the slaves expected certain rights and obligations from their masters. A surgeon in Albany, New York, discovered this to his cost. As he wrote to a friend, he was determined to sell one of his slaves even though he was a likely young fellow and used to hard country work. "His fault is, being born in the family with me, he thinks

I am not to use the same government with him as with one who wasn't, or at least he should be allowed as much privilege as he chooses, and knowing my disposition, that I cannot flog him, for the aforesaid reason, he has at length got the upper hand of me, by the advice of a free Negro wench who he would have for his wife, against my will."[15]

The closeness between master and slave made it possible that occasionally a slave with a strong personality and superior talents could dominate his master and the running of his master's household. The Reverend Samuel Palmer's slave Titus, for example, was said to be decidedly the boss of the two on his master's eighteenth-century Falmouth, Massachusetts farm.[16] Perhaps such relationships were more common between male masters and mature female slaves, as the regional literature of New England suggests. In *Oldtown Fireside Stories* Harriet Beecher Stowe recalls how Captain Brown's Guinea slave woman, Quassia, dominated her owner. Similarly, in *The Jonny-Cake Papers of "Shepard Tom"* Thomas Hazard records that his grandfather's Senegambian cook, Phillis, dictated to her henpecked master. Sometimes a slave factotum would (within defined limits) dominate an entire family. The Reverend Mose Parsons of Byfield, Connecticut, owned among his slaves a woman, Violet, who had grown up in the service of his family and was slightly older than her master's sons. Like many Yankee slaves she called the boys by their familiar names, even after they had become important men. Described as "the autocrat of her family, and the presiding genius of her household," she was indulged with all the spending money she wanted and was considered the best dressed member of the parsonage circle.[17]

Of course, masters need not tolerate a slave with an unseemly dominant personality. Although severe punishment was frowned upon, Yankee masters could always sell unruly slaves south, as they were reminded by advertisements in the Boston *Evening Post* and *Newsletter* in the late summer of 1761. These offered to exchange African children for Negro men who were "strong and hearty, tho' not of the best moral character, which are fit subjects for transportation."[18] After William Royall of Canton, Massachusetts, became so cowed by his black field hands that he was afraid to leave his house to direct them in their labor, he took his revenge as the new state constitution and the Quok Walker Decision were ending Bay State slavery. Shortly before the date of emancipation, he secretly hired a gang of men to surround his house and forcibly ship his hands off to perpetual servitude in

Barbados. Two of the slaves, Hector and Pero, escaped and afterward asserted that had they known of Royall's intention, he would not have lived to carry it out.[19]

Other Yankee slave owners must also have feared their slaves' responses to unwanted sales—whether by violence, escape, or an appeal to the community—because when they sold such slaves south they tried to effect the sale and removal without their slaves' knowledge. Cujo, for example, being feared by his Salem master, was ostensibly sent with a load of potatoes to the wharf, where the sailors had been paid to lure him aboard ship. They accomplished their deception by tricking him into fiddling for them until he was well at sea.[20] But intractable slaves were exceptions in New England, where most bondsmen grew up with the family of a single master and were considered part of the household.

The social and emotional distance between masters and slaves in household slavery was reflected in the physical distance ordered by the seating arrangements when master and slave gathered for shared meals. Among rural New England families class differentials between slaves and masters were often neglected, and the observant traveler, Madam Sarah Knight, disgusted at the great familiarity between the races on Yankee farms, reported that Connecticut masters allowed their black servants "to sit at table with them (as they say to save time), and into the dish goes the black hoof as freely as the white hand." J. Hector St. John Crèvecoeur noted that, although this was also the case in New York, there was still distinction made by the master, for "at the lowest part sat his Negroes, his hired men were next, then the family" and their guest. In the urban areas and among the upper classes, the family kitchen shared by blacks and whites maintained the exclusive distinctions we might expect, and the slaves had a separate table.[21]

For black servants a more familiar seating arrangement at dinner was generally stigmatized. As early as 1693 it was grounds for complaint that Thomas Shepard had let John Saffin's slave Adam eat at the Shepard family table. A half century later, the "proper" behavior for a slave still included discretion with regard to accepting a too familiar seating arrangement. When Lucy Prince, a respected African-born woman visited a white family in rural Deerfield, Massachusetts, in her old age, she is said to have refused a place at the table, saying, "No Missy, no, I know my place." Phillis Wheatley, although famed for her poetry and cultural attainments, always declined the seat offered her when invited to the homes of important whites, requesting instead that a side table be set for her apart from the rest. Since certain African societies similarly insisted on separating slaves during meals, the polite blacks who refused to sit at the head tables may have been upholding an Afro-American sense of propriety as well as deferring to white sensibilities.[22]

The emotional attachments within Yankee families between white and black were a complex and contradictory fabric, interweaving formal expectations of social roles with coarser strands of racial prejudice and finer threads of human affection. Many slave owners felt real love for their bondspeople; and many slaves returned this emotion. Yet masters went on exploiting their servants as chattel; and bondsmen continued to chafe under the discriminations of a hated slavery. Ebenezer Bridge tried to come to terms with the complexity of this relationship from the master's perspective following the death of his slave Venus in 1756.

> I think I can truly say that considering it as a loss of Estate, it hath little or no weight in my mind—but considering it as a death of one of my family—one that hath lived so many years with me; one that hath been so much trouble to me in her behavior and conduct (though one that hath gone through a great deal of hard service), one that hath provoked me and my wife a great multitude of times to rash and unjustified expressions and hard treatment of her, one that was so wicked and sinful, and one whose soul is as precious as any.[23]

Many other New England slave owners also saw the death of a slave as a personal as well as an economic loss. The Reverend Ebenezer Parkman bought a Guinea Negro who died during his first winter in 1728; Parkman mourned him as "the first death in my family." Likewise, when Professor John Winthrop's slave boy George died of the measles, "he was mourned as one of the family, not as an unfortunate investment." But sentimental Puritan masters were also parsimonious Yankees. When David Hall's Negro man expired, Hall noted, "He died like a saint but tis thought that I have lost . . . near 200 old Tenor [£200 in the older, inflated colonial currency] . . . by his death."[24] Slaves, too, mourned the loss of a kind owner. Prime Fowle, in fact, refused to give way to his master in the place of honor during the funeral procession of his mistress, sputtering to his surprised master, "Go tudder side ye sef, ye mean jade."[25]

Lieutenant Richard Herbert of Concord, New Hampshire, had a slave named Nancy whose history illuminates the complex experience of family slavery. Herbert purchased Nancy as a baby in 1768 for five dollars. Born in Boston, Nancy was given away at nine days of age to a man moving to Rumford, who later sold her to Herbert when she was eighteen months old. She grew up with the family, attending school sporadically to learn to read and recite the catechism. In her old age she supposed that she "was treated just the same as the other children."[26] Indeed, as Anne Grant reported in her memoirs, domestic slaves in northern families usually "shared the same religious instruction with the children of the family; and, for the first years there was little or no difference with regard to food or clothing between their children and those of their masters."[27] But as Herbert's Nancy explained, while material conditions were roughly similar, she "did not expect as much" as a white child would have. Nonetheless, she was relatively satisfied with her state and said she was never conscious of a wish she had been born white.[28]

Like most orphans, Nancy often wondered about her roots, especially when the Massachusetts constitution of 1783 abolished local slavery and threatened her relationship to the Herbert family. Having been told that she came originally from Boston, she inquired constantly about the city and the roads leading there, for she feared that she might have to return to Boston when she was given her freedom. When the great news of emancipation came, she was washing dishes; surprisingly, Nancy greeted the announcement with tears rather than joy. She knew no other existence besides that in Concord. The Herberts soon relieved her of her despair by telling her she could stay on as a hired servant, thus keeping her familiar role.[29] Black slaves such as Nancy often became part of their masters' families both emotionally and socially. Nonetheless, as slaves, no matter how well loved, they still could be sold or sent away at whim.

Slaves who became old in service to a white family often refused a "reward" of freedom because they felt at home in their master's household and because they could have assurance there that they would be cared for in their old age. Prince Jonar, an African-born slave owned in succession by Joseph Buckminster and his son Thomas, managed a farm in Framingham, Massachusetts, where he lived in a small cabin overlooking a meadow he had picked for cultivation because it reminded him of the soil of his native country. Offered freedom in his old age, Jonar refused by sagaciously citing a proverb common to Yankee slaves in this situation: "Massa eat the meat;

he now pick the bone." As William Brown, the son of a Rhode Island slave, explained, "The old bondsmen declared their masters had been eating their flesh and now it was the slaves' turn to stick to them and suck their bones." Mose Parson's slave avoided the African proverbial intricacies by commenting more bluntly: "You have had the best of me, and you and yours must have the worst. Where am I to go in sickness or old age? No, Master, your slave I am, and always will be, and I will belong to your children when you are gone; and by you and them I mean to be cared for."[30] Domestic slaves were especially apt to remain with their masters or return shortly after gaining freedom.[31] The refusal of freedom was, as might be expected, more common among older women since they would have greater difficulties outside the family and because they usually retained close bonds to the white children they had helped raise.

Many slaves came to identify with their white masters, relating as "family history" the history of the master's family (of course, this worked the other way around too). Henry Vassal's slave Tony, for example, felt himself part of the Vassal family and was remembered as being "delighted to expound to the younger generation the glories of grandiloquent description of the ancient splendors of 'the family' and his own Apollo-like magnificence on the box seat of the chariot when they drove to church . . . or into Boston for some stately function." In his old age, Tony's most cherished possession was said to have been a "pass" which guaranteed him a place in the Vassal family vault.[32]

In death many slaves remembered their masters' children in wills. For example, old unmarried Nero in 1733 gave them his prized possessions including his silver shoe and knee buckles; the base ones he gave to a fellow slave. In 1743 a similar will divided the legacy of a slave between his master's children and his own. Samuel Gipson, a slave originally from the West Indies, had by the time he died in 1795 at age thirty-four become a free and successful merchant. Prior to his death he had taken the son of his old master as a clerk, and when Gipson died he left the young man his entire estate.[33]

Oddly enough, slaves who identified with their masters' families sometimes even offered financial aid to their masters' children while still alive. Moses, while a slave of Priest Fowler of North Guilford, Connecticut, was so successful as both a businessman and farm manager that he sent his master's son Johnny to college, paying all the expenses. Moreover, it was not unusual for a slave to lend his master money to help him out during times of stress; unfortunately, such generosity sometimes proved costly to black bondsmen forced to sue for the return of the loan in a white man's country.[34]

When black slaves took their freedom they usually adopted the surname of their first or favorite owner.[35] This adoption of a master's name, although relatively common in the New World, was as symbolic of the connection between master and servant as it was useful for purposes of identification. Not all New England slaves felt close enough to their masters to want these names. Jack Lander, an African who served W. Lander of Salem as a chair-maker, took the name of Jack Southward at freedom. Southward may have been the name of Jack Lander's first master, but more likely he chose the name for other reasons.[36] A heady anticipation of freedom led nine among the forty-eight blacks in the Second Company of the Fourth Connecticut Revolutionary Regiment to take surnames well-suited to the cause of personal and national independence—Cuff Liberty, Cuff Freedom, and Jube Freedom, for example.[37] Other freed slaves apparently took their surnames from the names of their fathers, as did both Charles Prince and Tabitha Quamino at their marriage.[38] Interestingly, Paul Cuffe, a noted black merchant and philanthropist, became Paul Cuffe rather than Paul Slocum because the Slocum family denied Paul's father, Cuffe, the right to take their surname.[39]

Family slavery speeded acculturation in New England. Indeed, family slavery often fostered close and relatively humane relationships that sometimes approached a fictional kinship between masters and slaves—an effect noticed throughout the Americas wherever the ownership of one or two slaves per master was common. As Henry Koster noted of small-scale slaveholding during his travels in Brazil, "Africans who have been purchased very young . . . are frequently part of the family. . . . the difference of the feeling of one of these men towards his master, and that of the generality of the slaves which are owned by the great proprietors, is very striking."[40]

Nonetheless, the family slavery of New England which eased the assimilation of Afro-American bondsmen also developed a series of bitter internal inconsistencies. Chattel slavery, even in a New England family environment, could not resolve the basic contradictions inherent in treating humans as property. The artificial laws of paternalistic ownership could never successfully be reconciled to the innate laws of human spirit. The family system of slavery worked best with young slaves who could grow up as domestic servants in their masters' households, yet black children who were paternalistically integrated into white families had first to be taken from their own natural parents, just as African slaves had first to be separated from their native homelands. Those bondsmen who labored most faithfully for their owners discovered that full integration into their master's family usually precluded the development of independent black families for themselves. Loyalty to the one naturally conflicted with the time and responsibility needed by the other. The tension between family slavery and slave families ultimately fractured both institutions and gave the lie to the so-called civilizing mission of Christian bondage. This was poignantly noted in a petition from a group of Boston Negroes in 1774:

> The endearing ties of husband and wife we are strangers to for we are no longer man and wife than our masters and mistresses think proper married or unmarried. Our children are also taken from us by force and sent many miles from us where we seldom or ever see them again there to be made slaves of for life which sometimes is very short by reason of being dragged from their mother's breast. Thus our lives are embittered to us on these accounts. By our deplorable situation we are rendered incapable of showing our obedience to almighty God. How can a slave perform the duties of a husband to a wife or parent to his child? How can a husband leave master and work and cleave to his wife? How can the wife submit themselves to their husbands in all things? How can the child obey their parents in all things?[41]

While the closeness of master and bondsman often created ties of deep and abiding affection, the duty of the one to rule and of the other to obey led to unavoidable frustrations for both, frustrations which constantly chafed the ideal of paternalistic harmony. Functionally, family slavery was a successful institution for easing the first steps of assimilation; but since family slavery was unable to produce both obedient black servants and free and independent black Americans, it failed in the larger task of Americanizing New England's African immigrants.

Chapter 4

The Training of Servants

NEW ENGLAND slave owners never contemplated cultural autonomy for their black servants. Instead, Yankee masters arrogantly believed the opportunity to be educated in the traditions of English Christian civilization was recompense enough for the trials of Yankee bondage. New England's black population did become among the most assimilated in the Americas by the end of the eighteenth century; but, even putting the best light on the hypocritical motives of the master class, the subservient and limited roles of slavery were neither able to, nor intended to, prepare black immigrants for full participation in an open American society. However paternalistic New England's intentions, Yankee slavery, like bondage elsewhere, was worse than a poor school of Americanization; it was a school of miseducation creating a caste system that belied the region's proud democratic traditions.

New England slave owners had two major concerns in dealing with new slaves. The newcomers had to be sufficiently instructed to satisfy new occupational roles; and they had to be weaned from those prior life styles, values, mores, and ways of doing things that seemed alien or bizarre to Yankee sensibilities. It was expected that newcomers would adapt themselves to an English Christian social order and find a special niche in the families of their owners as faithful black servants. They were not being trained to be the equal of white New Englanders, only to be useful and accommodating slaves.

Since in New England black immigrants faced a dominant English culture which was more complex technologically than traditional African cultures and which, more importantly, belonged to a powerful and ethno-centric master class, it is not surprising that the basic flow of cultural change usually saw Euro-American patterns displace African behaviors. But since African immigrants were rarely passive or without choices, acculturation was always far from the enculturation envisioned as ideal by the master class. On the one hand, black newcomers clung to traditional values and patterns of behavior important to them, especially those they believed superior to, or found more comfortable or understandable than, the new alternatives. On the other hand, masters blinded by a narrow ethnocen-trism eschewed all compromise with what they believed to be uncivilized traditions. Accommodation between these extremes became possible, however, because while Yankee owners found African behaviors distasteful in their servants, they were also persuaded that too much acculturation could spoil a slave by destroying the illusion of inferiority and servility.

A new slave's receptivity to New World service and Euro-American culture depended on prior experiences. As a rule, new Africans were be-lieved more rebellious than Afro-Americans because Africans were accus-tomed to taking their own initiatives, making them, in the words of New York's Jeremiah Van Rensselaer, "proud and treacherous."[1] The proudest of the new slaves were bondsmen of noble or royal status; African nobility generally refused to participate in menial New World labor (and even when they did try, they were often unequal to the physical burden).

Upper-class Africans, as the Barbados assembly complained in 1693, were people "nursed up in luxury and ease, and wholly unaccustomed to work."[2] Many such men and women of royal birth or high status believed it beneath their dignity to work. As Captain John Stedman explained from eighteenth-century Surinam, "I have seen some instances of newly im-ported Negroes refusing to work, nor could promises, threats, rewards nor even blows, prevail; but these had been princes or people of the first rank in their native country . . . whose heroic sentiments still preferred instant death to the baseness and miseries of servitude."[3] Even when broken of their imperious ways, royal slaves made unaccommodating servants. An African princess in Barbados, for example, refused for twenty years to either eat or converse with fellow slaves.[4]

Samuel Maverick was probably the first New Englander to discover such royal obstinacy, when in 1639 his slave woman, who had been a queen in

Africa, adamantly refused the slave he had intended for her spouse, throwing the would-be suitor from her bed and taking the idea "in high disdain beyond her slavery." Similarly, Jin Cole of Deerfield, Massachusetts, was said to have been especially discontent as a slave because she was unwilling to forget her days as an African aristocrat.[5]

It is not surprising, then, that African slave merchants preferred to buy bondsmen who had been slaves from their infancy, noting that they made better, stronger, and more docile servants.[6] New World masters agreed, for as Hugh Jones of Virginia explained, "Those Negroes make the best slaves that have been slaves in their own country; for they that have been kings and great men are generally lazy, haughty, and obstinate; whereas the others are sharper, better humored, and more laborious."[7]

But Africans of low as well as high status faced a traumatic period of cultural shock in adjusting to their arrival in America, and for many, one of the first and greatest hardships was the problem of language. Since to be put ashore in New England could easily mean to be separated from all fellow countrymen, newly landed Africans often felt an intense isolation like that suffered by Chloe Spear who, long years after her arrival in Boston, remembered those first lonely days when she constantly "sighed and wished for death."[8] This alienation was also well described by Olaudah Equiano after his arrival in Virginia: "All my companions were distributed different ways and only myself was left. I was now exceedingly miserable and thought myself worse off than any of the rest . . . for they could talk to each other, but I had no person to speak to that I could understand."[9]

African slaves often first communicated with their masters and fellow bondsmen through gestures and signs.[10] At times, this naturally led to confusion, a confusion memorably captured in the New England anecdotal tradition. There was the story, for example, of the newly arrived Caesar Wilcox, who struggled to inform his Connecticut mistress of her husband's death from a fall in the barn. It was said, only after "a long time with help of signs" that he succeeded in imparting his unfortunate message.[11] Similarly, while the Reverend Peter Thatcher's Sambo still could only be communicated with by means of such signs, he ran away, almost dying of exposure in a nearby swamp before he was recaptured. Later, after learning sufficient English, Sambo explained that after seeing the flames in the mouth of Mrs. Thatcher's oven he had been afraid he would be eaten. This story was remembered as particularly funny in Boston, but it is probably literally true. West and Central Africans commonly believed white men to be cannibals who slaked their evil appetites by consuming the victims of the Atlantic slave trade.[12]

Most slaves who had been brought from Africa after infancy soon adopted a variant of English that combined an African grammatical system with an English vocabulary. Like other early observers, Cotton Mather misjudged the reason that this black English varied from standard English. Referring to the story he had received from Boston's Negroes about small-pox inoculation practiced in Africa, he said there were "a number of Africans in this town, who can have no conspiracy to cheat us. No body has instructed them to tell their story. The more plainly, brokenly, and blunderingly, and like idiots, they tell their story, it will be with reasonable men, but the much more credible."[13] The blacks were not speaking English like idiots, but like Africans; and they would have been able to communicate their story with fair success to the wide range of Afro-Americans in the English New World. In relating the manner in which he was first told of African inoculation, Mather also offered a sample of the pidgin English spoken by his "Guramantee-Servant."

> I have since met with a considerable number of these Africans who all agree in one story: that in their country *grandy-many* die of the small-pox. But now they learn this way: people take juice of small-pox; and *cutty-skin*, and put in a drop; then by an by a little *sicky-sicky*, then very few little things like small-pox; and no body die of it; and no body have small-pox any more.[14]

In the more intimate family servitude of New England, slaves picked up a functional grasp of their masters' language faster than elsewhere in the New World. Newspaper notices in New England for runaway slaves often noted that a slave spoke "good English."[15] Many of these blacks were probably native-born New Englanders, like eleven-year-old Hampton, who was advertised as "this country born . . . talks good English," or like twenty-nine-year-old Newport, who was "born in Newport, talks plain."[16] But some who spoke good English were Africans, like twenty-one-year-old London, who had "several negro scars on his face . . . speaks good English."[17] A *Boston Newsletter* advertisement of 1759 offered for sale a likely Negro boy who "has been about twelve months from the coast of Guiney, speaks good English," which apparently proves either that salesmen have not changed or that some young slaves could adapt to the new language quickly. Slaves who were isolated from their owners by living in outbuildings or who labored beside fellow Africans were probably much slower to master the new language. This was the case with twenty-two-year-old Cato, "a Popow Negro, has been in this country for 5 years, talks poor English," and thirty-year-old Jack, who was "not much of a talker."[18]

Some slaves who spoke broken English also spoke other European languages learned in their travels, on the islands off the African coast, or in the West Indies. Thus the "yellowish" Negro Jack could converse in French and Spanish, and a black advertised in 1774 as talking "but little English" contended he was a Portuguese (more likely he was a Cape Verdean), and offered his linguistic skills in evidence. Hamlet, a slave from Middletown, Connecticut, was said to have spoken French, Spanish, German, English, and his native African language; and twenty-two-year-old Dick rounded out the New World colonial background by speaking English "very fluently, also the low Dutch."[19]

For most African immigrants, learning to speak English was a severe trial, as is indicated in the importance of linguistic skills as an identifying device in runaway advertisements. Whether it was New England or Brazil, African runaways were distinguished by their manner of speaking the New World tongue; and New World masters generally agreed with the Reverend James Falconer of Virginia, who contended in 1724 that those "grown up before and carried from their native country . . . are never being able either to speak or understand our language perfectly."[20] Caesar Wilcox of West Simsbury in Connecticut, for example, spoke only a very broken English the fifty-three years he resided in New England; and the African-born Chloe Spear's use of English was said to have been "extremely broken; so much so, that she could never pronounce many words which are in quite common use," and this after some forty years in Boston.[21] The use of a Creole English was sometimes carried over to the second or third generations, although slaves isolated in the households of Yankee families usually moved more rapidly in their assimilation of English.

New slaves who did not learn to speak standard English well may have found it sufficient to communicate with fellow slaves in some form of black English. Moreover, most Africans also retained skills in one or more African languages. Bristol Yamma and John Quamine became assimilated enough to wish to return to Africa as Christian missionaries, yet both Newport blacks maintained their ability to speak their native tongue; in Quamine's case this was after some eighteen years of residence in Rhode Island.[22] Their fellow townsman Newport Gardner continued to speak fluently in his native language well into his eightieth year, keeping up his skills both so that he might receive a mission to Africa and so that he could converse with new arrivals from his homeland.[23] Fanny Saltar's reminiscences of old Daddy Caesar of Philadelphia capture the essence of such northern blacks. "In his dialect," she said, "there was as much African as English."[24]

The black immigrants' inability to speak "correct" English contributed to the opinion among the master class that Africans were stupid, while New World–born blacks, because of their higher level of assimilation, were viewed as more intelligent. As the Virginia House of Burgesses noted in 1699, "Negroes born in this country are generally baptized and brought up in the Christian religion but for Negroes imported hither the gross barbarity and rudeness of their manners, the variety and strangeness of their languages and the weakness and shallowness of their minds renders it in a manner impossible to attain any progress in their conversion."[25] Cotton Mather held to a similar, but more hopeful, opinion in regard to New England's blacks: "They are barbarous. But so were our own ancestors. . . . Christianity will be the best cure for this barbarity. . . . It may seem unto as little purpose to teach, as to wash an Ethiopian. But the greater must be our application."[26]

What did the new slaves think about such prejudices? An insight comes from the remarks of Ka-Le, one of the Africans who in a revolt for liberty took over the slave schooner *Amistad* in 1839. Hearing of the local reaction in New Haven to the *Amistad* case, he informed John Quincy Adams, "Some people say Mendi people crazy, Mendi people dolt, because we no talk American language. Merica people no talk Mendi language; Merica people dolt?"[27]

The immediate problem with a "new Negro," or "Guinea Negro," as they were often called, was occupational training. The adult slave was bought to work; and in New England this meant a wide variety of jobs besides farming or domestic service, since New England's diversified economy required a more skilled and versatile slave population than was needed for the plantation agriculture stressed elsewhere in the Americas. The majority of New England blacks found themselves in service to masters who could afford no more than one or two slaves to aid them in general housework and the running of a small farm or business. Gang labor was rare.

Outside the major cities black bondsmen often possessed a knowledge of all sorts of husbandry and general housework in addition to whatever special skills their owners required of them. Thus, when Colonel James Frye of Andover, Massachusetts, offered a twenty-year-old black for sale in 1770, he noted that the young man was both a good farm hand and skilled in iron work, that is, in "blowing and refining."[28] The prestige value attached to slave ownership was most enhanced by the use of slaves as proper body servants or as liveried coachmen. But in New England even a valet was often required to serve his master with practical labor too, so that a twenty-two-year-old black male offered for sale in Hartford, Connecticut, in March 1766 was thus advertised for his versatility: "can attend gentleman, employed several years making potash at works in Suffield."[29]

Historians have noted the wide range of skilled and unskilled labor roles filled by northern blacks in addition to agricultural and domestic work. A suggestive listing of such jobs would include: anchor maker, baker, barber, blacksmith, bloomer, bookbinder, brick maker, butcher, carpenter, chairmaker, chimney sweep, cook, cooper, ditch digger, distiller, doctor, dye maker, ferryman, fisherman, fox hunter, grocer, iron worker, joyner, mason, miner, nailor, porter, potash maker, pressman, rope maker, sailmaker, sawyer, seaman, sexton, shipwright, shoemaker, stave maker, soap boiler, spinner, tailor, tallow chandler, tanner, teamster, tinker, type setter, washerwoman, watchmaker, weaver, whitesmith, woodsman, and worsted comber. In the major coastal cities large numbers of blacks typically served as common laborers and in many facets of the maritime industry.[30] The acquisition and practice of such labor skills should have accelerated acculturation; if this was the case, the rapid assimilation of northern slaves may, in good part, be explained by their occupational versatility.

An exception to the general New England situation was found around the Narragansett region of Rhode Island, where landowners sometimes employed gangs of from five to forty slaves to tend stock or work in their dairies. Thus, the largest Yankee slaveholder was Newport's Abraham Redwood, a slave merchant who in May 1766 owned 238 slaves. He kept sixty-seven men and twenty-two boys in the field alongside seventy-nine women and fourteen girls. Eighteen of his slaves were too old to work. But the other thirty-eight were tradesmen, mechanics, or household servants displaying the versatility and skilled labor so common among Yankee bondsmen.[31]

Newly arriving Africans and Afro-Americans received industrial and social training in the homes of their first masters; if they learned well and were compatible they were seldom resold. The slaves were taught by example as they labored in shop, house, and field beside their owners. When a master was rich enough or ran a small business, black slaves also sometimes fell under the tutorship of fellow white servants.[32] In either case, new Negroes fresh from Africa required considerable instruction because of the difficulty in communications. The Reverend Ebenezer Parkman noted in his diary that he was not free to perform ministerial duties while his black servant, bought two weeks previously, was new and yet unable to do his work. Similarly, the Reverend Benjamin Colman bemoaned the many hours he spent teaching the African slaves he had purchased.[33] On a daily basis new slaves also learned from white children in the household, a relationship which was often institutionalized in regard to catechismal instruction.[34]

If a master already had slaves, the training and indoctrination of newcomers was usually placed in their hands. In New England this kind of slave acculturation was most common on the extensive farms of eastern Connecticut and in the Narragansett country of Rhode Island. Such training was probably similar to that in the American South, where new Africans were assigned to gangs under reliable, experienced black drivers who taught them a pidgin English and the necessary work skills.

New slaves could learn quickly under fellow blacks because there was not as great a linguistic barrier dividing African languages as there was separating African and European tongues. The general structural similarity in grammar, phonology, and semantics among West African languages meant that only a modicum of English vocabulary was required before the slaves could develop a pidgin black English similar to the trading languages long used on the African coasts.[35] In addition, this training of black by black not only refracted culture through an Afro-American prism; it also effectively mixed particular African traditions into a generalized Afro-American culture. Interaction between Africans and Afro-Americans was also common in New England's cities and villages during holidays and after working hours when the slave population could meet and socialize.

Since masters justified slavery as a school of civilization, it is both ironical and tragic that they retarded the assimilation process by severely restricting the opportunity of black immigrants to share in the most desirable aspects of Euro-American culture. Literacy, for example, had a great attraction for preliterate immigrants; yet throughout the United States, black literacy, the most appropriate tool of acculturation, was either suppressed or restricted. Although many New England slaves were taught to be able to read the Bible, and some to do simple writing and arithmetic, formal education of blacks was slight and primarily for children.[36] The chance of an adult African becoming literate was slim. In addition, many Yankee slave owners may have agreed with Chloe Spear's master, who forbade her instruction, she reported, "under penalty of being suspended by two thumbs, and severely whipped; he said it made Negroes saucy to know how to read."[37]

Those few blacks who attended school were often part-time students. Thus, William J. Brown's African-born grandfather remained an uneducated teamster, but his four children were able to attend school during the winter seasons in late eighteenth-century Rhode Island.[38] Prior to emancipation separate black schools were extremely rare.[39] Jeremy Belknap, one of the founders of the Massachusetts Historical Society, summed up the New England situation well when he noted in 1788 that black children were allowed to attend school in Boston, although he knew of none who exercised the right; and while Belknap contended that by the 1780s many of Boston's Negroes could read and write, he illustrated his point by relating that one of his blacks while at work received a note from another Negro which caused great laughter among the black workers—an implicit comment on Belknap's low level of expectation in regard to general black literacy.[40]

A few Yankee slaves were celebrated by the white community for their successful assimilation. Rhode Islanders were proud to remember that after the teenaged Occramer Marycoo (later known as Newport Gardner) was brought from Africa to Rhode Island in 1760, he taught himself to read after only a few lessons. Gardner became known for his abilities as a composer and as the director of a popular singing school in Newport; he could also cipher, write passable poetry, and speak French, and was highly regarded for his devotion to the Christian faith.[41] The teenaged Phillis Wheatley, another New England slave, won national recognition for her poetry with her first publication in 1770, only nine years after her arrival from Africa, and during the same year she entered into membership of the Old South Meeting House Church in Boston.[42]

Unfortunately, the limited upward mobility possible for a Wheatley or a Gardner was usually effectively denied free blacks. It was not considered threatening for bondsmen to rise to important positions of responsibility superintending their masters' farms, households, or businesses; but white society was hostile to free blacks adopting the same kind of job roles in their own interests; thus whites tried to make certain that freedmen took the menial jobs suited to a subservient caste. In 1831 Alexis de Tocqueville observed an American tradition of long standing in New England. Free blacks, he said, were "deprived of their rights in the midst of a population that is far superior to them in wealth and knowledge, where they are exposed to the tyranny of the laws and the intolerance of the people." Many, he pointed out, perished miserably; the others congregated in the cities, "where they perform the meanest offices and lead a wretched precarious existence."[43] In part, this was because free black shopkeepers and artisans faced obstacles they would not have encountered as slave agents of white masters; as another French traveler, J. P. Brissot de Warville, observed during his 1788 visit to the eastern states, "Those Negroes who keep shops live moderately, and never augment their business beyond a certain point. The reason is obvious; the whites . . . like not to give them credit to enable them to undertake any extensive commerce nor even to give them means of a common education by receiving them into their counting houses."[44]

William Grimes of Connecticut was probably typical in finding it more difficult economically to be a poor free man than a slave. He was twice driven out of business by white competitors who used the courts to advantage against him; moreover, several times he was warned out of town by the selectmen just as he was setting up business in a new city.[45] Poor blacks who migrated to the cities after emancipation were often warned to leave by the selectmen, ostensibly for fear that the newcomers might have to be buried at town expense. In 1791 almost 3 percent of the people warned out of Boston were born in Africa—at a time when only 1 percent of the Massachusetts population was Negro.[46] Some of these unfortunate freedmen, forced to fend for themselves outside of the cities and villages, ended their lives residing in root cellars, shacks, and dugout caves.[47]

Other blacks (mostly males), attracted by the urban centers' potential for economic and social autonomy, stayed on as city residents despite the selectmen's warnings to leave; but they, too, usually had to be satisfied with squalid housing or an old age "retirement" in the poorhouse. In 1742, the shocking truth was that over 7 percent of Boston's total black population were free but living in the almshouse; that is a racially comparative rate more than thirty-six times that of the white population, and if free citizens alone were compared, the rate would be astronomically higher.[48]

Free blacks who migrated to New England's cities lost the protective association with their masters that family slavery had provided. Thus, freedom could often bring a growing insecurity and a lowered potential for material rewards and comforts. In 1717 New London, Connecticut, even went so far as to deny Robert Jacklin, a free man of color, the right to buy any land in the city; it also persuaded the Connecticut colonial assembly to pass a statute to similar effect for the entire colony the following year, although it seems to have been seldom enforced.[49] Emancipation, like slavery, brought a cruel reversal of the American dream. Unlike other immigrant groups, who were remunerated economically and socially for their initiative and perseverance in assimilation, blacks were, more often than not, punished for such behavior by a white community that feared black advancement might threaten the stability of caste relationships.

Masters told themselves that they were fostering a program of positive acculturation to "civilize" their African slaves; in fact, they were restricting black attainment of the mores and values usually associated with Americanization, so that blacks could not share those parts of the American experience that might disqualify them for slavery or turn them away from domestic service and common labor. Whites sometimes recognized there was a problem; but, like Jeremy Belknap, they blamed the black freedmen for being crippled by their servitude: "Too many are impoverished and indolent. . . . Having been educated in families where they had not been used to provide for themselves in youth, they know not how to do it in age."[50] Clearly, the acculturation of New England slaves was not synonymous with Americanization as it is normally understood, for the submissive behavior inculcated into slaves proved a handicap for freedmen facing the competition of open American society. The slavery and racism of New England retarded a full Americanization for the region's blacks by restricting their economic experience and by limiting their mobility, literacy, self-improvement, and personal freedom.

Chapter 5

A Christianity for Slaves

YANKEE masters consoled themselves that in enslaving men they were freeing souls. In a region like New England, where slaves were few and dedicated masters were many, the conversion of black newcomers into good Protestants should have been swift and inclusive. Indeed, as early as 1641, only three years after the arrival of the first African in New England, a slave woman of the Reverend John Stoughton became the first black convert.[1] But surprisingly few conversions followed; after more than a century of slavery and slave proselytizing, the vast majority of New England's blacks were still outside the white churches, unconvinced and unconverted, as the eighteenth century ended.[2]

From the beginning only a tiny minority of blacks had joined the Yankee churches. In 1679 Governor William Leete of Connecticut reported only one-fifteenth of the colony's blacks christened; two generations later, in 1743, the Reverend Samuel Johnson informed the Society for the Propagation of the Gospel, which encouraged missionary work among black slaves, that there were "many unbaptized Negroes about" the area of Stratford, Connecticut. In the 1730s Dean Berkeley of the society noted that in Rhode Island "some few [blacks] are baptized, several frequent the different assemblies, and far the greater part none at all." Forty years later, in much the same vein, Ezra Stiles of Newport noted but seven communicants among the eighty or ninety blacks who attended his church; there were all told, he reported, "not above 30 professors out of twelve hundred Negroes in town."[3] Thus when the American Revolution arrived, less than 3 percent of Newport's blacks were Christians in good standing, while another

25 percent or so may have at least attended church. The situation was probably better in the small towns of New England, but nowhere was the record impressive.

In part, as we shall see in the next chapter, the reasons for this perplexing differential between New England's high potential for Christianizing black immigrants and its slender achievements began with the African immigrants themselves; but equally important was the way in which Protestant Christianity was offered to the new Americans. From the masters' perspective the religion preached to slaves sanctified the Yankee social system by emphasizing the servant's duty to obey; it was not until the slaves came to know scripture better that they found the Christian message could just as easily justify their own world view. But since the masters' interpretation remained the orthodox view as expressed from the pulpit throughout most of the eighteenth century, slaves seldom found church membership enticing.

At the beginning of the eighteenth century many New England slave owners, like their fellow English colonials, opposed the Christianization of Negroes. A few held that Africans were not intelligent enough to be converted, that they were an inferior breed unworthy of God's covenant. Such a view confused culture with intellect, as can be seen in the observation of the Virginia House of Burgesses near the beginning of the century: "For Negroes imported hither the gross barbarity and rudeness of their manners, the variety and strangeness of their languages and the weakness and shallowness of their minds render it in a manner impossible to attain any progress in their conversion."[4] Some masters attempted to disguise materialism with morality by arguing that since Christians could not lawfully enslave their peers, the conversion of bondsmen (but not slavery itself) was improper. Other slave owners openly contended that conversion was inadvisable because the education and status that came with Christianity would simply ruin good slaves by making them proud, saucy, and rebellious.[5] Such overt opposition to Christian training passed, but the economic interests and racial prejudices that had fostered it remained.

From the first, Cotton Mather had seen the danger that racial prejudice could taint the Christian message. In 1702 he cautioned his congregation against their tendency to despise the souls of their black servants; but such prejudice had not abated in 1743 when the Consociated (Old Light) ministers of Connecticut met in Bolton to decide that a vote in church discipline should not be given to either slaves who had otherwise been accepted as "savingly converted" and worthy of communion or males under twenty-one. In 1774 the Hartford *Connecticut Courant* summed up the continuing effects of Yankee prejudice: "Nothing is more common than for men to treat the Negroes, and to speak of them in the most contemptuous manner, as tho' they did not belong to the same species."[6]

Even in Christian worship New England's blacks were treated as second-class citizens. On their way to Sunday services black servants were expected to follow their masters at a respectful distance; once in church they found themselves segregated from other parishioners. Blacks were not allowed to sit at the altar rail; commonly their pews were raised in the rear of the church, in a porch, belfry, or attic gallery "on the beams," or even in "a pen near the ceiling." In at least one church, sensibilities were carried to such an extreme that the black gallery was boarded up "so that the Negroes would see no one and be seen by none." The location of the black pews at the rear of the church helped foster another demeaning practice—the serving of communion to blacks only after all other parishioners had finished.[7] Such separation and second-class citizenship hindered the conversion of black worshipers. As the African-born Chloe Spear of Boston remembered, the seats assigned to blacks were remote from the view of the congregation; since Spear and her friends did not understand the preaching, the young women took no interest in it, and instead spent their time playing, eating nuts, and enjoying other diversions.[8]

One reason that white New Englanders may not have paid more attention to the dismal record of black conversion is that less than one-half of Yankee whites were regular in church attendance, and fewer still "owned the covenant" as church members.[9] New Englanders never expected all men to be regenerate; they only required all citizens to be members in a Christian commonwealth, open to the possibility of conversion, and bound by a code of Christian conduct. It was enough for most masters to educate slaves with the essentials of the Christian message and to expect them to hew to the line of proper conduct. More than that would be more than they asked even of themselves.

Formal missionary work among New England's blacks was begun by John Eliot in the late seventeenth century. The Anglican Church's Society for the Propagation of the Gospel in Foreign Parts continued this missionary tradition in the eighteenth century, as did the Associates of

Dr. Bray, who founded a school for Negroes in Newport in 1760.[10] But neither the society nor Dr. Bray was a prime mover in converting congregational New England's slave population. Most conversions came through the work of individual ministers, families, or black Christians consulting informally with slaves they knew well.

Eighteenth-century New Englanders believed that slavery was part of God's plan for evangelicalism. Few would have taken the part of Judge Samuel Sewall, who argued that regarding the slave trade "evil must not be done, that good may come from it." Instead, most would have agreed with Judge John Saffin, who held the commerce in Africans to be virtuous because "it is no evil thing to bring them out of their own heathenish country [to] where they may have the knowledge of the True God, be converted and eternally saved."[11] Black New Englanders, of course, probably would have questioned Saffin's argument as a convenient hypocrisy, but once converted they apparently took a somewhat middle ground—albeit one which excluded any honor to the whites. As the African-born Chloe Spear explained, "[Whites] meant [the slave trade] for evil, but God meant it for good. To his name be the glory."[12]

Clearly, the immorality of slavery does not seem to have been recognized by most Yankee clergy, for most kept one or two household slaves.[13] Congregations often took up collections to purchase black servants for their ministers, and Andrew Eliot was unusual in refusing the gift unless the Negro were an indentured servant rather than a slave. Indeed, Eliot's radical idea so offended the sensibilities of his friends that they refused him the gift of a servant altogether.[14]

In Massachusetts, Cotton Mather defined the proper role for the conscientious slaveholding minister. In regard to his black servant Obidiah in 1718, he noted that "my Savior has committed him unto me, that I may bring him up to be a servant of the Lord." Indeed, Mather chided himself for less than full devotion to "exquisite endeavors for the instructing and restraining" of Obidiah.[15] Unfortunately many ministers fell short of the ideal, losing Christian patience and mistreating their servants. No doubt Mather would have considered the outcomes of these fallings away from grace as divine judgements.

When Parson Hall of Meriden, Connecticut, whipped one of his five slaves on a Sunday before church, his Sunday labor cost him a hay rick, which was burnt in revenge after the parson had left for his ministerial duties. Similarly, in 1764 the Reverend Leawitt of Walpole, New Hampshire, was dismissed from his parish after leading his runaway slave woman back home by a rope attached to his saddle and tied around her neck. By selling two feeble, old slaves who soon became town charges, the Reverend Nathan Webb of Uxbridge, Massachusetts, caused a committee of the Massachusetts General Court to propose legislation to forbid the disposing of elderly slaves by those who intended thereby to avoid the cost of keeping them.[16]

Most of New England's clergymen seem to have worked conscientiously to bring their black charges into the Christian flock. But since there were few green pastures or still waters in the Christianity preached to bondsmen, Yankee ministers were not above using the shadow of death as a theme for conversion. When a smallpox scare swept Boston in 1721, Mather saw it as an opportunity: "My *African* Servant, stands a candidate for Baptism, and is afraid how the Small-Pox, if it spread, may handle him. I must on this occasion use very much Application to bring him into a thorough Christianity." Chloe Spear similarly noted how her first serious impression of religion came when a young friend was dying.[17]

When the Reverend Edward Fells of Cromwell, Connecticut, recorded his baptisms, the first and last were those of Negro slaves, and the years between contained the names of his own black servants as well. Such dedication was probably typical, but even committed ministers were unable to greatly accelerate the process of conversion. In 1731 New London's Eliphant Adams was given a slave by his friends, but it was not until seven years later that Adams had his five black servants baptized and engaged for their Christian education. The Reverend Ezra Stiles worked twelve years with his slave Newport, who arrived from Africa in 1763 as a ten-year-old boy, before admitting him to full communion.[18]

The baptism of black slave children posed a difficult problem to the Yankee clergy because while the children were clearly part of the Christian family of their masters, the young candidates could not themselves be "federally holy" since their parents were native Africans or Afro-Americans living as heathens outside the Christian covenant. In 1722 Cotton Mather handled this question traditionally; only after Mather's slave Ezer was received into the church did Mather write to the Reverend Thomas Prince informing him that Ezer's child, lately born into the Prince family, was now "humbly recommended unto the Christian Baptism with you."[19]

But since this was not a workable solution for most slave children, the General Association of the Colony of Connecticut decided in 1738 that infant slaves of Christian masters could be baptized by right of their masters' covenants with God, and that such Christian masters had a responsibility to baptize their slave children and further their Christian education. In 1741 the church at Medfield, Massachusetts, pondered the same question—whether black children whose parents were outside the covenant could be baptized in light of their masters' grace—and again decided that they could be. Thirty-one years later in Rhode Island, the Reverend Ezra Stiles confirmed such decisions on the parish level when he baptized a black child whose parents were not baptized but whose master was. Such decisions on infant baptism point out the seriousness with which New Englanders took the responsibility and relationships of household slavery, since theologically a man's slave child belonged to the master's family rather than to the child's biological parents.[20]

In the English colonies adult slaves were required to demonstrate both a Christian demeanor and theological knowledge before baptism. In the southern colonies the test of baptismal knowledge for a slave usually included the ability to repeat the Lord's Prayer, the Creed, and the Ten Commandments or the Catechism.[21] But in New England ministers required more than memorization; as Cotton Mather proposed, "It is to be desired, that the *Negroes* may not learn to say their *Catechism* only by rote, like Parrots; but their instructors may put unto them such other Questions relating to the points of *Catechism*, that by their Answers (at least of Yes or No) it may be perceived, that they *Know* what they say." The black church members of New England had to give a good account of the hope for conversion that was in them as well as evidence that their everyday lives were in accord with Christian principles.[22]

Instruction of household slaves came during the period of family prayers, when all the household joined together for religious devotion. In addition, slaves were often taught to read the Bible during time set aside for religious instruction. Cotton Mather suggested to Yankee masters that Sundays be especially reserved for the religious improvement of their servants by "such means of Instruction, as may be afforded unto them." And although some masters may have agreed with the Cranston, Rhode Island, slave owner who worked his slave Sharpener in an iron mine on Sundays, explaining "there is but few negroes troubled with religion and no first days to furnaces," it was, nonetheless, common in Christian families to catechize slaves at Sunday noon, often questioning them over the morning sermon.[23] Harriet Beecher Stowe remembered joining such a typical domestic catechism lesson. The young Harriet sat at her aunt's knee along with her little cousin Mary to receive Christian instruction; black Dinah and Harry, the bound boy, were ranged at a "respectful distance" behind. Stowe's aunt always impressed upon her servants "to order themselves lowly and reverently to all their betters," and it was this portion of the catechism that always pleased Stowe as a girl because it insured the servants calling her "Miss Harriet."[24]

The informality of household instruction was reinforced by the more formal attentions of Yankee clergymen. Ministers like Cotton Mather and John Usher commonly inquired into the conduct of their black parishioners, continually urging them onward in the Christian life. Ministers also catechized groups of Negroes, preaching special sermons to the black members of their congregations and lecturing to black religious and social associations.[25] Night gatherings where local blacks would meet at a minister's house for a sermon and prayer were popular with slaves because they afforded an unusual opportunity to meet and socialize. Even religious meetings, however, could cause problems with white prejudice. Samuel Hopkins reported in 1780 that "a considerable number" of Negroes attended his Sunday evening lectures "and behave so well that the whites who are . . . present can't but speak in their favor." But this he feared would make many enemies, some whites apparently feeling that decorous blacks might mistake their place in society.[26]

The social aspects of Christian fellowship at first must have been more attractive to potential converts than the theology preached to the servant population. The religion tendered slaves was not the Weberian Puritanism of the protestant ethic; instead, slave religion inculcated servility and Augustinian acceptance of menial status and submission to authority. In New England, as throughout the United States, Protestant Christianity was presented to slaves as a defense of the status quo.[27]

Christianity, as Cotton Mather noted in his *Catechism for Negroes*, made better servants, since blacks who knew God would also know their proper place.[28] The original rules of the Negro Society of Boston, written under the guidance of Mather, reveal the essentials of the Christianity offered to most of New England's black church members.

IV. Wee will, as often as may bee, obtain some wise and good Man, of the *English* in the Neighborhood; and especially the *Officers* of the Church to look in upon us, and by their Presence and Council, do what they think fitting for us.

V. If any of our Number fall into the sin of *Drunkenness*, or *Swearing*, or *Cursing* or *Lying*, or *Stealing*, or notorious *Disobedience* or *Unfaithfulness* to their Masters, wee will *admonish* him of his Miscarriage. . . .

VII. Wee will, as wee have Opportunity, sett ourselves, to do all the good wee can to the other *Negro-Servants* in the Town; and if any of them should *run away* from their Masters, wee will afford them *no shelter;* but wee will do what in us *lies*, that they may bee discovered and punished. . . .

VIII. None of our Association, shall be *absent*, from our Meeting, without giving a *Reason* of the Absences; and it bee found that any have pretended unto their *Owners*, that they came unto Meeting, when they were otherwise and elsewhere emplo'd, wee will faithfully *inform* their owners. . . .[29]

In answer to Mather's proposed catechism, the Negro who wished to serve Christ would reply, "I must love God, and Pray to Him, and Keep the Lord's Day. I must Love all Men, and never Quarrel, nor be drunk, nor be unchast, nor steal, nor tell a ly, nor be discontent with my condition."[30]

The sermons of Yankee clergymen to their black congregations continually evoked the servant-master relationship. When Ezra Stiles preached to eighty or ninety blacks who met in his home in Newport during 1772, he lectured on Luke 14:7–24, the parable of the great supper. In the text the poor were called as well as the rich, but only those who were willing to give up worldly concerns were chosen. Thus Stiles was able to present both the universal message of Christian salvation and the particular message of passivity preached especially to slaves. The condescending flavor of many of these special lectures is also preserved in a fragment from Parson Jonathan Ashley's evening lectures to the Negroes of Deerfield, Massachusetts, in 1749. Ashley saw the blacks as poor, ignorant, and despised:

> On the other hand there are some who are ready to think God will not have mercy on them because they are such poor miserable creatures. It may be they are poor and despised, and will *God* think on *them* the world will take no notice of? Or it may be they are ignorant and can't know and understand like other men . . . or it may be they think they are servants and they han't time or advantages, and they are such poor creatures that it is not likely they shall ever obtain mercy. But let us take notice of the riches of grace to the children of men.

The poor may be rich in faith and heirs of Glory. The ignorant may understand and know God in Christ, whilst the wise perish in their own understanding. Servants who are at the dispose and command of others, who it may be are despised in the world, may be the Lord's freemen and heirs of Glory.[31]

Even preaching the equality of the human condition under God, slave-owning divines like the Reverend Ashley never meant to claim equality of condition in this world. The whites' emphasis on obedience rather than freedom in God compounded the already difficult process of achieving slave conversions.

Nonetheless, in Christianity black slaves sometimes found an explanation that gave solace for the injustices of bondage. When Chloe Spear felt herself unjustly treated, she found consolation in the hope of a redress from the higher power of God. Indeed, her favorite Bible verse was Psalms 71:4: "Deliver me, oh my God, out of the hand of the wicked, out of the hand of the unrighteous and cruel man." For her, the Bible was clear. In the next world social status would be reversed; cruel masters would be punished and their humble servants would be exalted. Thus, when she explained herself in metaphor—"Brudder, don't you know, when anybody bow to me, I always *drop*"—we must not see pride in subservience so much as preparation for revenge. Other slaves probably saw in the yearly foot-washing ceremony observed in local churches a promise of the life to come, as the whites were momentarily humbled into washing the feet of their black servants. Christianity clearly promised that though a chosen few might be asked to endure great suffering, they would have a day of final redemption.[32]

Those blacks who were converted to Christianity worked hard to convince their fellows of the wisdom of following the religious path, although very few were permitted to become active preachers during the colonial and revolutionary eras. In a letter to her friend Obour Tanner of Newport, Phillis Wheatley represented the interest of her fellow black Christians in observing, "it gives me great pleasure to hear of so many of my nation, seeking with eagerness the way to true felicity." Ezra Stiles recorded a typical effort of these black Christians when he reported in his diary the death of Phyllis, a slave of the Rhode Island governor, Josiah Lyndon.

This day died Phyllis a Negro Sister of our church: I hope she had chosen the better part. Her Husband Brother Zingo, upon becoming religious and joyning my church, had an earnest Concern for his Wife and Children, and labored greatly to bring her into a saving Acquaintance with her Redeemer; and I doubt not his Endeavors and prayers were blessed to her saving conversion. She was brought hither out of Guinea in 1759 aet. 13 or 14, and has lived in Gov. Lyndon's Family ever since. She was always free from the common Vices—and expecially since her profession has walked soberly and exemplarly.[33]

Often the principal actor in a slave conversion was the slave himself. The slave John Quamine (or Quamino), for example, not only became a Christian but dedicated the rest of his life to an attempt to bring Christianity back to his African homeland. Quamine was brought to Rhode Island from Anomabu on the Gold Coast in 1754 or 1755 at about ten years of age. In 1761, about seven years after his arrival in New England, "he fell under serious Impressions of Religion," according to the Reverend Ezra Stiles, "and thenceforward sought to God by secret prayer about three years. At length it pleased God that he experienced as he hopes a divine change." Since he would not learn to write until 1772, Quamine dictated a formal account of his experience to a female fellow servant; after presenting the paper to Madam Osborn (possibly his owner), he offered a copy to Deacon Coggeshall for consideration. In 1765, more than ten years after his arrival in New England and two years after what he felt was his conversion, Quamine made his Christian profession formally in church, and was baptized by the Reverend Inall and admitted to membership in the First Congregational Church of Newport.

After purchasing his freedom, Quamine visited the Reverend Ezra Stiles in 1773 to be examined as a candidate for an African mission. Stiles judged him unready because of his poor ability to read scripture, a decision that points out white New England's overestimation of sermons and scripture in the conversion process. Quamine retained his Fanti tongue, and the English-educated Fanti missionary Philip Quaque confirmed Quamine's family connections were still strong on the Gold Coast; nonetheless, the ethnocentric Stiles assumed all conversion should be done New England style. Quamine died in 1779 on a privateer attempting to win prize money to redeem his wife from slavery, and a great missionary opportunity was lost. Yet in the personal history of this man is reflected both the arduous process of Christianization facing Africans in Protestant New England and the commitment of black Christians to their faith and their people.[34]

In New England those blacks who accepted Christianity often took their own initiative in forming religious welfare societies. Cotton Mather condescendingly recorded in his diary that in December 1693 "a company of poor Negroes, of their own accord, addressed me, for my Countenance, to a design which they had, of erecting such a meeting for the welfare of their miserable nation that were servants among us."[35] Such Afro-American societies were probably partially shaped by the memory of traditional African mutual aid associations, but to win acceptance by the master class, New England's black associations had to be connected to religious activities. At a time before black churches were permitted, these African societies offered a semblance of religious autonomy as well as practical social benefits.

It was odd for a Boston Negro to be offered for sale in 1734 for joining a "rascally club of Negroes," because black societies were generally formed by an elite, described by the Salem minister William Bentley as "many grades above the common blacks."[36] This was the case in 1742 in Gloucester, Massachusetts, where the Reverend John White reported that the members of the local religious society of Negroes were baptized members of the church.[37]

Black Masonry began in 1755, when Prince Hall, a member of the Congregational Church of Boston and later a Methodist minister, attempted with some fellow blacks to seek admission to the St. Andrew Masonic Lodge of Boston; denied membership, they applied to the Grand Lodge of England for a warrant to set up an independent lodge, which they received in 1787. Although African Lodge 459 remained isolated by the prejudice of white lodges, it generated the fellowship of Negro Masonry in the United States, and in 1799 issued a warrant to the blacks of Providence, Rhode Island, to form another black chapter.[38]

In 1780 a group of Newport, Rhode Island, blacks had met at the home of Abraham Casey to form the Newport African Union Society for the physical and moral welfare of Newport's Negro citizenry; they reorganized in 1783 at the home of Newport Gardner to form a religious society and then turned toward becoming a separate church. Six years later in 1789, Samuel Hopkins characterized them as "a number of religious blacks . . . who wish to be formed into a distinct church or religious society, and to have a black appointed pastor"—an ambition they later achieved as the nucleus of the black Union Congregational Church of Newport.[39] The blacks of

Providence, Rhode Island, also formed an African society, which then supported an emigration scheme to Africa; and in 1792 and 1796 African societies were likewise begun in Boston with forty-four and forty-six members respectively. By the turn of the century many of these African societies, like the Newport group, became active in formally instituting the separate black churches that their social organizations had already implied.[40]

However, such black religious organizations were the exceptions rather than the rule. Most black Yankees were not members in good standing with any Christian group. Neither did the proselytizing efforts of black or white believers make significant headway in colonial New England. The general failure of New England to produce a black Christian community in the eighteenth century resulted from a blind and overbearing ethnocentrism. Slave owners piously denied their bondsmen opportunity to practice the pagan beliefs so feared and despised by Christian overseers, but offered no satisfactory alternative because slaves were rarely permitted to achieve the level of acculturation needed to appreciate the highly literate Protestantism of New England.[41]

The black subculture was considered by white New Englanders to be at or near the bottom of the social scale. Slaves had little time for the refinements of upper-class life or the bourgeois style of the middle class; in general the social environment of hard labor, enforced ignorance, and poverty proved more powerful than the efforts of individual masters, ministers, and Christian blacks. This, indeed, was the conclusion of Newport Gardner, who in his old age supported a return to Africa because the young people of the Negro race, he said, "can never be elevated here. I have tried it for sixty years . . . it is in vain."[42]

New England's blacks were frustrated by the hypocrisy of their Christian slave masters. In petitioning for release from bondage, a group of Boston Negroes argued that without freedom, even the most religious black Christians had little to gain from their efforts in this world. "How many of that number have there been and now are in this Province, who have had every day of their lives embittered with this intolerable Reflection that, let their behavior be what it will, neither they, nor their children to all generations, shall ever be able to do, or to possess and enjoy anything, no not even life *itself*, but in a Manner as the beasts that perish."[43]

In the end, New Englanders failed to convert more than a tiny minority of their slaves because the Protestant churches were unwilling to accommodate their preconceptions of religion to those brought by their African bondsmen. It was not so much that Yankee masters did not tell their servants about Christianity, but that the Christianity they offered was self-serving and neither emotionally nor intellectually satisfying to most Africans and Afro-Americans.

Part 3

The Blending of Traditions

Chapter 6
The Great Awakening: What Might Have Been

T HE conversion of black New Englanders to Protestant Christianity would have come more easily and rapidly if the white master class had presented their religious instruction, ceremonies, and preaching in a style more congenial to African religious practices. African immigrants were in many ways apt candidates for religious conversion. Religion was a pervasive part of their everyday lives, and almost all traditional African institutions and actions were deeply imbued with religious meanings. African ethics often paralleled Christian mores; and many African concepts of good and evil, of spirits, the soul, and of God could be reconciled with similar Yankee beliefs. Moreover, such reconciliation of religious differences was common among West Africans, who traditionally accommodated new deities possessing power or other useful attributes.

Many of the newly arriving immigrants were thus eager to gain the good graces, the rewards, and the protection offered by the Christian god. Unlike the disciples of the Judeo-Christian god, who rejected all other religious ideas as false, Africans believed other peoples would naturally worship gods of their own countries. Excluding the Muslims among them, most African immigrants were therefore reconciled to making some religious accommodations in the New World.

Afro-Americans were also ripe for religion because, by promising justice in the next world, Christianity presented a message of hope for the downtrodden. As black preacher Jupiter Hammon assured his New York brethren in 1787, "Our slavery will be at an end, and though ever so mean, low, and despised in this world, we shall sit with God in his Kingdom as Kings and Priests, and rejoice forever." In the New World, Christianity offered slaves an approved institution of status and cultural cohesion, one that could give a legal outlet for many of the emotional and social needs of the black community.[1]

From the beginning, New England's ministers unintentionally discouraged black religious participation by emphasizing the preached gospel over the music and psalmody so attractive to their black parishioners. When Newport's Ezra Stiles let his black congregation sing, he noted "they sang very well," but he was more satisfied in recording that his meetings were "very serious and devout."[2] A more perceptive minister might have noticed that the slaves found the musical activities the most attractive and meaningful feature of the services. The Reverend Samuel Davies of Virginia struck a cultural chord when he recognized that local blacks were especially fond of Watts's *Psalms and Hymns*. "I cannot but observe," he reported, "that the Negroes, above all the human species I ever knew, have an ear for music, and a kind of ecstatic delight in Psalmody; and there are no books they learn so soon, or take so much pleasure in, as those used in that part of the divine worship."[3]

Psalmody not only permitted illiterate bondsmen to participate immediately by having a leader read the psalms line by line for the congregation to follow; it also comfortably paralleled the African call-and-response manner of singing. Moreover, since there was no printed music, black congregations could improvise within the limits allowed by the white clergy so that the effect was, as Samuel Davies reported from Virginia, "a torrent of sacred harmony, enough to bear away the whole congregation to heaven."[4] Psalmody thus had enormous potential as an aid to conversion.

In almost all other areas of religious practice, the spare New England style of religiosity inhibited the transfer or transformation of African beliefs and practices into corresponding Christian rituals. In the Catholic Americas, black newcomers often achieved a cultural accommodation by placing African deities and beliefs under a pantheon of nominal Catholic ritual and form, and Indians were permitted to respond to attractive verbal and behavioral forms introduced by the Jesuits long before learning their deeper meanings. In New England there were few opportunities for similar syncretisms.[5]

Had Yankee ministers changed their style to place greater emphasis on psalm singing, communal catechizing, and emotional give and take between minister and congregation, the results of their work with Afro-Americans would have been more successful. In New York, for example, the Reverend Elias Neau noted that by adding psalm singing to his Negro services in 1707 he greatly encouraged black interest, with blacks competing to be the best singers.[6] A similar report by the Reverend George Wilson Bridges from early nineteenth-century Jamaica suggests why the revival pattern of preaching engendered during New England's Great Awakening had so much greater impact on the black population than did the more typical stolid sermons of the local clergy. Bridges noted that the sectarians of Jamaica, "aware of the power of melody over the Negro mind, have introduced vocal music amongst their congregation with peculiar effect: for so susceptible are the Africans of the influence of that art . . . that they will scarcely give any attention to a religious speaker who possesses a harsh or discordant voice." Bridges also reported that when the largest parish obtained an organ, "the negroes left the dissenting chapels; and deserted even the Sunday market; their attention was fixed on the service, and the public registers proved, that during the ten months which followed the revival of a neglected form of worship, the conversions to Christianity were more numerous than ever, and the rites of marriage more frequently applied for."[7] But in New England where organs were few, the black population continued to find more enjoyment and release in Sunday markets and amusements than in Sunday services.[8]

Given their Puritan heritage, it is not surprising that New Englanders never considered altering the forms of their religious institutions to accommodate the African immigrants; nonetheless, inadvertently they achieved somewhat the same results during the fiery Great Awakening of the 1730s and 1740s, when an emotional style of preaching appeared that more closely approximated the religious patterns to which Afro-Americans were predisposed. Across New England, believers responding to New Light preachers like Jonathan Edwards and George Whitefield manifested their faith in overt physical and vocal responses such as screeching, fainting, convulsions, visions, and possession by the holy spirit. The cold, inhibited

Yankee style of religion was momentarily transformed as the Awakening emphasized felt religion and opened the possibility of conversion without so much attention to doctrinal niceties or closely scrutinized preparation.[9]

In moving the emphasis of conversion from an intellectual catechism to a more immediate emotional response, the Great Awakening created a Christianity better suited to the slave population. Preliterate African immigrants and illiterate or barely literate second generation Afro-Americans lacked the education and religious tradition to make an easy conversion to New England's Calvinistic Christianity. But when the emphasis changed, allowing a more emotional response, members of New England's black community became better candidates for conversion. African immigrants, whose traditional religions included possession patterns somewhat similar to revival Christianity's, found the new religious style more familiar, while Afro-Americans suffering the repressions of bondage were psychologically refreshed by the emotional outlet of New Light enthusiasm.[10]

Reflecting on the Awakening of New England, Jonathan Edwards noted "many of the poor Negroes also have been . . . wrought upon and changed," a striking phenomenon also observed by the traveling revivalists, the so-called Grand Itinerants of the revival circuit. George Whitefield, a leader of the revivalists, had quickly discovered that American Negroes were exceedingly moved by his preaching. Gilbert Tennent found the same to be true of his own ministry; in a letter to Whitefield in April of 1741, Tennent proudly reported that at Charlestown, Massachusetts, "multitudes were awakened, and several received great consolation, especially among the young people, children, and Negroes." At the same time, James Davenport was converting 100 people in Stonington, Connecticut, doing especially prodigious work among the blacks there. In 1742, Boston's fiery Presbyterian, John Moorhead, noted the special effect of the Awakening on hitherto resistant groups: "I can't express the wonderful things God is doing and has already manifested amongst Indians, Negroes, Papists, and Protestants of all Denominations."[11]

Part of the New Light success in converting the black population was due to the inclusiveness of the preachers' appeal, a sincere invitation which in great measure also accounts for the later success of Methodist and Baptist evangelizing among the black populations of the North and South.[12] It was this aspect of George Whitefield's ministry that inspired Phillis Wheatley in her eulogy on the death of George Whitefield. Whitefield, she recalled, offered hope to the black nation saying, "Take him, ye Africans, he longs for you; Impartial Savior is his title due."[13]

But it was more than the opening of Christianity to the lower orders and the less educated that gave Whitefield success among his black converts. Whitefield accepted and encouraged an emotional response that was in resonance to traditional African and Afro-American religious patterns. Black response to revival Christianity was African, not in theology, but in physical, emotional, and cultural style. The Awakening permitted a religious response that helped bridge the cultural gap between African and English religious styles. Both new slaves and American-born blacks found revival Christianity better suited to their primarily oral culture and to their native religious heritage than the traditionally more literate and reserved forms of Protestant Christianity. This internal resonance was reinforced by the external democratic appeal of the Great Awakening.

The freer expression of the Great Awakening allowed New England blacks to respond in a style closer to the ecstatic spirituality common to Afro-American folk religions. Both black and white observers noticed the strong physical manifestations of black folk worship. Two Virginia descriptions can serve as examples: "Their religious services are wild, and at times almost raving." "They commonly are more noisy in time of preaching than the whites, and are more subject to bodily exercise, and if they meet with any encouragement in these things, they grow extravagant."[14]

New England's anecdotal tradition has preserved a feeling for the black response to revival preaching. It was said that in 1742, during Massachusetts's Great Awakening, the Reverend Peter Thatcher's African servant, Sambo, joined the First Church of Middleboro. Learning that the Reverend George Whitefield was to be in Plymouth, Sambo was said to have walked twenty miles to hear the famous preacher. Unfortunately, Whitefield did not appear, and an itinerant of lesser lights replaced him on the pulpit. During the service Sambo was very affected and he cried out so loudly that one of the deacons asked him to be still. Sambo was said to have replied, "I cannot be still; Massa Whitefield preach so, he nearly break my heart." "But," said the deacon, "it is not Whitefield." "Not Massa Whitefield? Den I hab made all dis hubbubboo for nothing."[15]

This anecdote was remembered by white New Englanders for its lampooning of what many whites felt was the emotional excess of the black religious response to the Awakening. It seemed a source of humor to whites that black Christians found the emotional participation of the congregation as important as the message of the preached word. And while the anecdote was meant as a satire, it contains, like many another traditional anecdote, more than a grain of truth in its assertion that for Yankee slaves the form of the religion was as important as its content.

New England's Negroes found the Christianity of the Great Awakening in tune with their own assumptions about the proper style for religious celebrations. As the Reverend Whitefield had noted, Yankee blacks were "exceedingly wrought upon," and "in an uncommon manner" by the revival preaching. The Reverend Eleazer Wheelock also recorded in his diary of November 1741 the marked response with which local Negroes reacted to his message.

> To Taunton Massachusetts. Preached there, Job XXVII/8, one or two cried out. Appointed another meeting in the evening, Hos. XIII/13. I believed 30 cried out; almost all the negroes in town wounded, 3 or 4 converted. A great work in the town . . . Col. Leonard's negro in such distress that it took 3 men to hold him. I was forced to break off my sermon before I had done, the outcry was so great.

The same year the Reverend Williams of Lebanon, Connecticut, likewise found the blacks a peculiarly affected audience, with "a great many groaning and crying out."[16]

The emotional agitation of black Christians probably differed from that of whites in both physical motor patterns and intention; where possession in the European pattern usually prescribed a swoon, trance, vision, or disability, among Africans and Afro-Americans possession more often meant convulsive motion or dancing.[17] Many Afro-Americans doubtless responded to revival Christianity by blending in African practices of vocal call and response and possession—practices which in their traditional forms were unacceptable to Euro-American sensibilities. As the Reverend Isaac Browne of Brookhaven, New York, sarcastically noted in 1743, the blacks "who were lately called Heathens, seem many of them now to be a miraculous compound of Paganism and Methodism."[18] The Reverend Joseph Travis of Wilmington, North Carolina, reflected the generality of white response to this Africanization of religion when, a century later, he warned of the dangers of what was clearly an African possession pattern.

I make it a point to guard them against fanatical expressions, or wild, enthusiastic gestures. On one occasion, I took a summary process with a certain black woman, who, in their love-feast, with many extravagant gestures, cried out that she was 'young King Jesus.' I bade her take her seat and then publicly read her out of membership, stating that we would not have such wild fanatics among us.[19]

So great was the excitement among the lower orders in New England that the Reverend H. A. Brockwell complained to the secretary of the Society for the Propagation of the Gospel that "the very Servants and Slaves pretend to extraordinary inspiration, and under the veil thereof cherish their idle disposition and . . . run rambling about to utter enthusiastic nonsense."[20] Charles Chauncy, Jonathan Edwards's chief antagonist, also lamented the growth of so many exhorters, arguing that the Awakening led to a perversion of religious response; things were so bad, he complained, that "young *Persons*, sometimes *Lads*, or rather *Boys:* Nay *Women* and *Girls;* yes *Negroes*, have taken upon themselves to do the Business of Preachers."[21] One Negro who did just that was advertised as a runaway in the *Boston Weekly News-Letter* in July 1742; he was identifiable by being "very forward to mimick some of the strangers that have of late been preaching among us."[22] It sometimes seemed to the conservatives that the worst fears of Brockwell and Chauncy had come true, and the old Antinomian heresy had returned in a black light whereby slaves in a state of grace thought themselves above the laws of their masters. The Reverend Jacob Eliot recorded in his diary such horrible effects of the New Light in Lebanon, Connecticut:

Tisdel's correcting his servant (for lying &c) & his brother & a maid in the house justifying of him and condemning ye Master, crying out what a vile thing it was for a Reprobate to correct a child of God—what would they come to—of Bristol's stealing—Flora's getting drunk & Webster's Caesar exhorting at Smith's & then attempting to lie with an Indian woman telling her to entice her to commit Lewdness with him that Hell was not so dreadful a place as had been described, neither was it so difficult to get to heaven as he had set forth.[23]

Despite the Awakening, black preachers remained a novelty in New England. The revivals had given blacks the opportunity to hear the calling;

but society only permitted them to take advantage of the opening in small numbers. The Boston *Gazette* reported in April of 1765 that one Negro converted by Whitefield "preached to crowded audiences," but it was more typical for black ministers to take up missionary work since the opportunity to gain a stable parish in New England was slight. One of the black converts of Lorenzo Dow became a preacher in the West Indies, and four Rhode Island blacks were trained in the Episcopal faith for a possible return to Africa as missionaries.[24] While the egalitarian implications in Protestant Christianity were never more apparent in New England than during the Great Awakening, the movement was still unable to reverse the growing trend toward racial separation. Although the black minister Thomas Paul was soon able to preach to the First Baptist Meeting of Salem, his own Third Baptist Meeting of Boston remained unrecognized by Boston's white Baptists.[25]

The Great Awakening had quickened black interest in Christianity just as it had the interest of white New Englanders, but by the end of 1743 the emphasis on emotional response was passing, and with it passed the opportunity for a syncretic Afro-American pattern within northern Protestantism. Instead, New England blacks had to continue to conform to the religious demeanor defined as pious and correct by their masters, a restriction that seriously impeded a transference of traditional African religious response to a Christian setting. It frustrated the revivalist James Davenport, for example, that his "new Negro" Flora was deeply affected by Eleazer Wheelock's sermon but unable to "give but a broken account" of her religious experience.[26] In general, Yankee clergymen were unable to adjust their highly intellectualized attitudes about conversion to the changing realities of the nonliterate, emotional appeal of Awakening religion. Thus New England developed a style of response well adapted to fostering the religious acculturation of black slaves, but never realized its potential.

Ministers, however, did notice the positive effects of emotionalizing their sermons and improving the vocal qualities of their deliveries. As they spoke before the awakened congregations of black and white worshipers, the awakened clergy began to develop a new style of preaching, correlated to new expectations about audience response. To a certain extent in New England and to a considerable extent in the American South, this change in emphasis was shaped by the strong feedback given to awakened ministers by their black congregations and listeners. And to this extent, the changes in religious style engendered by the Greak Awakening were at least partly a product of the Africanizing of American culture. W. P. Harrison noted this among Methodist preachers in South Carolina:

> There was a peculiar *unction* that descended upon the preacher in the presence of these sable children of Africa. While they were not good judges of rhetoric, they were excellent judges of good preaching, and by their prayers and that peculiar magnetism which many have felt and none can explain the power of the Holy Ghost seemed often present in the preacher and the hearer.[27]

Unfortunately, in the Yankee colonies the black community was too small and too weak to effect a permanent accommodation, and so the Great Awakening remains only a suggestive incident, illustrating the potential receptivity of New England's black community to the Christian faith.

Yankee Christianity remained literally a religion of the book; its finely reasoned and plainly styled Calvinism was designed to separate saints from sinners rather than to entice conversions among an immigrant subculture. Except during the Great Awakening, the ceremonies that permitted Afro-Americans in the Catholic New World to syncretize African traditions to Christianity were missing in Protestant New England. To make matters worse, the emotional essence of religious celebration was also generally downplayed. Throughout the eighteenth century most of New England's Africans and Afro-Americans judged Yankee Protestantism an elitist and sterile faith, far removed from the participatory aesthetics of song, music, and dance which defined African religions south of the Sahara. Instead of converting, they practiced in that invisible institution—the folk religion of their own.

Chapter 7

An Afro-American
Folk Religion

HABIT, an old African proverb tells us, is "a full-grown mountain, hard to get over or pull down." So it was for Africans in the New World. As a Barbados master complained in 1750, slaves were "very tenaciously addicted to the rites, ceremonies, and superstitions of their own countries, particularly in their plays, dances, music, marriages, and burials. And even such as are born here, cannot be entirely weaned from these customs."[1] Yankee slaves, like other New World blacks, fused their ancestral beliefs in the afterworld, in witchcraft, protective charms, divination, herbal medicine, evil spirits, devils and ghosts to surrounding Euro-American traditions; in doing so, they created their own Yankee version of the Afro-American folk religions found throughout the Americas.

Across the New World many of those Africans who held most tenaciously to their native religions chose a suicidal martyrdom designed to return them to their ancestral shores and families. As Zephaniah Swift explained in 1791, "to them the prospect of terminating life furnishes the pleasing consolation of terminating their wretchedness—to them the messenger of death is an angel of peace and they fondly believe that they shall have a day of retribution in another existence in their native land."[2] One of New England's truest, if least recognized, religious martyrdoms was neither the execution of a disgruntled Quaker nor the exile of an Antinomian rebel, but the 1733 suicide of a black Salem woman who, in an act of hope and despair, cut open her stomach, saying she was returning to her own country.[3] Likewise, when Parson Stephen Williams's slaves Cato and Tom drowned themselves, their deaths were likely the result of a common Afro-American conviction that drowning could be a supernatural method for returning to Africa—as well as affording an escape from slavery.[4]

In her old age, Boston's Chloe Spear explained the kind of feelings and one of the beliefs that led to such suicides. She remembered the overpowering loneliness and isolation that greeted her in New England in 1762. In a constant depression, she pined for the death she felt certain would return her to her homeland. For just as "a young moon [would] appear after the old one was gone away," she said, so too would "the first child born into a family after the decease of a member be the same individual come back again."[5]

In his journals Henry David Thoreau recorded how an African-born Concord slave named Casey dealt with his own solitude. Casey had been taken from Africa at about twenty, leaving a wife and child behind; according to Thoreau's informant, Casey "used to say he went home to Africa in the night and came back again in the morning." Thoreau believed Casey was dreaming of home, as indeed he was; but for Casey these night visits were more than dreams. Many West Africans believed the soul could wander out of the body at night and then return to the slumberer in the morning; so Casey's "dreams" were really "soul visits" home.[6]

Until the new slaves had established a sense of belonging and place in the New World, they continued to maintain familiar African conceptions of the universe. The Atlantic crossing had only physically separated slaves from their homelands; years of immersion in Euro-American culture and the development of New World families and connections would be necessary to effect the same separation intellectually and emotionally.

Many of the Africans who were unwilling to return to Africa immediately by suicide probably believed they would, nonetheless, return home after death. After nearly a lifetime of service in the family of Parson Ashley of Deerfield, Massachusetts, Jin Cole, for example, still retained faith that with her last breath she would miraculously return, possessions and all, to the Africa which she had left as a twelve-year-old girl in 1715.

> She fully expected at death, or before, to be transported back to Guinea; and all her long life she was gathering, as treasures to take back to her motherland, all

kinds of odds and ends, colored rags, bits of finery, peculiar shaped stones, shells, buttons, beads, anything she could string. Nothing came amiss to her store.[7]

Strings of cowrie shells and other valuables like those she collected were used as money in West Africa. Jin must have explained this to her son Cato who, although he had spent all but the first few months of his life in the Ashley household, continued until his death in 1828 to gather such possessions for his own translation to Africa.[8]

Other Africans, perhaps with less to gain by returning home, soon modified their traditional conception of the afterlife as a continuation of worldly status in the hereafter to fit the description of heaven given them by Christian New Englanders. Thus when Ginny, a Guinea slave owned by the Reverend William Worthington of Saybrook, Connecticut, requested on her deathbed to speak to the Reverend Doctor Goodrich of Durham, she was said to have described her vision of paradise to be much like her former life in Saybrook:

> "Yes, Massa Goodrich," said Ginney, "when I die I shall go right to heaven, and knock at de door, and inquire for Massa Worthington. . . . Massa Worthington will come right to me; and I will say, 'Ginney's come. I want you to tell God that Ginney was always a good servant. She never lie, never steal, never use bad language.' And then he will come back to the door and say, 'Ginney, you may come in.' And I will go right in, and sit in the kitchen."[9]

When old Aaron, the African-born slave of the Morton family of Middleboro, Massachusetts, asked to be buried near the house so that he might "hear de chilluns' voices when dey be playing," he, too, was voicing a belief very African in its conception of the "living dead" watching over future generations—a belief that is African as well in suggesting the house site as a place of burial.[10] Yet Aaron must have believed that the years he had spent with the Morton family in New England destined him to an eternity in the new land where he had long since set down his roots.

Nonetheless, the conception of heaven as a homeland did not disappear. Hagar Merriman, a third generation Afro-American, recalled that for her mother, heaven, like the heaven of black spirituals, became a "home hereafter"—a true home for the American Negro. "I often think of my poor old mother, when she was alive," Merriman reminisced. "I used to say, 'I'll go home,' and she would say, 'This is not our home.' "[11] Unlike New England, heaven would be a true Zion, a place of justice where blacks would be recognized as God's children and a place from which hypocritical and sanctimonious slaveholders would be barred.[12]

At first, slave funerals and burials were conducted by Yankee blacks much as they had been in Africa. Since it was believed that the dead would return to the ancestral continent, the original style and meaning of the ceremonies continued. As the Reverend John Sharpe complained from New York, the blacks were "buried in the common by those of their country and complexion without the office, on the contrary the Heathenish rites are performed at the grave of their countrymen."[13] African music, dancing, and singing serenaded the departing otherworldly travelers, and liquor and material offerings were made to comfort them on their journey. Africans felt that the dead were especially honored and delighted by the celebration and merriment that accompanied their funerals.[14] Therefore, in the New World too, as Zephaniah Swift remarked, "The funeral rites of a slave are performed by his brethren with every mark of joy and gladness— They accompany the corpse with the sound of musical instruments—They sing their songs and perform their dances around the grave and indulge themselves in mirth and pleasantry."[15]

Such funeral celebrations disturbed Christian New Englanders, whose faith in hell made Yankee obsequies somber and didactic affairs; white observers, therefore, misinterpreted and generally disapproved of the high spirits that accompanied black funerals. William Bentley, for example, explained the traditional African aspects of a Salem funeral in 1797 in materialistic terms:

> We had this day, the funeral of a young Black, born of African Parents, according to the rites of the Church of England. The appearance was pleasing to humanity. Tho' the number of men was not great yet that of the women was so. All of them were clean and they were dressed from common life up to the highest fashions. We saw the plain homespun and the rich Indian Muslins and trail, so that they completely aped the manners of the whites and in happiness seemed to surpass them. They did not express so much sorrow at the funeral, as real gratification at appearing so well, a greater sympathy with living happily than the bereaved.[16]

The noise, merriment, and drinking of less Christian funerals especially grated on the sensibilities of the New England magistrates. In 1721, for example, Boston's selectmen limited the number of bells that could be tolled for Negro funerals to one in order to cut down on attendance; and they ordered the funeral processions to stop wending their way all over town and to take the most direct route to the grave.[17]

These wandering funeral processions were an African custom. In West Africa, funeral corteges would zig and zag so as to pass every house in a village until the mourners were satisfied by the actions of the corpse that God would punish the hidden malefactors who had done the deceased ill.[18] This continued in the New World, as Griffith Hughes reported from Barbados in 1750:

> There are few Negroes who believe that they die a natural Death, but rather that they are fascinated or bewitched. The bearers, in carrying the corpse of such a one to the Grave, when they come opposite to, or in the sight of the House of the Person who is supposed to have bewitched the Deceased, pretend to stagger, and say, that the corpse is unwilling, and will not permit them to carry it to the Grave, until it is suffered to stop near, or opposite to, that House: After this is complied with for a few minutes, the corpse is, as they think, appeased, and then the Bearers, without Difficulty, carry it to the Grave.[19]

Since such African customs were slow in dying, the selectmen of Boston were forced to remind the city's sextons in 1735 "to take care, that the by-law of the town, for preventing and Reforming Disorders at the funerals of Negroes &c. be duly comply'd with."[20] And although the African or "heathenish" elements of the funeral rites continued to disappear, it was still noteworthy to William Bentley in 1809 that there were in Boston "80 Blacks capable of dressing themselves in good fashion and conducting [a funeral] with great solemnity, without the ignorant state and awkward manner of a new situation."[21]

Since the white Christian majority of New England considered it their duty to repress any practices they clearly recognized as pagan or "savage," there were few public displays of undisguised African religious behavior in the Yankee colonies. Individual blacks were often seen to practice what to Christians seemed religious aberrations, but actions like those examined in the following pages were usually recorded in local anecdotal traditions as examples of African superstition and eccentricity. In the eighteenth century these religious practices were seldom understood for what they were, but in retrospect their connections to African religion seem clear.

When Cotton Mather admonished Yankee masters to be heedful of their slaves' religious lives and secret prayers, he recorded an example of an African faith surviving intact in North America, even if he misunderstood what he saw: "Very many of them do with Devilish Rites actually worship *Devils*, or maintain a magical conversation with *Devils;* and all of them are more *Slaves* to Satan than they are to *you*, until a Faith in the *Son* of *God* has made them free."[22] Charles Eliot, in his *New England History*, similarly reported from family tradition that when one of his own ministerial Yankee forebears found his slave Cuff bowing and mumbling before a rough stone god, he asked sharply, "What's this Cuff?" Cuff's answer burns through the hypocrisy of the Christian slave trade. "White man steal nigger, nigger no like white man's God. Cuff make his own God and den he know 'em."[23]

When African slaves were brought to the New World there was little reason for them to suppose that the Atlantic crossing would involve a total break with the spiritual world. After all, even Christians and Indians believed in gods, ghosts, spirits, and charms. It was simply a matter of adjusting native traditions to an American interpretation.

Sometimes African and American religious beliefs could simply blend into one another. In New England, black servants were taught as children that thunder was God's voice. The theologian Cotton Mather explained God was "the high thunderer . . . who hath both good angels as well as evil ones, to the executions of his judgements in his thunders." Such ideas would have seemed familiar enough to Africans acquainted with Shango, the Yoruba thunder god who targeted adulterers, liars, and thieves for destruction. During New York's 1741 slave uprising Afro-American conspirators stepped into a chalk circle to swear their loyalty "by thunder and lightning"; and later in the century the man appointed deputy governor of Connecticut's Negroes began his election day inaugural grace honoring the newly elected black governor by recognizing the same power: "Tunder above de Hebens, Litnin' on de earth, Shake de tops of de trees." Similar beliefs may clarify the actions of Phillis, a slave woman of Suffield, Connecticut, whose remembered terror of thunderstorms probably stemmed from a guilty conscience and a fear of punishment by lightning. Shortly before her death Phillis requested burial near a great beech tree where she said "the lightning [will] never find me."[24]

Beliefs in the power of amulets and talismans to protect wearers from illness or misfortune were widespread in Africa, and such traditions crossed the ocean almost intact. Many a Yankee slave felt there were evil spirits all about, and so wore charms for protection. If a slave was sick, the devil was believed the cause and had to be driven out by some sort of incantation or ritual. The typical slave, it was said, had "many gods, mostly unkind," which had to be propitiated. "In one form or another," a Yankee observer reported, "fetish worship . . . was almost inherent." Even when Afro-Americans adapted to the idea of a supreme Christian god and devil, the spirits of good and evil remained African in essence with "as many moods as all the gods and goddesses in Valhalla to be appeased every one, by some self-prescribed infliction." This is visible in the attitudes of Titus Kent, the Christian slave of the Reverend Ebenezer Gay of Suffield, Connecticut, regarding his charms:

> In a mild sort of way he became a fetish worshiper. . . . He always carried
> a frog's foot in his pocket to keep off the colic demon, for he thought there was a
> special imp for each disease. Around his neck he carried four rattle-snake's
> buttons, so suspended as to hang over his lungs. These he considered a
> sovereign remedy for consumption, and of course valued them highly, as most
> of his best friends had died of that dreaded disease. On one occasion he lost
> them and it is a mild statement to say that he made things lively in the neighbor-
> hood. He bored every one he met about "dose buttons," until at last one of the
> boys found them for him, or at least killed another snake; and so gave him a new
> set which he wore to the end of his days.[25]

Given such beliefs, it is not surprising that in the seventeenth century African slaves joined other New Englanders in their fear of witches; indeed, the flying witches of Africa who rode victims during the night seemed to be visiting Massachusetts as well. Because of the similarity of beliefs, New England's black population added little new to the white witchcraft traditions. While they were occasionally accused of witchcraft, blacks were not singled out for alien beliefs or heathen practices. As early as 1656, Old Ham was called one of three male witches at Strawberry Bank, New Hampshire, by Elizabeth Rowe. During the infamous Salem trials of 1692, four local blacks were suspected of witchcraft. Old Pharaoh, the slave of Zaccheus Collins of Lynn, was accused of being one of those who came to torment and entice Mercy Lewis during the trials. Mercy Lewis also was among the girls naming Mary Black, the Negro slave of Nathaniel Putnam, as a witch. Of course, the most famous of the accused was the much romanticized Tituba, an Afro-Carib slave from Barbados, who may have taught several local girls some West Indian conjuring tricks.[26]

A more likely candidate as a real conjurer was Candy, a slave and fellow islander of Tituba's, who was accused of witchcraft by Ann Putnam. At her trial, Candy denied any such heritage, explaining that in Barbados neither she nor her mother had been witches; she said that she had become a witch in Salem only under the instruction of her white mistress. But since Candy did show the court a conjuring aid with clear African and Afro-American parallels—"a handkerchief wherein several knots were tied, rags of cloth, a piece of cheese and a piece of grass"—it is possible she may have known about, and practiced, conjuring techniques.[27] Nonetheless, despite Candy and the others, the evidence is much too slim to find significant Afro-American origins or impetus behind New England's witchcraft hysteria. For the most part it was local white citizens, rather than the exotic black newcomers, who were chosen the scapegoats of the witchcraft madness.

Blacks, like the other citizens of Massachusetts, found themselves the victims of witchcraft. In December 1679, Wonn, a black slave belonging to John Ingerson, helped indict Bridget Oliver for witchcraft by testifying in the Salem quarterly court that the month before, she had bewitched the horses of his sled so that they "ran down the swamp up to their bellies." When he returned to the barn, he said, he saw her sitting "upon the beam with an egg in her hand"; and later at dinner, after seeing two strange black cats, he was mysteriously pinched. During the Salem troubles a little over a decade later, Peter Tuft of Charlestown complained that his black woman was being persecuted by acts of witchcraft committed by Elizabeth Fosdick and Elizabeth Paine.[28] According to a letter left by Rhode Island's Willet Carpenter, his maternal great-grandfather Powell "protected" his slave, Peter, in a very different manner:

> [Powell] was a Newport merchant, and made frequent journeys to Boston and Salem, attended by his Negro servant, Peter, who, whilst at one of these places, went into the Court-house, where some of the witches were on trial. On his return to the house where his master lodged, he was taken apparently with convulsive fits, falling down in great agony, and the people of the house called him bewitched, but Mr. Powell, who had expressed much indignation at the scenes he had lately witnessed, declared with much energy that nobody would

be hanged for Peter, for he would himself undertake his cure. Accordingly, he applied his horsewhip to Peter (but for the first and only time), with such effect that he gladly returned to his duty.[29]

Unfortunately, such a cure was not used on the girls of Salem.

The most interesting reference to Afro-American conjuring practices in New England comes from the local traditions of late eighteenth-century Narragansett, traditions which have been romantically embellished in Alice Morse Earle's *In Old Narragansett*. Tuggie Bannock, the conjurer of Earle's tale, was a slave of Rowland Robinson and the daughter of an African woman given the name Abigail. Abigail was well known in local tradition as a woman of royal status, who with the support of her owner returned to Africa to find the son from whom she had been separated. Mother and son returned to Rhode Island, where the boy subsequently became a governor of the black community.[30] Like other Afro-Americans of her day, Tuggie respected and feared the supernatural power of conjuring; in Earle's words she was "far more afraid of being bewitched than she was confident of bewitching." To protect herself from evil spirits, Tuggie wore her petticoats inside out and hung a bag of eggshells around her neck. To work revenge on an enemy she would place a dough heart or dough baby on the victim's fence or doorstep. She might also "burn a project," as she once did, to give Bosum Sidet "the misery," using incantations handed down to her by her mother, Queen Abigail.

According to Earle, "Everyone in Narragansett knew that when a project began to boil, the conjured one would begin to suffer some mental or bodily ill." One of Tuggie's projects was once broken up when the door of her cabin crashed open and she was knocked to the floor by a heavy object that she at first believed to be a terrifying "moonack" or devil. In actuality it was the bobsled of some local boys.[31] The literal truth of such anecdotes cannot be established, but the fact that such conjuring practices were well enough known to be part of the local folklore is important; indeed, we can only wonder how much of the true Afro-American folk culture of New England has been censored from the white records.

Afro-American conjuring practices were often confused by white observers with poisoning, as can be seen in the 1748 description by Peter Kalm of the witchcraft "poisoning" of black collaborationists by their fellow slaves in New York:

Only a few of them know the secret, and they likewise know the remedy for it; therefore when a negro feels himself poisoned and can recollect the enemy who might possibly have given him the poison, he goes to him, and endeavors by money and entreaties to move him to deliver him from its effects. But if the negro is malicious, he not only denies that he ever poisoned him, but likewise that he knows an anecdote for it. This poison does not kill immediately, as I have noted, for sometimes the sick person dies several years afterward. But from the moment he has the poison he falls into a sort of consumption state and enjoys but few days of good health. Such a poor wretch often knows that he is poisoned the moment he gets it. The negroes commonly employ it on such of their brethren as behave well toward whites, are beloved by their masters, and separate, as it were, from their countrymen, or do not like to converse with them. They have likewise often other reasons for their emnity; but there are few examples of their having poisoned their masters. Perhaps the mild treatment they receive, keeps them from doing it, or perhaps they fear that they may be discovered, and that in such a case, the severest punishment would be inflicted on them.[32]

Such "poisoning" is an almost perfect description of "voodoo death" (the psychosomatic effect of the fear of being bewitched), a syndrome common throughout the culture areas of Africa and Afro-America. As Griffith Hughes explained from eighteenth-century Barbados, "If once a Negro believes, that he is bewitched, the Notion is so strongly riveted in his Mind, that, Medicine seldom availing, he usually lingers till death puts an End to his Fears."[33]

Whether the three blacks arrested in Newport in 1772 for allegedly poisoning a fellow slave woman were conjuring or using real poison is unclear, but frightened by the fiendish reputation of Africans as master poisoners, white Americans kept a wary eye against possible revenge by disgruntled house servants. Sometimes the vigilance may have paid off, as in 1735 when Yaw, a Negro man, and a black boy named Caesar were apprehended for attempting to poison the Humphrey Scarlett family by putting arsenic in their breakfast chocolate. Twenty years later the slaves of John Codman of Charlestown, Massachusetts, conspired to poison him in order to gain new masters and be free of his harsh rule. Mark, the leader of the conspiracy, had been trained as a Christian; but this was not sufficient protection for his master. Mark read the Bible through in order to discover how Codman could be killed with impunity and concluded that according to scripture it could be done if the act was accomplished without bloodshed.[34]

An African retention much more important to the folk beliefs of New England than conjuring or witchcraft was the use of divination. Here there could be an easy syncretism since fortune-telling was a popular pastime with white colonials, and the exotic nature of Afro-American seers made them especially believable. At first, black diviners followed traditional African patterns, with little emphasis on fortune-telling per se, but whites tended to frown upon such practices as quackery. Indeed, as early as 1709, authorities took a complaint to the Bristol county court about "Negro-Mancy," arguing that certain black seers were "pretending to discover lost or stolen goods and to find out the persons that have them."

Despite court action other black diviners continued to find employment for their occult skills in New England. A black man in Newfane, Vermont, was remembered to have "told fortunes, discovered lost property, and performed strange feats." Similarly, in 1795, the Reverend Paul Coffin reported that a Negro in Gilmanton, New Hampshire, consulted about missing property, divined that there was a theft, and successfully put a spell upon the white culprit. As Coffin explained, "A man in Gilmanton lost a bar of iron and suspecting such a neighbor, a negro quack gave him directions to find it. These followed, tormented the suspected man, and his brother paid for the iron."[35]

Well into the nineteenth century, Jude, an African woman of Salem, Massachusetts, and Silvia Tory, an African-born slave of Narragansett, Rhode Island, continued to profitably dispense charms and fortunes. It was said that the "obscure rites and ceremonies" Silvia had brought with her out of Africa gave her tea readings an especially exotic allure. Silvia also received certain older applicants who understood the value of the more African aspects of her hidden powers. "Did a cow stray beyond boundaries, or was a horse stolen, the bereaved owner hastened to inquire to Silvia, who would obligingly furnish him with various occult directions, by a strict adherence to which, the lost might be found."[36] Many of the black women of New England who told fortunes also gathered and sold herbs, a calling facilitated by traditional African, Afro-American, and Indian expertise in herbal medicine.[37]

In an interesting reversal of roles, folk tradition recalls one perceptive master who used his servant's belief in divination for his own purposes. Phineas Sprague of Melrose, Massachusetts, convinced his slaves that by using arithmetic as a kind of white man's magic, he could divine any mischief they had been up to.

When a neighbor made a complaint that he had reason to believe a certain negro had stolen a cart chain, Sprague called the negro up and told him he suspected he had been doing wrong, and unless he owned up, he (Phineas) should figure it out. There being no confession, he would then take his chalk and board and sit down to cipher. In a few moments he would musingly say, "Links three inches long; links three inches long, what does that mean?" Then turning to his "boy" he would say, "Pomp," or whatever his name might be, "Pomp, you have been stealing sausages," Pomp astonished at such arithmetic, would say, "No, Massa, me no steal sausage, me steal cart chain."[38]

While this story was remembered as a kind of black "Polish joke," the anecdote also reveals a Euro-American adaptation of an African method for discovering criminal behavior.

Another African religious retention that helped shape Yankee traditions was a strong belief in ghosts. Fear of ghosts was common to Afro-Americans through the New World; as Francis Varnod reported from South Carolina in 1724, "Some of our negro pagans have . . . dismal apprehensions of apparitions."[39] Such beliefs had been carried from Africa and seemed even more frightening in a land filled with strange new spirits, where the benevolent protection of sympathetic ancestors could be of no avail. Thus both Rhode Island and South Carolina blacks wore their clothes inside out as a protective device during night journeys, when they felt especially vulnerable to ghosts.[40] Since the dread of ghosts was reinforced by parallel ideas common among the Euro-American population, it is not surprising that the "African imagination" was given credit for several Yankee traditions that certain houses or sections of the New England countryside were haunted.[41]

It is at first perplexing that so many folk beliefs of New England's Afro-Americans contained strong African survivals in a culture which had a puritanical devotion to the ideal of a Christian commonwealth. The explanation lies to a great extent in the similarities of folk religions in Europe and Africa. Black folk beliefs were close enough to white traditions to make them seem relatively harmless superstitions in the eyes of the white authorities. In addition, the Narragansett region, where the retention of African ideas was strongest, was an island of concentrated black population safely ensconced in the religiously tolerant colony of Rhode Island. Many African religious ideas also survived because they remained functional; indeed, white New Englanders as well as blacks visited black mediums and diviners, both feared the power of ghosts, witches, and conjurers, and both believed in the efficacy of herbal medicine and carried protective fetish charms for good luck. Thus, while it might seem surprising given the general perception of Yankee folklife, the folk traditions of white New England met and blended with those of Africa to reinforce one another in a new Yankee folklore—a folklore that may have looked Euro-American, but was instead a complex, intercontinental alloy.

Chapter 8

To Build a Family

ERHAPS the strongest institution of cultural cohesion and informal education is the family, which passes the core values of a culture down from parent to child. But the new American slave families formed by New England's black immigrants were poor substitutes for the powerful corporate associations that defined African kinship. Indeed, for the newcomers one of the most destructive breaks with African tradition was the immediate loss of the large extended families made possible by unilineal descent. In unilineage, brothers, sisters, cousins, second cousins, and even more distant kin all share a common ancestor. Even if the slaves had been able to return to African kinship forms, such extended families would have taken generations to rebuild.

Since the slave immigrants were from a variety of African societies and ethnic groups, their New World marriages were, effectively, "mixed marriages"; and no common precedent dictated kinship affiliation for their children. Couples from different African backgrounds had to work out new arrangements on their own; and it should not be surprising that Yankee blacks soon adopted a bilateral system of descent like that practiced by white New Englanders. But this change entailed a considerable cost, for typical American bilateral descent—where only full siblings have identical kindred—destroyed the cohesion upon which the large extended families of Africa had built their stability.

The institution of marriage itself was also weakened. In Africa, marriage was a matter of family consultation. The appropriateness of the union had to be examined, and the interests of both parties and their families considered before consent could be given. Since even remnants of families seldom crossed the ocean intact, it was a rare Yankee bridegroom who could obtain a traditional approval from the lineage of his wife-to-be through a series of premarital negotiations between the two families. Without this traditional family guidance, and without the bond insuring good treatment symbolized by a bridewealth payment, sexual desire may have often replaced long-term considerations of compatibility in preparing for the success of the union. The isolated American nuclear family simply could not replace the interests of African kinship as a foundation for family development and a stable marriage.[1]

The transition to new sexual mores and matrimonial patterns was eased in most New World areas by the wide latitude left to the blacks over control of their own sexual lives. In the early years polygyny was common almost everywhere in Afro-America and, as Codrington Plantation manager Abel Alleyne confessed from Barbados in 1741, as "impossible to prevent as any one thing in the world."[2] Yet it was precisely this impossibility that Yankee clergymen sought. In New England, monogamy was required by law, and slave marriages were contracted under the watchful eyes of paternalistic and god-fearing masters.[3]

In reality, black sexual relationships in New England never approximated the ideal propounded by the white clergy. As might be expected in a society that had many more men than women, the sex lives of bachelors were rarely examined unless charges of bastardy resulted. As Boston's Samuel Sewall explained in 1700, "It is too well known what temptations masters are under, to connive at the fornication of their slaves; lest they should be obligated to find them wives, to pay their fines."[4] Many masters believed enforcement of sexual codes was impossible with "lawless" bondsmen, although ironically they expected enforcement in regard to other slave delinquencies.

Even among slaves owned by the Yankee clergy, premarital and extramarital sexual activity was common. In an attempt to change this situation Cotton Mather had placed special stress on the sinful nature of fornication in his rules for Boston's Negro Society.[5] But there is little evidence that his or other ministers' efforts were rewarded with a change in the slaves' value system. In Rhode Island, for example, the Reverend James MacSparran complained that his servant, baptized Maroca Africa in 1725, would not keep her promise of chastity. The Reverend Peter Thatcher of Milton, Massachusetts, had the same problem with his Negro woman, Hagar, who in 1719 "made her confession of her sin of fornication and entered into the covenant with God," being baptized with her sons Sambo and Jimmie. Hagar had been married to Sambo, a slave of Mr. Brightman of Boston, in 1716. She apparently had another child after Sambo's death or departure from the area by 1719, for in 1722 she baptized a daughter Hagar. Similarly Juno Larcom, the slave of a proper Beverly, Massachusetts, master, had four children by Jethro Thistle prior to their church marriage in 1756.[6]

Since there were many African societies wherein young people were encouraged to engage in sexual play before marriage, and where prenuptial pregnancy was the norm, some of the so-called promiscuity of black slaves was less the result of moral decay than a reflection of different standards for premarital conduct.[7]

When in 1713 the Reverend John Sharpe reported from New York the existence of what he called "negro marriages," he described a situation familiar to New Englanders. The marriages of the blacks, he explained, "are performed by mutual consent without the blessing of the church." Some slaves, he went on, were kept from Christian marriage "because of polygamy contracted before baptism where none or neither of the wives will accept a divorce." Since Yankee slave spouses seldom belonged to the same master, opportunities for multiple marriage increased if one mate was sold to a new owner far away. When there was no hope for reconciliation of the "negro marriage," and the remaining spouse lacked the desire to remain single, then a "Christian marriage" might be performed, but even this could cause scandalous problems. As Sharpe noted, some slaves agree "to break by mutual consent their negro marriage . . . and marry a Christian spouse. In these cases it's difficult how to proceed without giving scandal or matter of temptation."[8] Indeed, in the West Indies black men often married their oldest or first wives in a Christian ceremony while keeping younger wives in relationships unacceptable to the church.[9]

In 1725 John Bartow complained to the Society for the Propagation of the Gospel from his Rye, New York, location that he could not "be very zealous to baptize slaves because . . . they will not or cannot live up to the Christian covenant in one notorious instant at least, viz., matrimony, for they marry after their heathen way and divorce and take others as often as they please."[10] Eight years later, from Boston, Elihu Coleman warned Yankee masters against suffering their slaves "to take husbands and wives at their pleasure, and then leave again when they please, and then take others again as fast and as suddenly as they will and then leave them again."[11] In fact, much of what was transpiring in New England might be better described as serial monogamy rather than as polygyny or promiscuity.

Despite enforcement of laws against fornication and adultery, there remained three states of sexual relationship among Afro-Americans in New England: Christian marriage, "negro marriage" (i.e., common-law marriage), and less formal attachments.

The reality of the looser marriage bonds among slaves supplied a condescending Yankee anecdote about Chatham Freeman of Wallingford, Connecticut, who was freed in 1782 with his common-law wife and child.

> When at last he became a free man he told his former master Noah Yale that he
> wanted to be married just like white folks. . . . Some little time after the
> marriage he came to Mr. Yale and said he wanted to be "unmarried as I never
> can stand it to be married to that woman." On being told that there was no
> remedy—that now he was married he must stay so, he went away exclaiming,
> with uplifted hands, "Oh Massa what I gwine do, what I gwine do?"[12]

The freer sexual connections of slave society reflected the vulnerability of relations under bondage, where lovers or mates were always at risk of separation. Nonetheless, they were only partially the result of a breakdown of social and moral standards; many Afro-Americans freely and rationally chose a more African structure for their premarital and marital life styles. The marriage ties of Africa generally allowed for more protection for the woman, and greater freedom of separation, divorce, and selection of sexual partners than did the restrictive Christian practices of Euro-Americans; therefore it is not surprising that many newly arrived black women were disposed to enter less confining bonds than the Christian European ideal of their masters.[13] Moreover, since stable marriage was difficult, if not impossible, in slavery, many African immigrants must have seen little value in church marriage except to please their masters.[14]

In the New World, marriage lacked the institutional underpinnings that offered sanction and stability in Africa, where matrimony was a sacred union horizontally connecting two families and vertically connecting the ancestral past to both present and future. Many Afro-American men felt less attachment to the conjugal institution since they lived separated from their families. Further, children no longer symbolized the immortality of the patrilineage. In Africa a man needed sons to care for his spirit after death, and it was also often believed, as we saw Boston slave Chloe Spear explain above, that children were the reincarnation of deceased family members.[15] But, in America, few supposed their African antecedents would choose to be reborn as slaves in an alien land.

Moreover, New World monogamy removed one of the African male's most important potential status symbols, the possibility of supporting several wives and many children.[16] New arrivals, therefore, often re-worked the polygynous ideal into unsanctioned relationships outside of the monogamous household. The symbolic and psychological meanings of "polygynous" keeper relationships accorded Afro-American men at least part of the status which multiple marriage had given to those able to afford it in Africa.[17]

In American marriage, black women lost the security they usually enjoyed in Africa. The bridewealth payments which legitimized and bonded African marriage were abandoned in the New World. Only small remnants of the form occasionally remained, as in the following North Carolina example in which the bride received a small marriage gift.

> Their marriages are generally performed amongst themselves, there being very little ceremony used upon that head; for the man makes the woman a present, such as a brass ring or some other toy, which if she accepts of, becomes his wife; but if ever they part from each other, which frequently happens, upon any little disgust, she returns his present: These kind of contracts no longer binding them, then the woman keeps the pledge given her.[18]

In the marriage model offered by Christian masters, most wives had less economic autonomy and social rights than they would have had in traditional African cultures. Moreover, since a woman's children were owned and supported by her master rather than her spouse, slave women were less tightly bound to their husbands than would have been the case in African society. Indeed, under slavery, marriage often placed women under the control of mates beneath their own status, who had less to offer in providing security or potential freedom than a good master.[19] This was not lost on New England's black women, and is typified by Obour Tanner's observation on her friend Phillis Wheatley: "poor Phillis let herself down by marrying."[20] In New England, brides who were purchased to live with their husbands were better off in many respects, but they still lacked even the safeguards of Euro-American marriage; their insecurity has been captured in the anecdote of Boston Carpenter's purchase of a "wife":

He had been a slave and bought his freedom. Then he bought a slave named
Lillis, who was familiarly known by the name of Lill. They lived together as
man and wife, though it was said they never married. He used to say to her that
if she did not behave well, he would put her in his pocket (or, in other words, he
would sell her).[21]

If, in general, the break from traditional African marriage patterns
destroyed much of the meaning and security of matrimony, the situation
was not without certain opportunities for women from patrilineal and
patrilocal societies to improve their positions. In the New World, women
were not removed in marriage to a husband's village and clan. Instead, they
often remained at home among familiar friends and relations, where they
were relieved of living under the direction of in-laws and co-wives. Women
often responded to this new situation by creating matrilocal, almost matrilineal, support systems such as that noted in Susan Snow's remembrance of
her childhood in nineteenth-century Alabama: "All de niggers on de place
was born in de family and was kin . . . I don't 'member nuthin' about
havin' no pa . . . in dem days husbands and wives didn't belong to da same
folks."[22] The key for New England is that Yankee women, like their sisters
elsewhere, often put themselves at the center of their new family arrangements. Sometimes this could become almost matrilineal, as is reflected in
a naming pattern common throughout early Afro-America. In the same
manner that in Barbados, Quashey, son of Maudlew, took the name
Quashey Maudlew, in New England Dick Violet and James Dinah gave
themselves matrilineal surnames. In Africa such naming was used to distinguish particular mother-child relationships in polygynous families; but in
New England it suggests the matrilineal conception of kinship held by some
black Yankees.[23]

Freed from African restrictions, Afro-American women were loath to be
reburdened with the inferiority of the wife's role as defined by Judeo-
Christian monogamy. Accordingly, black women in the New World often
thought Christian marriage a mark of subordination: after marriage they
would be forbidden to leave their husbands if treated badly, while the
males, for their part, could claim total economic control of the family's
assets.[24]

Since a slave mother and her children were supported by a master, she
was often freer than other women to avoid or terminate an unwanted mar-

riage; and given the unbalanced sex ratio of the early years, the slave woman often found her favors widely sought by both white and black suitors. Throughout the Americas, female slaves took advantage of such situations to improve their material conditions, gain their freedom, and, most importantly, improve the situation of their children.[25] Nonetheless, they were still vulnerable to sexual abuse from the master class; even worse, their children and mates could be sold away at whim, as Juno Larcom of Beverly, Massachusetts, discovered when deaths and financial difficulties led to the sales of three of her children and her husband.[26]

In New England it was a fortunate slave who could marry a fellow servant of the same household, and many slaves must have tried to persuade their masters to buy them spouses or intended mates. But for many Yankee masters the purchase of even one extra servant was an expensive luxury—so expensive that Richard Smith of Essex County, Massachusetts, agreed to give eventual freedom to his slave Jo rather than purchase him a wife.[27] Few slaves were able to amass sufficient funds to make purchase a viable way of building a family household. The idea of purchasing a mate, however, may not have seemed particularly alien to Africans acquainted with the custom of making substantial bridewealth payments as part of the bonds of marriage. When Samson, a slave of Archelaus Moore of Canterbury, New Hampshire, worked for a year under William Coffin of Concord to buy Coffin's slave Lucy for a wife, he was following a traditional African pattern.[28]

Free black men, also, when they were financially able, tried to purchase wives and children. In 1724, Scipio, a free Boston black, paid fifty pounds for his fiancee and her apparel; during the Revolution, Wethersfield, Connecticut's Abner spent forty pounds for his wife; and when slavery was ending, twenty-one-year-old Andrew Dewner gave up his freedom gift of a horse in exchange for a Marlboro slave girl.[29] In an interesting turn of this tradition, Harriet Beecher Stowe relates in *Oldtown Folks* how Aunt Nancy Prime by hard labor treated herself to an expensive luxury in the shape of a husband. He was a heavy drinker and a bad buy; and Aunt Nancy was often heard to declare, says Stowe, that "she would never buy another nigger."[30]

Most slave spouses in New England were forced by the circumstances of bondage to live apart from each other, either in separate households under different masters or in separate cities. Marriage partners were able to visit only during limited periods of free time. Even then, such visits often lacked any real privacy. When, for example, Quaco visited his wife Phoebe, a Massachusetts slave woman, she had to entertain him in the garret of her master's home, a section of the house that served as the common resident for all the family's slaves, both male and female.[31] Under such conditions of slavery black men and women could not form the typically American nuclear family; indeed, only in those marriages where husbands were free and able to purchase the freedom of their families could black marriages have a real chance for normal stability.[32]

Nonetheless, the New England slave family maintained a certain autonomy despite constant intrusions by the demands of bondage. While almost nothing is known about the internal relations of family members, what evidence we have suggests black mothers and fathers often loved their children fiercely, and gave their offspring pride in a black heritage. Consider Hagar Merriman's mother who, it has been noted, threatened to "spill her last drop of blood" rather than be separated by sale from her daughter. Merriman also recalled that her mother sternly insisted Hagar follow a code of manners (or was it pride?) that forbade the child to ask for the coins offered her for dancing before several white ladies; and she insisted that Hagar never refer to the house Hagar shared with her owner as "home." In another example presented earlier, Jin Cole, isolated in a white ministerial family in a small town in western Massachusetts, nonetheless taught her American-born son to save valuables for his eventual translation to her family in Africa after his death. Since, boy and man, her son was surely indoctrinated with the beliefs of Christianity, his adoption of his mother's faith (in all its matrilineal implications) marks the power of even isolated slave families to resist absorption by the surrounding white culture.[33]

In the Atlantic crossing and in American slavery, African newcomers lost the social cohesion of traditional marriage within the extended family. At the same time, they found many of their standards of morality and premarital sexual mores rejected out of hand by a puritanical master class. As compensation, black slaves were offered only an inferior and vulnerable imitation of Christian marriage lacking the autonomy of its Euro-American original. Little wonder, then, that Afro-Americans in New England, as elsewhere, experimented with alternative living and sexual arrangements.

Many of the Afro-American sexual relationships that appalled Christian observers as immoral deviations from lawful monogamy were in reality attempts to blend African mores with the new social realities of American bondage. Unfortunately, no matter which traditions were used or how they were recombined, solid marriages simply could not be fostered without economic and social autonomy for the family units. Given the insecurities and separations of slavery, not even a carefully nurtured Christian morality was sufficient to create a stable Christian family life.

Chapter 9

Aspects of Black Folklife

T HROUGHOUT the eighteenth century the folklife of black New England was more Afro-American than Yankee. In work habits and labor skills, in culinary and musical arts, as in dress, entertainment, and folklore, slave immigrants maintained their own traditions or blended them with Yankee ways to create a truly Afro-American folk culture. This black subculture reinforced the immigrants' sense of community and self-worth; its skills generated much needed personal income; and, at times, black folkways shaped the lives of white New Englanders as well.

The extent to which black folklife in predominately white New England maintained a strong African essence may be surprising. However, in retrospect, the surprise comes not from the internal logic of the process of acculturation, but from the way that studies of the Yankee intelligentsia and ruling class have shaped our perceptions of New England. By emphasizing the lives of the literate elite, historians have drawn attention away from the very different life-styles and attitudes of more common sorts of people, white and black.

Slaves, like other common men in eighteenth-century New England, spent most of their waking hours in hard physical toil. When the bondsmen were given tasks similar to those they had undertaken in Africa before their arrival in New England, they preferred to follow their old work routines if it were possible. Thus, when African laborers were brought to Dorchester, Massachusetts, during the 1740s to excavate a hill, they carried away the dirt on trays balanced on their heads—the traditional manner of carrying heavy loads in the forest zones of Africa. Anglo-American observers, ignorant of the efficiency of the method, thought to speed up the work by substituting wheelbarrows; but "to the amusement of passers by, the laborers were seen, at first, with the barrows on their heads."[1]

Across the New World, whites misunderstood the resistance of African workers to new (and sometimes less efficient) Euro-American methods of labor. The master class generally blamed the immigrants' conservatism on stupidity; but the African newcomers were simply choosing to exercise their own expertise. Doubtless, they wondered about the pigheadedness of their white bosses. Edward Kimber captured the situation in this comment from plantation America:

> To be sure, a new Negro, if he must be broke, either from obstinacy, or which
> I am more apt to suppose, from greatness of soul, will require more hard
> discipline than a young spaniel: you show him how to hoe, or drive a wheel-
> barrow, he'll still take the one by the bottom, and the other by the wheel; and
> they often die before they can be conquered.[2]

Not understanding that African hoes were short-handled and African hoeing required considerable bending, New World masters issued long-handled varieties and then ridiculed the slaves for their "incorrect" grips and awkward postures. Yet, Africans were skilled with their short hoes and refused to give up hoe agriculture despite their masters' insistence on Euro-American plow techniques so destructive to the humus of the thin soil of the tropics. As the agent of the St. Kitts legislature noted in 1789, "Wheelbarrows, dung pots, three wheel carts . . . and plows, have been introduced at times; but the negroes . . . very soon laid them aside."[3]

The old African ways of doing things continued across a range of labor skills. For example, when Old Dinah, an African-born slave of Dr. Paine of Salem, Massachusetts, did her spinning, she rejected the American wheel of her mistress and continued to spin yarn in the African fashion—on a stick centered on a plate.[4] Similarly, it was probably a West African finger counting tradition like that of the Malinke (which makes six, *wolo*, by adding five, *wo*, to one, *lo*) that led Dinah, the bondswoman of Samuel Ham of Portsmouth, New Hampshire, to plant corn in the hole by counting "three kernels, and then two" instead of five at a time, or directed Jack Lee of

Rowley, Massachusetts, to use a system of threes to count cattle.[5]

In the same context, it is not too speculative to suppose that New England dairy farms may have profited from herding skills brought by slaves from the West African grasslands, or that some of the Negroes working in the iron beds and forges of Hope Furnace and Cranston, Rhode Island, carried useful mining or smithing skills with them from the Old World.[6] Such a hypothesis would explain, for example, why it was a new slave and not a European who discovered the copper deposits of nearby New Barbados Neck, New York, in 1710.[7]

Unlike white immigrants, Africans from the forest regions were especially artful in the use of snares and traps for capturing small game. Black men not only improved their diets with supplements of small game, they also impressed the children of both races with their skills as hunters. Harriet Beecher Stowe, for example, remembered the slave Caesar for his ingenuity in trapping squirrels; New York's Washington Irving recalled another Caesar for his trapping of quail. Since crows and other small animals also fell victim to African techniques, small white boys across New England made themselves eager disciples of the slaves, who showed them how to build snares and trap fish, as well as how to make whistles—things their own fathers did not know. Certain Yankee blacks won local renown for their hunting skills, like Black Nim the deerhunter or Roswell Quash the "scourge of foxes."[8]

New England's Afro-Americans were also excellent basket makers. Here again, a traditional African craft could be put to work to supplement a freeman's meager income or a slave's ration. When Charles Danforth of Norfolk, Connecticut, lacked the funds to pay the minister who performed his son's marriage, he paid the debt by weaving a clothes basket. Peter Salem, likewise, earned a spare livelihood in his old age making and mending baskets and bottoming chairs. When their days as slaves were over, they simply returned to older skills to make their way in the world.[9]

The traditional African interest in herbal medicine continued to produce root and herbal specialists in the Yankee black community. Although Afro-Indian women were believed to be the region's most skilled herbal practitioners, black women like Barrington, Rhode island's "Doctress Phillis" also won local recognition for their expertise in the traditional Afro-American medical arts.[10]

Another African medical carry-over important to New England was the use of variolation to protect against smallpox. As was noted in Chapter 4, Cotton Mather learned about smallpox variolation from his "Guramantee" (probably "Coromantee," an Akan people) servant. In checking the report in Boston, Mather found "a number of Africans in this town" who vouched for the technique's effectiveness. Apparently the Akan peoples had used variolation to protect against yaws and followed the same procedure against smallpox. The technique proved successful and helps account for the black population's superior resistance to smallpox noted in the Boston statistics of 1752.[11]

Mather was unusual in listening seriously to his slave. Akan immigrants in the New World had been protecting their own children while their masters continued to face the scourge of smallpox in ignorance. Cadwallader Colden of New York explained the matter in 1753:

> It is not to be wondered at, since we seldom converse with our Negroes, especially with those who were not born among us; and though I learned this but lately when the smallpox was among us last spring, by some discourse being accidentally overheard among the Negroes themselves, I have had the same Negroes above 20 years about my house, without knowing it before this time.

Other whites did not ask and therefore misunderstood what they saw. The early nineteenth-century historian James Stewart mistakenly believed Negro mothers in Jamaica "wilfully infected their children with yaws that [the children] might be released from their labour." But a more sensitive observer, Bryan Edwards, an eighteenth-century historian of the West Indies, inquired about the treatment and was told by one of his Akan women that the technique was used on the Gold Coast to inoculate children with infectious matter from the yaws to give them a mild case of the disease and thereby provide resistance later in life.[12]

Tired of masters who seldom understood them, former slaves too old to work left their Yankee masters' families and congregated in little settlements of free blacks. Archaeological evidence from the settlements of black freedmen in Andover and Plymouth, Massachusetts, indicates that their homes were designed on Afro-American or African twelve-foot floor patterns, rather than following the sixteen-foot floor length common to Anglo-

American homes. Moreover, the small mud-and-post storage sheds the freedmen constructed are especially reminiscent of West African house building traditions.

These retentions of an African aesthetic, even given their overlay of Anglo-American materials and style, bespeaks the continuity of African values, a continuity that is also suggested by the communal nature of these small settlements where the dwellings were built one right next to the others. Similarly, the use of floor fires in these little houses which lacked fireplaces was unusual for New England but common enough in Africa.[13]

One of the most interesting retentions of Old World culture was the perfection of memory skills in the manner common to the griot castes of Africa. Old Blind Caesar, who likely came from such a family in Africa, had been a carpenter in slavery, but in his old age he made his living off his remarkably trained memory. As William Bentley remembered, "Twenty years ago I gave him the age of my parents and kindred of three generations with the promise of a reward upon notice of their birthday. I have never known that he lost one or confounded it with any other." Rosanna, a Gambian-born Narragansett slave, used similar skills to entertain her less talented white acquaintances: "When members of the family applied to her, as they often did, in real or feigned perplexity concerning the exact date of any past occurrence, however trifling, she was able to reply that it took place so many days before or after the time of the last (or whatever) Meeting."[14]

Since African immigrants had to learn the new Anglo-American ways from scratch and often resisted what they considered odd or inferior practices, it might have been expected that Afro-Americans would have made mediocre chefs. In their own cooking, for example, archaeological evidence suggests Yankee blacks preferred to use an African pattern of cutting and serving meat for stews rather than sawing the meat for roasts as favored by the master class.[15] This African predisposition for "butchering" meat could cause problems at the master's table. Consider this description by Fanny Kemble on her visit to the American South:

Such is the barbarous ignorance of the [black] cook . . . that I defy the most expert anatomist to pronounce on any piece (joint they cannot be called) of mutton brought to our table . . . Remonstrances and expositions have produced no result whatever, however, but an increase of eccentricity in the *chunks* of sheeps' flesh placed on the table; the squares, diamonds, cubes, and rhumboids of mutton.[16]

Nonetheless, black cooks more than made up for their different styles of preparation by their superior knowledge of spices and other culinary artistry. It was, said Fanny Kemble, "a natural gift with them, as with Frenchmen."[17] William Fowler, an early New England historian, agreed the situation was the same in the northern colonies: "In many families, Negroes had an important position, especially as cooks. As compared with the Indians or the Irish, they were epicures. They generally took care to know what they carried upon the table, being their own tasters."[18]

Black New Englanders seem to have long retained other African predispositions about food and eating, preferring to eat communally from bowls, for example, rather than individually from plates. African tastes showed up in the ordering of tamarind fruit from the West Indies by the freedmen of the "New Guinea" district near Plymouth, Massachusetts; moreover, these sweet lovers stored the dried fruit in jars almost identical to West African pottery and unlike anything in the New England tradition.[19]

Whites appreciated and, within the limits of their own tastes, encouraged the Afro-American artistry in cuisine; the Marine Society of Salem, for example, chose to hire a black chef to oversee the preparation of their important turtle feast. Black cooks were celebrated in local histories for their cakes, pastry, and gingerbread—even though these arts were usually learned under Euro-American guidance. New World cooking, even then, was best defined as a blending of different traditions. When Thomas Hazard memorialized Phillis, his grandfather's African-born cook, for her "jonny-cake" (johnnycake was a Yankee version of the American hoe cake), the artistry he was immortalizing probably combined African and American Indian techniques.[20]

A blending of styles and tastes also marked the dress of black New Englanders. The slaves brought an African eye to their Euro-American materials and created something new out of their owners' used clothing and their own purchases. The black style of dress in New England, as elsewhere, celebrated life in bright colors, demonstrating joy in physical attractiveness. The boldness of this affirmation was generally considered unseemly by white observers, probably because it belied what they believed should be the humble demeanor and position of bondsmen. New

England was not unique in this; throughout the Americas white writers commented on what they regarded to be the excessive emphasis Afro-Americans placed on colorful and stylish dress during their Sunday and holiday promenades.[21] Indeed, in their own folklore, Afro-Americans satirically blamed the African love of red cloth as the cause of their being lured into slavers' chains.[22]

The black Yankees were as resourceful as their brothers and sisters elsewhere in turning their masters' used clothing, local dyes, and their own purchases into a special kind of sartorial splendor. Harriet Beecher Stowe has given us a portrait of one well-dressed black Connecticut woman who strolled to church in a typically Afro-American ensemble. Her yellow gown was boldly set off by a red petticoat and a red, African-style kerchief turban; to accent her wardrobe she chose a string of golden-colored beads and African-style, gold hoop earrings. She cut a fine figure, especially as she was a large woman, plump in accord with African standards of beauty.[23]

The clothing tastes of the region's black men may be surmised from a runaway notice for an escaped slave from Hebron, Connecticut. Tony took with him his new coat and claret-colored vest (worn with mixed red, white, and yellow buttons), a worn grey coat with a red and white striped vest, a pair of deerskin breeches, a pair of checked long trousers, two Holland shirts, a striped shirt, and one checked shirt. Tony's tastes were nothing if not bold.[24]

Even if the slaves of New England left no diaries, we still know something of their personal pride, their zest for life, and their rejection of their masters' values by the language of their Sunday dress. It is true that in their everyday wear most bondsmen and bondswomen looked drab and tattered; but when they put on their best, the old African immigrants among them knew their sartorial splendor outdid that of even the coastal elites of Africa.

An important commercial and social carryover from Africa was the slaves' Sabbath markets. It appalled the sensibilities of pious Boston that during the first half of the eighteenth century black bondspeople swarmed into the churchgoing city not with prayer books but, as the selectmen complained, "with corn, apples, and other fruit of the earth to the great disturbance of the public peace and scandal of our Christian profession." The Negro markets of the slaves were a source of common complaint throughout the Americas; but nowhere, even in New England, was the master class able to suppress them. As Abel Alleyne explained from

Barbados, "Nothing could keep the blacks from their markets short of locking them up."[25] Only at such markets could black women maintain their traditional role as traders; and, of course, the market was no small social attraction. It is ironic, given the free enterprise heritage of the United States, that whites so constantly tried to discourage this central institution of black economic initiative.

Since the Sabbath markets were a place for socializing as well as business, they probably fostered surreptitious drinking and gambling among the men. Gambling was a favorite pastime for most of the black Yankees. Indeed, a young ship's steward named William Reed memorialized this attraction with his explosive anger. When he wasn't given leave to partake in the gaming of Boston's election day festivities, Reed blew up two casks of gunpowder, destroying the stern of his ship. His deed ignited what became a local folk chant: "Who blew up the ship? Nigger! Why for? 'Cause he couldn't go to 'Lection and shake paw paw."[26]

Paw paw (also called "pa pa" and "props") was a popular gambling game in New England which was played with cowrie shells. Since Paw Paw was also a common name for slaves from the Dahomean port of Popo, the game may well have been brought to the northern colonies by Africans from that region.[27] The game probably stems from African divination techniques. The Igbo of eastern Nigeria practice divination by throwing four cowries; they interpret four shells with their openings down as a favorable omen and see three-and-one combinations as disastrous. In New England's paw paw, four shells were also shaken, with evens winning and odds losing.[28]

By the middle of the eighteenth century this African game had become a favorite of whites as well as blacks throughout the coastal cities of the North. Thus, in gambling as in other folk ways, African traditions continued in New England. However, in the case of paw paw, the tradition was not only able to maintain itself, it expanded to fill what may have been a void in the local white culture: it remained the most popular form of gambling in the northern ports until at least the Civil War.

Music was another element of folklife heavily influenced by African culture. New England's black immigrants brought with them the musical technology to make African three-string fiddles, flutes, banjos, tambourines, drums, and various idiophones. As Isaac Norris of Philadelphia noted in 1719 of his bondsman Peter, "Thou knowest Negro Peter's ingenuity in making for himself and playing on a fiddle without any assistance." In New England, as elsewhere in the New World, African-style drumming was discouraged; but Hamlet, an African-born slave from Middletown, Connecticut, was still able to get around the informal prohibitions by putting his traditional craftsmanship to use in his old age by manufacturing "toy" drums which were not threatening to the master class.[29]

The musicians performing at many Yankee celebrations were men whom the whites called "the natural musicians among the slaves"—that is, men who had learned their musical arts in Africa or from fellow bondsmen. Here was another traditional skill which could be put to a profit by former slaves; this was noted in a runaway advertisement from Boston in 1743 which warned masters against allowing Cambridge, who "plays well on a flute, and not so well on a violin" from teaching their servants his skills.[30] The musical talents of Occramer Marycoo were so apparent that he was allowed while still a slave to open a singing school in Newport. Under the name Newport Gardner, Marycoo became a composer and dance master, and near the end of his life wrote the anthem "Promise" for the Newport Colored Union Church's missionary expedition to Liberia.[31]

New England's black community produced numerous maestros of the fiddle: Concord's Samson, East Guilford's Caesar, Wallingford's Cato, Meriden's Robin Prinn, and Narragansett's Polydore Gardner all profited from their Afro-American expertise in the musical arts. And the description of West Simsbury's Simon Fletcher is apt as a general characterization: "Simon was what is called a second or third rate fiddler, and the same may be said of a great share of the men of color of those times."[32] The best of these black fiddlers (or was it those who best assimilated Euro-American musical styles) played for the dances of both the white and black communities.[33] As fiddlers, it is likely that black musicians were more energetic in their playing and more expert in the popular jigs and reels because of their African taste for energetic music.[34] Indeed, given the ubiquity of African-born fiddle players in the early United States, it is extremely probable that the American fiddle playing style carries a strong African influence.

In New England, as in the American South, the improvisational and satiric humor of African song was perfectly suited to the development of a special Afro-American expertise in the calling of dance figures. Like many of his race, Pomp, the slave of William Bucknam of Malden, Massachusetts, was fiddler and caller at local country dances. Two couplets dating from

1777 of one of Pomp's humorous lyrics to the tune of "The Black Swan" are said to be still extant in the following lines:

> Theare was five cobblers made a frolick
> An one was taken with the collick
>
> The fiddlers name was pomp or seser
> And david danced with a mop squeser.[35]

Dancing, as might be expected by those familiar with Africa, was a major part of the way Afro-Americans in New England celebrated their informal get-togethers, husking parties, and other holidays. When William Grimes, for example, opened an upper room in New Bedford, the black community flocked to his establishment with their families so as to dance late into the evenings—much to the annoyance of Grimes's neighbors. The constant noise finally cost Grimes his lease.[36] While many New Englanders, white as well as black, enjoyed tripping the light fantastic, it would seem fair to surmise that the emphasis given to the dance by Yankee blacks stemmed from a continuation of African custom. Black Caesar, as described by Harriet Beecher Stowe, was a representative figure: "He could sing and fiddle, and dance the double-shuffle, and was *au fait* in all manner of jigs and hornpipes." Caesar's abilities in the double-shuffle and jigs sounds suggestively African, as does the dancing of the light-hearted women who Jane Shelton recalled "shuffled and tripped to the sound of the fiddle" on election day.[37] Thomas Hazard's description of Sam, "who had a way of his own of fetching a terrific screech like a catamount, and then dashing forward to the middle of the floor," sounds like the Africans whom Pierre de Laussat observed celebrating Christmas holiday in South Carolina; they, he said, danced by "distorting their frame in the most unnatural figures and emitting the most hideous noises."[38]

Little specific is known about black vocal music in New England. Singing was part of the communal celebrations of elections, and much of it may have been African, as it tended to be elsewhere in the New World during similar holidays. The accompaniment of singing with hand or percussive fingernail drumming on boards, such as was noted as part of black Cato's songs in Deerfield, Massachusetts, was doubtless an attribute of Afro-American style.[39]

Many whites recalled the singing of their families' black servants. Thomas Hazard reminisced that as a boy, "Old Mose's Guinea songs sounded in my ear a thousand times more divine than [any] I ever heard from the throat of Jenny Lind." White children often loved the black servants of their families and so made a most appreciative audience—often absorbing far more than their parents suspected. Henry B. Stanton, for example, dated his abolitionist concerns to his New England infancy, when he learned of the white treachery that had sent Miantonomo, chief of the Narragansett, to a cruel death in 1643:

> In my childhood we had a Negro slave whose voice was attuned to the sweetest cadence. Many a time did she lull me to slumber by singing this touching lament. It sank deep into my breast, and moulded my advancing years. Before I reached manhood I resolved that I would become the champion of the oppressed colored races of my country.[40]

Folk narratives joined folk songs as part of the moral armament of the slave population. In African fashion blacks used the tales for instruction of their own and their masters' children, as well as relishing the stories for their entertainment value. Tales of cruel enslavement were favorites commonly told to impressionable white children, for in the children alone the slaves recognized a fair-minded audience. As Jupiter Mars explained in regard to the white infant Mary Oakley, "My black skin does not make any difference to her."[41]

Even after he grew up, John Tower could clearly recall how his family's slave, the African-born Cuffee Josselyn, looked as he told of his childhood, of playing innocently in the surf of his homeland while his mother watched so that no harm should befall him. Without warning, sailors from a large ship seized the boy "while his mother stood on the shore wringing her hands and screaming for her little boy that she was never to see again." Jinny Cole poignantly summed up a similar experience to her wet-eyed audience by stressing "and we nebber see our mudders any more."[42] Black children were, of course, even more affected by such tales; Jeremiah Asher remembered listening "with feelings of unmingled grief when my grandfather related the story of his capture,—stolen away as he was, from father, mother, brother and sister."[43]

Memories of enslavement were only a small part of the immigrant repertoire. Much more popular were exotic stories of the African homeland. Many young Yankees spent long New England evenings sitting by the fire while old African-born servants enthralled them with tales of witches and hobgoblins intermixed with humorous anecdotes and sunny reminiscences of their African youths. Thomas Hazard, a great Yankee yarn-spinner in his own right, never forgot the "splendid stories these old nigs, gathered from all quarters of Narragansett [for the Christmas holidays] used to tell me and the six little nigs and niggeresses." Many a time he sat "scrooched up" in the kitchen corner "trembling all over with fear, listening to their stories of big lion, and giants, in Guinea." And, recalling the effect of those stories, he commented, "Even now that I am in my eighty-third year, I seldom see a wild-grape vine loaded with fox grapes, that I do not think of Old Mose's story [of a black girl "cocht" by a Guinea monster], which I devoutly believed in, into advanced boyhood."[44]

Senegambia, the grey eminence of the slaves of Willet Carpenter of North Kingston, Rhode Island, never tired of relating the praises of his African "family" history. His father, he said, was a powerful king in Gambia, living in a great palace with gold stepping stones, a silver door, and a "gold-iron" dog-shaped knocker. At the end of a long entrance hall was a golden throne on which his father sat dressed grandly in European garments given to him by British sea captains. The king, he boasted, maintained a fleet of gigantic ships on the Gambia, bigger than any made in England.[45] Senegambia, who may have been from a griot caste rather than a royal family, embellished his narrative of noble birth with tall tale flourishes typical of the American story-telling style; but the larger truth he intended to illustrate, the power and prestige of the Gambia River kings— of Africa itself—comes through clearly.[46]

Senegambia's riddles were equally intriguing; they also seem suggestively alien to the Yankee riddle tradition, but at home with Afro-American ones. For example, he asked, what is "a woman dressed in grey, that goes crying 'round the house, and throws her black veil in at the window?" It was the rainstorm, as his Narragansett audience was pleased to remember.[47]

Throughout the New World, blacks were noted for their satiric wit, which they based on African traditions of improvisational humor, proverb, and metaphor. As Bryan Edwards observed of the West Indies, "I have sometimes heard them convey much strong meaning in narrow compass . . . such pointed sentences as would have reflected no disgrace on poets and philosophers." Indeed, white New Englanders recalled Chloe Spear precisely for her inventive skill in "conveying her ideas in metaphor which originated in her own mind."[48]

Yankee slaves were remembered for the content as well as the style of their observations. In satiric and critical commentary lampooning the New England ministry and landed gentry, the bondsmen turned the social world on its head with such wit that whites as well as blacks passed on the Afro-American perspective in humorous anecdotes. Jesse Sherburn, a Negro bootblack, was recalled for jokingly pointing out to the Reverend Mr. Woods of Newport, New Hampshire, the supposed similarity of their missions: "Sir, you *shines* the souls of men; I shine their uppers!" Often, the humor had more of a bite to it. It was said that on a fishing outing, Parson Parker of Pawtucket Falls, Massachusetts, planned to have some fun at the expense of his stereotypically dozing slave by tying a rat onto the unwatched line; but the sly Caesar turned the tables by noting as he pulled in his prize that he appeared to have caught a minister—"it was something with a black coat."[49]

Often the humor hung on the black response to Christianity. For example, one anecdote recalled that the Reverend Chauncey of Durham, Connecticut, had a meadow called the Burnham lot on which the hay crop had failed for a number of years because of heavy rains. When drought subsequently threatened Connecticut, the minister prepared to attend a midweek prayer meeting to invoke the Almighty God to send the necessary showers. Chauncey's slave, Devonshire, playing the innocent, is said to have asked, "Is it Sabbath Day to-DAY, Massa?" "No," replied Chauncey. Then why, Devonshire wanted to know, was Chauncey going to meeting?

> Mr. C. in reply said earnestly, Devonshire, Don't you see all our fields, meadows and gardens are drying up for want of rain? God is the author of all our mercies, and we meet to pray that *He* would send down rain to water the earth. O-o, said Devonshire, with a curious twinkle of the eye. *Rain*, Massa, *rain*, THAT'S what you want. Better go an mow the Burnham lot; get RAIN quick THEN.[50]

In anecdotal tradition, as they had in reality, slaves were recalled as humorously questioning the basic assumptions of Yankee society. Vance Coit, a black man from Newport, New Hampshire, was remembered for humorously mocking both the sacredness of the Sabbath and Christian beliefs about hell:

A neighbor, having some hay in a condition in which it would spoil unless taken care of on the Sabbath, applied to Vance for help, offering him a pound of sugar if he would assist in getting it in. Vance, with much apparent indignation, replied, "Do you think I would have my soul fry in hell to all eternity for a pound of sugar? No!"—then added, "Give me two pounds, and I will risk it."[51]

Another Negro wit pointed out how Yankee society looked from the bottom up. At the celebration marking the erection of the steeple of the East Windsor, Connecticut, meeting house, the speakers were extolling on the grandeur of the edifice constructed after sufficient funds were collected by subscription from the parishioners. Black Primus Manumit responded by roasting the self-satisfied deacons with a satiric and poetic sentiment:

> Big church, high steeple,
> Proud Committee, poor people.[52]

These traditional black witticisms found their way into Yankee anecdotal traditions and local histories because out of the black irritation with sanctimonious slave masters came pearls of humor that whites, too, appreciated. Consider the story told of the stereotypically "kind" master who planned to reward his slave in the hereafter with the honor of lying next to him:

An old gentleman, at the point of death, called a faithful Negro to him, telling him that he would do him honor before he died. The fellow thanked him, and hoped "Massa would live long." "I intend, Cato," said the master, "to allow you to be buried in the family vault." "Ah! Massa," returns Cato, "me no like dat. Ten pounds would be better to Cato. Me no care where me be buried; besides, Massa, suppose we be buried together, and de devil come looking for Massa, in de dark, he might take away poor Negro man in mistake."[53]

A reader who doubts the wisdom of folk humor would do well to note how this anecdote encapsulates the essential black rejection of the slave owners' rationalization of bondage as a path to eternal life for those of African descent; indeed, for the bondsman who went beyond pointing out the hypocrisy in the Christianity of the master class, slavery meant the eternal damnation of masters rather than the salvation of slaves.

White narrators kept these stories alive because the humor was too good, the relationships too revealing, to be totally censored or forgotten. Consider the slaves' reaction to Yankee justice as captured in an anecdote similar to the Cato story above.

> Cuff, a slave of Mr. Torrey, was taken up for breaking the Sabbath, tried before Justice Joseph Greenleaf . . . and fined. After he had paid the fine, he asked for a receipt of the justice. The justice asked him for what purpose he wanted the receipt? Cuff answered, "By-and-by you die, and go knock at the good gate, and they say, 'What you want, Cuff?' I say, 'I want to come in'; they say I can't because I broke the Sabbath at such a time. I say, 'I paid for it.' They will say, 'Where is your receipt?' Now, Mr. Judge, I shall have to go away down to the bad place to get a receipt of you, that I mended him, before I can enter the good gate."[54]

Just as many of the slaves suspected the hypocrisy and rejected the justice of Christianity as it was preached to them, they also made fun of their masters' puritanical approach to sexuality. Consider the story of the slave, Devonshire, who had for too long endured the pious preaching of his master:

> On returning from church (after hearing a discourse from the text [Ephesians 2:1] "Dead in trespasses and sins"), [Devonshire] found the barn door open and the "Old Ram" on the hay satisfying the demands of nature. He returned immediately to the house exclaiming, "Massa, Massa, the Old Ram is dead!" Mr. Chauncey followed him to the barn and found as above stated, and then, in a reproving manner said, "Devonshire! How came you to say so?" Devonshire replied quickly, "Dead in trespass and sin, I guess, Massa."[55]

Likewise, work experiences and the different perspectives of master and man over labor were naturally topics of humor among the bondsmen. The Reverend Mr. Chauncey of Durham, Connecticut, was said to have received his comeuppance when, after visiting a hay field, he remarked in a familiar and paternalistic way to his men that "many hands make light work." Devonshire, his slave, who was raking behind two others and thus saw the harvest from a different perspective, retorted, "No, no Massa, not when you'r rakin' behind." A similar anecdote recalls that Lieutenant Governor Gill of New Hampshire had both hired men and a slave to tend his farm. Gill, the story goes, rose early with his laborers and, praying before breakfast and work, he thanked God that he had preserved them through the night and had given them to see another morning. At the close of the prayer his slave chided, "No morning yet, Massa." The worker's viewpoint also appeared when Prince Youngey was offered his freedom in his old age so that his master, Deacon Thomas Buckminster of Framingham, Massachusetts, could avoid the cost of keeping him. Youngey pithily declined the tainted offer with the sagacious Afro-American proverb that fit the occasion: "Massa eat the meat; he now pick the bone."[56]

The slaves often disguised antiwhite sentiments and moral judgments in pretended misunderstandings of the Christian platitudes of their masters. Hidden in the self-deprecating humor of this feigned ignorance were unmistakable barbs of criticism. An example of such stories is found in a description of the encounter of Aaron, an African-born slave of the Morton family of Middleboro, Massachusetts, with the devil. His white audience made light of Aaron's beliefs about Satan. But Aaron simply placed himself within a symbolic protective circle, like those traditionally drawn on the ground in certain areas of Africa, and began to explain his vision of Satan:

"Now, here is de ring wid old Aaron in de middle, de Lord is wid him here; de devil is on de outside, now keep your distance, Massa debil, and do not dare to come into dis ring." Then with a heavy blow with his cane he would say, "Go your way, Massa debil, and do not come hangin' 'bout here to eat old Aaron up." Some one would banter him by asking how the devil looked, and he would say that he "had a head like a nigger's, only with horns, and eyes that kep' a-rollin' like dis (rolling his own), and a mouth dat would eat you up in a minute. He go about to ketch wicked niggers; he ketch white folks too, some o' dem," casting a significant eye on those who were taunting him. "Mistress read about him in de Bible, and Aaron has seen him hisself."[57]

The Afro-American folk wisdom of New England emphasized the illusory nature of worldly status. As Hagar Merriman put it, "All must die, and I feel it better to die poor, like Jesus, than be rich [like the whites], and have no fear of God, and no peace."[58] In their folklore the blacks inverted the value system of the Yankee slaveholders, contrasting Christianity as practiced by the master class with the Christianity they preached; thus, in

Afro-American eyes it was the slaves who most often followed the heavenly path of Christian humility, while the sanctimonious and hypocritical masters blindly paced the road to damnation.

If the hypocrisy of the master class was clear enough to the slaves, it was not an easy message to get across to their owners. Nonetheless, during the Revolutionary War, it was said, a slave named Jack approached his clergyman master with such a message. The master, a zealot in the cause of patriot liberty, still continued to hold his African servant in bondage.

> Jack went to his master one day, and addressed him in the following language: —"Master, I observe you always keep preaching about liberty and praying for liberty, and I love to hear you, sir, for liberty be a good thing. You preach well and you pray well; but one thing you remember master,—Poor Jack is not free yet." Struck with the propriety and force of Jack's admonition, the clergyman, after a momentary pause, told Jack if he would behave well in his service for one year longer, he should be free. Jack fulfilled the condition, obtained his freedom, and became a man of some property and respectability.[59]

Of course, such messages were usually too dangerous to say right out; therefore, in the best of African tradition, slaves often played the fool. As William Fowler observed, "In many towns, some Negro, by his drollery and good nature, was a great favorite, affording the people as much amusement as the king's fool. . . . they were very willing to be the fool of the play."[60] But this foolery was not a Sambo-like submission. The wit for which the blacks were so noted, as we have seen, was scathing and sarcastic under its droll cloak. Like Africans who traditionally used satire as a social control directed against those in power, slaves in the anecdotal tradition were usually remembered as deflating the proper world of their masters with barbs of wit.[61]

Since whites also chafed under the paradigms of virtue set forth by the Yankee upper class, they joined with the blacks in enjoying tales which punctured the pretensons of the upper orders. Thus it was the whites who took over and remembered Black Jack Lee's metaphorical description of the gentry of Rowley, Massachusetts: "One dog bark, set another barking, by-and-by all the dogs in town bark, sake of hearing themselves bark."[62]

James Fenimore Cooper had believed the black Yankees were "so ground down in the Puritan mill, that they [were] neither fish, flesh, nor red-herring, as we say so . . . nondescript."[63] But the truth was otherwise.

Black folklife, when shucked from its husk of white anecdotal tradition, reveals kernels of a true Afro-American culture. Even in predominately white New England, a black folk culture still grew. If the roots of black tradition had to crack puritan granite for sustenance, the bloom was still there to be seen, a black American hybrid flowering, against the odds, in the chill Yankee air.

Part 4

In Celebration of Afro-American Culture

Chapter 10

Black Kings and Governors

I n Puritan New England, election day was the most important holiday of the year.[1] It is not surprising, then, that the occasion was also adopted by Yankee slaves for annual festivals to honor the Afro-American community. Beginning in the mid-eighteenth century and continuing in places for almost a century thereafter, black New Englanders used the holiday both to elect governors and kings of their own and to celebrate the inauguration of the new officials. While outwardly it may have seemed that the slave population was simply imitating the election festivities of their masters, in actuality Yankee bondsmen were creating an important celebration of black awareness which, like similar holidays elsewhere in the Americas, borrowed from African forms and satirized white society as much as it imitated Euro-American institutions.

Such celebrations in New England may stem back to informal holidays organized by the slaves themselves to honor the royalty common among them.[2] For example, King Pompey, a slave of Thomas Mansfield of Lynn, Massachusetts, had been born a prince in Africa. When Pompey became too old to work, he was given his freedom to move to the forest east of the Saugus River. There each year, as had been the custom for many years previously, he was host, guest of honor, and master of ceremonies for a commemoratory holiday in honor of Africa celebrated by fellow slaves from all the neighboring towns. These memorial celebrations near Lynn may explain the entry of May 27, 1741, in the diary of Benjamin Lynde of Salem. It notes Lynde giving "Scip 5s and Wm 2s 6d" for a "Negro's hallowday."[3]

The formal election of black kings and governors in New England, however, probably began in the early eighteenth century in the capital cities of the charter colonies. Slaves who accompanied their masters into town for the colonial elections decided to use their free time together to elect leaders and hold celebrations of their own. Such elections were being held in Newport, Rhode Island, by 1756, and had been held for some time prior to 1766 in Hartford, Connecticut.[4] Whites seem to have gone along with these black elections because they hoped they could use the resultant black governors and kings as indirect enforcers of social propriety; moreover, since the whites saw the black elections and festivities as humorous, non-threatening imitations of white traditions, they did not perceive the celebrations as a threat to the social order.[5]

By the 1770s black election celebrations had expanded to include Norwich, Connecticut, and Salem, Massachusetts. When the eighteenth century ended, similar institutions were found in Derby, Durham, Farmington, Middletown, Oxford, Wallingford, Waterbury, and Wethersfield in Connecticut; Danvers, Lynn, and North Bridgewater (and perhaps Boston) in Massachusetts; Portsmouth in New Hampshire; and North Kingston, South Kingston, and Warwick Neck in Rhode Island. Additional Connecticut towns like Seymour, Woodbridge, and New Haven were hosting Negro elections in the early nineteenth century, and probably began the tradition in the late eighteenth century.[6]

There may well have been additional election day observances elsewhere in New England; but since these activities were of primary interest only to the slaves, the records of the master class overlook them. In any case, as the celebration of Negro election expanded to more and more localities, the jurisdiction the black rulers claimed contracted to smaller regions of the colony or state, and even to single towns.[7]

The difference in title between the black "kings" and "governors" usually stemmed from the location of the celebration. In Connecticut and Rhode Island, where white citizens were permitted to choose their own governors in the colonial era, black rulers were elected and, like their white counterparts, usually called governors; whereas in the royal colonies of New Hampshire and eighteenth-century Massachusetts, where white governors were appointed, the elected Negro leaders were called kings.

There was no universal form for the procedure of electing a black government; but it is possible to put together a composite representation of the election, celebration, and functioning of black government in eighteenth-century New England. The elections were made possible by the necessities of white election day activities. When the white masters came to town or took the day off for the local election, the slaves were generally allowed their own time for amusement. The masters probably did not have much choice in this because, as William Bentley observed in his diary, slaves "were too restless at home to be of any use till [the election holidays] were over."[8]

In Massachusetts, the black election was on the last Wednesday in Easter term (later the last Wednesday in May), and the celebrations ran from the Monday prior to election to the Saturday night following it. In Rhode Island, black elections took place around the third or last Saturday in June, while in Connecticut they fell on the day after the white elections, and the celebrations continued through the following Saturday.[9]

In early Newport, the franchise requirements (at least as far as the master class recalled them) were stiff: only those Negroes who owned a pig and a sty were allowed to vote. But, generally, informality was the rule, and the manner of choosing a governor or king followed the wishes of the incumbent and the candidates.[10]

Some insights into the nature of these elections comes from a controversy that arose in Connecticut during the American Revolution. In May 1776, Governor Cuff of Hartford abdicated his office as governor of the Negroes of Connecticut. He bypassed normal election procedures by appointing John Anderson as the new governor. Anderson was the slave of Phillip Skene, a British officer, and Cuff's friends advised him that as a Tory, Anderson could not be elected. Therefore, Anderson was appointed. Meanwhile the Tory party tried to assuage the electorate by the judicious expenditure of a twenty-five-dollar campaign fund for dancing and entertainment on the Friday after the appointment. The irregularity of this procedure led to an investigation by Connecticut's white governor and council, who had apparently feared some kind of Tory intrigue. But since the majority of Connecticut's blacks were loyal to the patriot cause and since the black leadership supported Governor Cuff's action, nothing came of the inquiry.[11] The key to the Negro elections is not to be found in the democratic processes they engendered. As the Hartford incident suggests, recognition of the office, its formalities, and the festivities honoring the leadership of the black community were what mattered most to the slave population.

Slaves dressed to the nines for the holiday. Clothes were borrowed from masters and mistresses; and the owner of the governor-elect was expected to help provide provisions, decorations, and liquor for the celebration. Wealthy landowners often surrendered even their horses to the use of black celebrants, who "with cues, real or false, heads pomatumed and powdered, cocked hat, mounted on the best Narragansett pacers, sometimes with their master's sword, with their ladies on pillions . . . pranced to election."[12]

It says much about the relationships of Yankee bondage that the slaves were able to persuade their masters to contribute so lavishly to their servants' election day displays. Indirectly the bondsmen increased these contributions by making it clear that the festivities not only reflected the position of the black candidates but that they were a conspicuous display of the economic status of the candidates' masters. It was said during slavery that the rank of the master was the slave's rank as well. Since slaves in their own society assumed the status of their owners, it became degrading to the reputation of masters if their slaves appeared shabbily dressed or had less money to spend on election treats than slaves of other masters.[13] Thus, family slaves came to enjoy a much better bargain than poor whites who had to hire uniforms and horses to be worthy of regimental review as members of the New England Training Day militias.[14]

For the masters, the whole process of black elections could become quite expensive. E. R. Potter, a state and federal legislator of Narragansett, Rhode Island, found the canvassing of his servant John excessive in cost, even if successful in effect: "Soon after the election, Mr. Potter had a conference with the Governor, and stated to him that one or the other must give up politics, or the expense would ruin them both. Governor John took the wisest course, abandoned politics and retired to the status of private life."[15]

On the morning of election day, the beating of drums and an occasional random gunshot quickened black pulses and announced the impending festivities. Although there was little if any work to be done, no one tarried; across New England the bondsmen hurriedly put on the best outfits they owned or could borrow, for many faced a long walk to reach the scene of the holiday festivities. Most slaves received their special holiday clothes as hand-me-downs from their masters; nonetheless, once the garments were cleaned up and matched with an African eye for color, they became ensembles of real style and flair. Looking their best, the bondsmen gathered into a procession to escort their incumbent king or governor to the polls. The appearance of this honor guard, which so pleased the blacks, struck more staid white eyes as being "anything but uniform," and, indeed, "somewhat fantastic." Imagine, for example, white attitudes toward the exotic sartorial style of Governor Eben Tobias of Derby, Connecticut, "caparisoned with gay feathers, flowers and ribbons, of red, white, and blue."[16]

The physical location of the elections approximated African choices in such matters—a suitable area of open grounds abutting a large spreading tree. Favorable conditions were found near the Collins farm in Danvers, at Hawkins Point in Derby, on the Neck near the North Burying Ground in Hartford, near Potter's Woods or Pine Hill in South Kingston, and at the head of Thames Street in Newport.[17]

The voting had been preceded by weeks of politicking by the ambitious candidates, and often party spirit was rife. Once at the polls, the aspiring politicos harangued the voters one last time and then invited their friends to sample the refreshment they provided. While only the men could vote, the women actively lobbied on behalf of their own favorites during these last crucial moments.[18]

At the end of some three hours of combined electioneering and celebration, the vote was taken. There was no single method used throughout New England. In Newport there was formal balloting; in Narragansett the chief marshal and his assistants requested the populace to form two lines behind their respective candidates so as to tally the vote; in Derby, Connecticut, a voice vote was used.[19]

After the votes were counted and the results declared, a general shout announced that the struggle was over and the inaugural parade would soon begin. Unlike New England's white elections, which often ended in the broken heads and bloody noses of party strife, black elections usually ended without mishap.[20] This was, in part, because election day was more a social statement and festive occasion in the black community than a dividing of real power and spoils.

Soon every voice among the celebrants was said to have risen to its highest key: "All the various languages of Africa, mixed with broken and ludicrous English, filled the air, accompanied with the music of the fiddle, tambourine, the banjo, drum, etc." The whole crowd joined the train of the governor-elect and proceeded in grand style to his master's house, where the postelection festivities would be held.[21]

In Connecticut the new governor rode through town "on one of his master's horses, adorned with plaited gear, his aides on each side *a la militaire . . .* moving with a slow majestic pace." To make their ruler's appearance even more impressive, new governors were usually honored with a sash, and kings were given crowns or other emblems of royalty.[22] The Hartford governor was escorted by "a troop of blacks, sometimes a hundred in number, marching sometimes two and two, sometimes mounted in true military style and dress on horseback." In close escort with the governor were his officials, which in Hartford included a lieutenant governor, sheriff, deputies, and a justice of the peace. These important personages were ceremonially armed with guns and swords provided by their masters, and in African style they fired off salutes as the procession advanced.[23]

The noise of the celebration and the impropriety of so many bondsmen carrying arms greatly annoyed some of the townspeople of Salem, Massachusetts. On March 7 and again on May 16, 1758, they petitioned the city fathers that "as great disorder usually exists here on Election days by negroes assembling together, beating drums, using powder and having guns and swords, a bye-law may be made to prevent these things."[24] But most New England towns with black election celebrations learned to live with the tumult and did not fear impertinence from the armed bondsmen.

What especially distinguished the black inaugural parades from the escorts that white New Englanders gave to honor their own incumbent governors prior to general elections (the whites did not have inaugural parades until around 1830) was not the types of officials or the order of march; the distinguishing features of the black parades were the random gunfire and, most especially, the raucous music. Indeed, the prototype for the American political parade probably owes more to these black processions in New England than to any corresponding Euro-American institution of the same era. Whether the black king or governor "was escorted by an indefatigable drummer and fifer of eminence" or preceded by a whole informal band of musicians with tambourines, banjos, brass horns, drums, fifes, fiddles, clarinets, and every "sonorous metal" that could be found "uttering martial sound," the music and flying colors made the black election parades something special to white and black New Englanders alike.[25]

At the home of the owner of the new governor or king, the gentlemen newly elected hosted an inaugural dinner paid for by the proud master. According to the custom in Rhode Island, the ceremonies began with the chief marshal introducing the defeated candidate, who would offer and drink the first toast to the new governor. After the toast, the defeated candidate sat at the right hand of the new governor, who presided over a long table of honor. At the governor's left sat his lady, and that whole table was usually shaded under several large trees.[26] After the feasting and carefully moderated drinking, the new governor would rise with an air of dignity and, surrounded by his aides, pass through the well-wishers to his quarters. There he would receive congratulations and, at least in Hartford, make his official appointments creating ceremonial military positions, sheriffs, and justices of the peace. The rest of the afternoon and evening was spent in dancing, drinking, and general socializing.[27]

The governor's inaugural party was, as might be expected, staid and formal compared to the amusements that characterized the rest of the week's activities. One of William Pynchon's diary entries for 1788 captures the flavor of the rest of the Salem holiday by noting that even on the third day "carousing, music, etc., etc., go on with spirit."[28] A crude poem about Boston's election day from about 1760 similarly describes the bustle of the holiday and the rowdy army of revelers attracted to the black activities on the common.

> The city swarms with every sort
> Of black and white, and every sort
> Of high, low, rich and poor;
> Squaws, negroes, deputies in scores
> And ministers & Counsellors
> Are seen at every door.
>
> Long before Phoebus looks upon
> The outskirts of the horizon,
> The blacks their forces summon.
> Tables & Benches, chairs, & stools
> Rum-bottles, Gingerbread & bowls
> Are lug'd into the common.

> Thither resorts a motley crew,
> Of whites & Blacks & Indians too
> And trulls of every sort.
> There all day long they sit & drink,
> Swear, sing, play paupaw, dance and stink
> There Baccus holds his court.[29]

The play activities of Negro election were a blend of Euro-American and Afro-American amusements: From the white holiday traditions came quoits and pitching pennies, while from Afro-American customs came pawpaw and African forms of wrestling, stick fighting, and dancing; in addition, the running races and jumping contests common to both cultures gave young men opportunities to display their prowess before the maidens, who would join them in what William Bentley called "the most fatiguing dances" under "the never ceasing sound of the violin."[30]

All the excitement made election day a very special holiday in New England, a rare occasion when the slave community was free to gather for fellowship and fun outside of the purview of white masters and mistresses. It was a day of cultural pride when bondsmen formally recognized and honored their own autonomous leadership class, a day when in joyous parade they could even strut, if they wished, before their erstwhile masters and social betters.

The strong similarities between the basic ceremonies of New England's black election and those of white New England led the region's historians to emphasize the mimetic quality of the Afro-American celebration. But viewed from the wider New World perspective of Afro-American culture, the New England holiday seems a great deal less Yankee and more Afro-American. To understand this requires some acquaintance with the black holiday traditions of the Americas.[31]

In 1706, years before the first Negro election in New England, the coronation of a black king in Pernambuco, Brazil, highlighted a series of popular plays Brazilian blacks called *Congos*. The form of this coronation bears striking similarity to the eighteenth-century Yankee pattern.

These plays employed titles drawn from the Portuguese monarchial system in which kings, queens, secretaries of state, masters of ceremony, heralds, ladies in waiting and guards of honor, a military service with marshals, brigadiers, colonels and all the other positions and ranks were to be found. The use of the terms *Majesty*, *Excellency*, and *Sir* were customary. Those of high rank received the title of Dom and were supported by the public authorities in their attributes of quasi-sovereignty. Each district or parish had its own king and queen with a court, the coronation taking place on the feast of our Lady of the Rosary, the crown being placed on the head of the fortunate Negro by the parish priest. This was the pretext for sumptuous banquets and African dances at the sugar plantation to which the king belonged.[32]

To gain greater attendance at church, the Catholic authorities of Brazil were willing to give permission for their African immigrants to appear in native costume and perform old country songs and dances during public festivals. In the early 1700s, a Jesuit priest advised Brazilian slave owners not only to permit such goings-on, but even to encourage their slaves in these celebrations: "You should not make it difficult for them to choose their king, and to sing and dance as they desire on certain appointed days of the year."[33] Many Brazilian slaves celebrated Kings Day (Epiphany or Twelfth Night) with a festival called *Rei do Congo* in which they elected and crowned a king and queen of the Congo; the annual March festival of Our Lady of the Rosary (patroness of Negroes) also served for a similar occasion, according to Henry Koster's description of 1810:

At this period is chosen the King of the Congo nation, if the person who holds this situation has died in the course of the year, has from any cause resigned, or has been displaced by his subjects. The Congo negroes are permitted to elect a king and queen from among the individuals of their own nation; the personages who are fixed upon may either actually be slaves, or they may be manumitted negroes. These sovereigns exercise a species of mock jurisdiction over their subjects which is much laughed at by the whites; but their chief power and superiority over their countrymen is shown on the day of the festival. The negroes of their nation, however, pay much respect to them. The man who had acted as their king in Itmaraca (for each district had its king) for several years, was about to resign from old age, and a new chief was to be chosen; he who had been fixed upon for this purpose was an old man and a slave, belonging to the plantation of Amparo. The former queen would not resign, but still continued her post. . . .

We were standing at the door of the church, when there appeared a number of male and female negroes, habited in cotton dresses of colours of white, with flags flying and drums beating; and as they approached we discovered among them the king and queen, and the secretary of state. Each of the former wore upon their heads a crown, which was partly covered with gilt paper, and painted of various colours. The king was dressed in an old-fashioned suit of divers tints, green, red, and yellow; coat, waistcoat, and breeches; his sceptre was in his hand, which was of wood, and finely gilt. The queen was in a blue silk gown, also of ancient make; and the wretched secretary had to boast of as many colours as his master, but his dress had evident appearances of each portion having been borrowed from a different quarter. . . .

   As the king belonged to Amparo, the eating, drinking, and dancing were to be at that place.[34]

In the French West Indies, as in Brazil, the church supported the institution of royal elections and coronations in an attempt to win converts. This worried and annoyed the civil authority to the extent that in 1758 the governor of Martinique wrote the French king to complain of what he felt was an indecent Corpus Christi Day procession by the blacks. The historian Lucien Peytraud explains:

As the procession was in imitation of those of the whites, the blacks tried to rival them in pomp. A large number of Negroes were suited in arms (albeit wooden ones) and their discipline appeared remarkable to him. "Several others were richly dressed to represent the King, Queen, all the royal family, even to grand officers of the crown. The Governor was even assured that in one of the parishes of the island, the priest had the year previously introduced the two darkies who imitated the King and Queen into the sanctuary where they were both placed into the chairs."

The governor requested that such processions be banned in the future because he feared that Martinique's blacks, gathered and trained as they were at these festivals, needed only a disgruntled leader to arise. The French monarch at first approved the prohibition because the Negro processions seemed to him indecent and bad for discipline; but in response to the intercession of the monks the king relented, on the condition that the slaves not dress for the occasion or in any other way appear above their station.[35]

In Cuba, too, the blacks elected regional kings whom they honored in holiday celebrations. A description from Güines in 1844 catches the dignity of the day:

Almost unlimited liberty was given to the negroes. Each tribe, having selected its king and queen, paraded the streets with a flag, having its name, and the words *viva Isabella*, with the arms of Spain, painted on it. Their majesties were dressed in the extreme of fashion, and were very ceremoniously waited on by the ladies and gentlemen of the court, one of the ladies holding an umbrella [an African symbol of royalty] over the head of the queen. They bore their honors with that dignity which the negro loves so much to assume, which they, moreover, preserved in the presence of the whites. The whole gang was under the command of a negro marshall who, with a drawn sword, having a small piece of sugarcane stuck on its point, was continually on the move to preserve order in the ranks.[36]

Public holidays in early nineteenth-century Jamaica had a similar air:

Each of the African tribes upon the different estates formed itself into a distinct party, composed of men, women, and children. Each party had its King or Queen, who was distinguished by a mask of the most harlequin-like apparel. They paraded or gambolled in their respective neighborhoods, dancing to the rude music, which was occasionally drowned by the most hideous yells from the whole party by way of chorus.[37]

One might note here a difference between the New England institution and its New World counterparts. Elsewhere queens and other female officials were elected and held positions of considerable importance. Apparently the male dominance of New England's white society was mirrored in the black Yankees' decision not to grant office to women despite the traditional respect accorded women in many African and Afro-American cultures. Since this is one of the most striking differences between the New England black governments and those elsewhere, it is frustrating that no historical evidence illuminates the matter further.

Whatever the case in regard to the suppression of black queens, the key issue here is that festivals honoring Afro-American royalty were extremely common in the Americas. Antigua, Argentina, Barbados, Brazil, Colombia, Connecticut, Cuba, Guadeloupe, Guiana, Haiti, Jamaica, Martinique,

Massachusetts, Mexico, New Hampshire, New Orleans, New York, Panama, Peru, Rhode Island, St. Croix, Saint Domingue, St. Lucia, Tobago, Trinidad, Uruguay, and Venezuela all had their black royalty or governors.[38] Therefore, the institution of New England's Negro election day must be understood as not only Yankee but as African and Afro-American in inspiration. This will become clearer as we examine the functions of New England's black governments and celebrations as well as the characters and qualifications of the men who held the executive offices.

Chapter 11

The Functions and Character of Black Government

A N African essence to the office of king or governor within the black community of New England is suggested by the election of many leaders with strong connections to the old country. Both King Pompey of Lynn and Prince Robinson of Narragansett were African-born and of royal lineages, while governors Tobiah and Eben Tobias in nineteenth-century Derby, Connecticut, were the grandson and great-grandson respectively of an African prince.[1] King Nero Brewster of Portsmouth, New Hampshire, and governors Boston of Hartford, Quosh Freeman of Derby, and London of Wethersfield, Connecticut, were all native Africans; in addition the names of Hartford governors Cuff and Quaw (both day names) and Boston Trowtrow of Norwich, Connecticut, seem to indicate that these men were of African birth, just as the classical, slave cognomen "Caesar" commonly given to "new negroes" marks King Caesar of Durham, Connecticut, as of likely immigrant status.[2] Of some thirty-one men identified as black kings or governors in New England during the eighteenth and early nineteenth centuries, the eleven of probable African birth or African royal heritage constitute more than one-third of the office holders.[3]

Nonetheless, since African birth and even royal lineage were not uncommon in eighteenth- and nineteenth-century New England, other attributes were also necessary for a man to be elected a leader of the black community. One of the most important qualifications for office seems to have been a politically successful master wealthy enough to support the financial costs incumbent on a successful candidate for governor or king. There seems no doubt that within the serving class the political prestige of the master was shared by the master's man.[4] Consider, for example, a few of the offices held by several of the most important masters.

The African-born Governor London of Wethersfield was a slave of Colonel John Chester, a county court judge and a member of the Connecticut General Assembly; Governor Quaw of Hartford belonged to Colonel George Wyllys, town clerk and secretary of the colony of Connecticut. The master of Governor Sam Huntington was a member of the colonial General Assembly of Connecticut and later president of the Continental Congress of the United States. Peleg Nott's owner, Colonel Jeremiah Wadsworth, was a United States congressman and a member of the Connecticut state legislature, in addition to being the wealthiest man in Hartford. General David Humphreys, who was the master of governors Jubal, Nelson, and William Weston, was on George Washington's general staff during the Revolution and was later sent on diplomatic missions to Great Britain and France; in addition, Humphreys served as a member of the Connecticut General Assembly. Elisha R. Potter of South Kingston, Rhode Island, owned at least one (and probably two) of the state's black governors; he also was thirty years in the state legislature and four times a United States congressman. The evidence is clear that the masters of other governors and kings were, likewise, men of considerable local political prestige.[5]

Despite the prominence and honor New England accorded its clergy, none of the known masters of the black rulers was a minister. Perhaps Yankee ministers disapproved of the Negro election day festivities, but more likely ministers were either unable or unwilling to fund the political activities of their bondsmen or host the inaugural celebrations. The lack of political prestige accorded the slaves of clergymen may also have reflected the growing secularization of Yankee society.

In addition to having an African heritage and a politically important master, most successful governors also relied on their own personal qualities. Among the slave population, which prided itself on its hard physical labor, it is not surprising that physical strength was often an important attribute. Thus, while the African-born Quosh (or Quash) Freeman of Derby, Connecticut, may have gained prestige for being the slave of the prominent and wealthy Agar Tomlinson, he was best remembered as being the largest and strongest man who ever held executive office in the state:

> He was a man of herculean strength, a giant six-footer, and it is said of him that he could take a bull by the horns and the nose and at once prostrate him to the ground. No one ever dared to molest or tried to make him afraid, and when he was approaching from a distance he awakened the sense of a coming thunder cloud.
>
> Tradition has it that one dark night he was out with his son Roswell, on the Ousatonic, fishing, and a party from the other side came in collision with his skiff and were much damaged. They sang out: "There is a lot of niggers over this side and if you don't keep your net out of our way we will come over and flax you out." Quosh curtly replied, "Nigger this side, too." Enough was said; they knew his voice and dared not trouble him.[6]

Another leader in the Quash mold was King Ring of North Bridgewater, Massachusetts, who was remembered as being such a tyrannical autocrat that it was said about him that "he whipped the apple trees to make them grow." Fellow Bay Stater King Mumford of Salem was recalled as "a big, burly, powerful fellow," while Governor Eben Tobias was described by his son as "of the very finest physical mold . . . over six feel tall and admirably proportioned."[7]

The men who were elected kings and governors were also often noted for their own achievements and cosmopolitanism. Peleg Nott was well traveled from driving a provision cart during the Revolution; his success was such that after the war he was appointed the supervisor of his master's farm in West Hartford. Governor Quosh Freeman had been similarly placed in charge, as a kind of headman of Agar Tomlinson's large Derby Neck estate. Guy Watson, who was both chief marshal and governor in Rhode Island, had in his early years distinguished himself in Rhode Island's slave regiment, which fought under Colonel Christopher Greene at Red Bank and Ticonderoga; indeed, at least one source gives Watson credit for the capture of Colonel Richard Prescot.[8]

The office of governor or king of the blacks bore no salary; its few emoluments seem to have been only tokens of prestige and small favors received. But the office did confer great honor and dignity; and honor and dignity were important attributes to New England's Afro-American bondsmen.

We might think slaves would have little pride; but it was only unfortunate circumstance that had dictated their low class position in the New World. The immigrants and their children did not interpret this fall in status as a personal failure; indeed, many Africans recognized themselves as coming from a social class above their masters, while others saw themselves as morally superior.

The black governors personified this dignity of the black community, and the bearing of the rulers reflected the personal self-respect and pride of the men chosen. Governor Quaw of Hartford was said to have "enacted the Governor . . . to great satisfaction" and was remembered by an old gentleman as the stiffest and proudest "Darkie" he ever saw. Governor Peleg Nott was recalled as "a first rate feller" who was "remarkable for his exact dress and military bearing."[9]

Whites were made uncomfortable by the dignity which the black rulers adopted, and they attempted to belittle black leaders by means of condescension. The nineteenth-century historian Francis Caulkins, for example, continued in this tradition by presenting the stately demeanor and African-style honors of the governor as an amusing pretension:

> This sham dignitary after his election . . . puffing and swelling with
> pomposity . . . moving with a slow, majestic pace, as if the universe was
> looking on. When he mounted or dismounted, his aides flew to his assistance
> . . . bowing to the ground before him. The Great Mogul, in a triumphal
> procession, never assumed an air of more perfect self-importance than the
> Negro Governor at such a time.[10]

Similarly, white old-timers in Hartford recounted a humorous, demeaning anecdote about Governor Peleg Nott. As the whites told it, no sooner had the newly elected governor "mounted his horse, booted and spurred, than his impatient and fiery steed started at once for a pond, and plunging headlong into it, bespattered his excellency from head to foot with mud and water."[11] The same kind of anecdote was told about King Nero of Portsmouth. According to the white raconteur, Nero was slender in the calf, and so required padding in the back of his borrowed silk stockings to give a proper contour to his royal person. As his procession moved along, one of his escort left the ranks to run forward; bowing to the King, the commoner was said to have damped Nero's glory by informing him that his "calf has got afore."[12]

The similarity of these two stories in their effect is apparent; uneasy as spectators to the dignified bearing of Negro royalty or rulers, white New Englanders prefereed to remember what they felt was the proper comeuppance for black hubris. But if whites maliciously intended such anecdotes simply to put the "darkies" in their place, their actual effect is more complicated: such tales give corroborating evidence of the threatening dignity of the office-holding blacks.

In personal reminiscences, Yankee whites remembered the black governors as men worthy of respect. Writing in 1851, Isaac Stuart described Hartford's Governor Boston, a native African, in this way: "All who remember him, and there are many, concur in giving him the character of a 'stable, respectable man.' " Boston's exemplary life brought him honors in death, and the former governor was buried with the symbols of his office after a memorial service at Hartford's South Congregational Church.[13] The imperious Quosh Freeman, although a slave to Agar Tomlinson, was remembered in the Tomlinson family as bossing his master. Indeed, after Quosh's election to the governorship, "his dignity and self-importance were so sensibly affected that it was commonly said [by Derby whites] that 'Uncle Agar lived with the Governor.' "[14]

The honor of a man like Governor Quosh was even higher in black eyes. Quosh's daughter-in-law fondly recalled how "awful proud" she had been to marry the "Gov'nor's" son. This son, Roswell, became a governor in his own right in the nineteenth century; and Roswell Freeman and his wife Nancy were noted figures among both the black and white populations of Derby. "No one," it was said of Roswell, "had a higher standard of right, better principles, kinder instincts as a friend and neighbor, was more respected in his position, or more worthy of the good esteem of his contemporaries."[15]

Many of the black governors were men of ready wit and keen intelligence. According to his grandson Eben D. Bassett, the United States minister to Haiti during the Grant administration, Governor Tobiah of Derby, Connecticut, was recognized as "a man of tact, courage, and unusual intelligence," and his son Governor Eben Tobias was "ready of speech and considered quite witty." Eben Tobias's clever sayings were known throughout the region, and he was still quoted at Republican League reunions after his death. The same kind of political savvy led King Mumford of Salem, Massachusetts, to use his prestige and political wiles to become a Democratic party "wire puller" in the early years of the nineteenth century.[16]

Besides chairing the executive office of the black community, the Negro governors and kings of New England, like their African forebears, often filled a judicial function as well. In Newport, Rhode Island, the black governor heard cases on appeal from lesser black magistrates and judges who were part of the informal system of black government. Henry Bull explains:

> Masters complained to the Governor and magistrates of the delinquencies of their slaves, who were tried, condemned and punished at the discretion of the Court. The punishment was sometimes quite severe, and what made it the more effectual, was that it was the judgement of their peers, people of their own rank and color had condemned them, and not their masters by an arbitrary mandate.
>
> The punishment was by bastinado, with a large cobbing board, the number of strokes ordered by the sentence. Execution was done by the high sheriff or his deputy—and what made it more salutary in restraining the immorality, infidelity, petty larceny, or other delinquencies, was the sneers and contempt of their equals.[17]

An account has come down of a similar black government in Hartford, Connecticut, conducting a trial for a local Negro accused of theft. The presiding justice of the peace, Squire Neptune, found the defendant guilty and ordered him to give up his tobacco and gun as restitution. In addition, the defendant was sentenced to thirty lashes on his bare back to be carried out on the South Green by candlelight.[18]

In Portsmouth, New Hampshire, a stolen axe led to a case under either the African-born King Nero or his fellow African, Viceroy Willie Clarkson (who was fittingly the slave of a white judge). Prince Jackson, the accused, was found guilty and given twenty lashes at the town pump on the parade ground. The lashes were laid on before a crowd of blacks by the Negro deputy sheriff; Jackson was then warned out of town on penalty of a similar punishment by the high sheriff, the African-born Jack Odiorne. Jackson did not reform, however, and he was later found guilty of larger thefts and placed under the cognizance of the white county court.[19]

Such black courts were not unique to New England; and while masters in many colonies may have seen the usefulness of an indirect court system, it is doubtful that they created the judiciaries, since typically the courts were connected to black institutions outside the masters' purview. In colonial Cuba and Brazil, for example, it was the kings of the African tribal societies who heard complaints about individual subjects. According to James Stewart, headmen among the slaves in Jamaica set up courts on the estates without their masters' permission to deal with disputes among the bondsmen; the African initiative seems to account for similar courts established in Alabama in the nineteenth century.[20]

The indirect rule of the black courts of New England seems to have ended with the abolition of slavery there; but the Negro governors retained the prestige requisite for informal social control in the black community. The governor, it was said, was respected by Negroes throughout the state and obeyed almost implicitly.

> He was consulted as to the settlement of many petty disputes among his black brothers, and his decision was law. His office thus had a certain power, and commanded some respect among white people, who through him could obtain small settlements and adjustments, and arrange many matters in their relations with the negroes, without the trouble of personal effort.[21]

In addition to his role as a kind of small claims court, general arbiter, and court of last appeal, the black governor was a final authority on matters black, and, as has been discussed earlier, director of the holiday festivities of the black population. The nineteenth-century local historian Isaac Stuart summed up the qualities possessed by the men who held this demanding office; the man selected as governor, Stuart explained,

> was usually one of much note among themselves, of imposing strength, firmness and volubility, who was quick to decide, ready to command, and able to flog. If he was inclined to be a little arbitrary, belonged to a master of distinction, and was ready to pay freely for diversion—these were circumstances in his favor. Still it was necessary he should be an honest negro, and be, or appear to be, "wise above his fellows."[22]

The autocratic style of the governors probably owed as much to African standards of leadership as it did to the duties of the office; but because New England's black immigrants were from a mixture of African cultures, no one political model dominated. The black governments of New England were not direct carry-overs from Africa, but neither were they simple imitations of the institutions of white Yankees. They were a new Afro-American blending. Quash Piere knew as much when he carried his gold-headed cane with the engraving "Quash Piere, Governor of Connecticut." Such canes were symbols of authority and status in Africa and the Afro-American West Indies; but they also fit the bill for the dandies in Yankee New England as well. [23]

Just as New England's form of slavery lived comfortably with black kings and governors, so too it permitted the training of informal black militias connected to the Negro governments. As in the case of elections, the blacks attached their muster to the parallel white Training Day. From the mid-seventeenth century, New Englanders had been drilling militias as part of the colonial self-defense effort. By 1750, muster, or Training Day as it was known, had become an important holiday assuming social as well as military significance. [24] In Connecticut and perhaps elsewhere, black trainings also became a part of the holiday. Those black trainings of which we have record all came after the American Revolution; perhaps armed black militias were acceptable then because of the blacks' loyal participation in the war.

It is possible, however, that the trainings date back to the black inaugural parades of the mid-eighteenth century, since even during slavery the escorts of the black governors were armed and reviewed. In nearby New York as early as 1740, Long Island authorities discovered "the Negroes had there formed themselves into a company about Christmas last, by way of play or diversion (as they would have it thought) had mustered and trained with the borrowed arms and accoutrements of their masters." New York's slave owners feared the worst, and "the Negroes were accordingly chastised for this daring piece of insolence." [25]

The Long Island blacks may have been no more guilty of planned insurrection than their New England counterparts, but since the muster came only several months before the New York Conspiracy of 1741, it is possible that these were preparations by the rumored reinforcements from Long Island mentioned during the conspiracy trials. Both insurrections and "plays" during the Christmas season were common enough in Afro-America to support either interpretation, although in the Long Island case it is noteworthy that the bondsmen, like those in New England, were

loaned weapons by their masters, who seem to have seen an innocent intent
in the matter.

In New England the Negro trainings were clearly put on by way of play
or diversion. As in the black elections, the troops often borrowed their uniforms, horses, and weapons from their masters; and as in elections, the
black militia took great pleasure in their gallant appearance.

> At one time subsequent to the Revolution, training was held at Picket's Tavern
> [in Windsor, Connecticut]. . . . General Ti, a slave belonging to Captain
> Ellsworth commanded on that occasion. His master, being a captain of the
> cavalry, furnished him with his own uniform, accoutrements, and watch, to
> the chain of which he added several huge seals, and set him upon his own war
> steed. So General Ti rode forth that day, "the observed of all observers."[26]

Both whites and blacks enjoyed attending these musters. As in the elections, the whites found the proud black official a source of amusement; also
comical to them were the motley dress of the black troops and their ignorance of infantry maneuvers:

> When the attempt was made to form the regiment, there was no little difficulty
> in arranging the soldiers so as to make the best appearance—for most had some
> bit of uniform, but no two alike. The general, anxious to put the best foot
> forward, hit upon a plan, and issued his orders accordingly. Rising in his
> stirrups, he shouted, "All you what got white stocca, rocker shoe, stand in
> de front." This order was readily understood, and the front rank was soon
> formed of those who were equipped with shoes and stockings. Then came
> another order from the chief, "All you what got rocker shoes and no white
> stocca, stand in de rear"; and then, with the self-satisfied air of one who felt that
> he had "gone and done it," the general exclaimed, "Now you niggers what got
> no white stocca, and no rocker shoe, stand out de way."
>
> During some of the evolutions of the day, which were badly performed, the
> general's passions got the better of his dignity, and he exclaimed, with heart felt
> bitterness, "A nigger allus will be a nigga, don't know nothing, and allus did."[27]

This anecdote with its deprecating humor belongs in the genre of others
belittling New England's black leadership.[28] Nonetheless, the awkward-
ness of black troops with Euro-American drilling was real enough. In fact,
the farcical nature of the trainings was often precisely the design of the men

who participated. When, for example, Governor Eben Tobias drilled his black escort, the command "Fire and fall off!" was said to have been interpreted literally by some of the men, who threw themselves from their horses.[29] It was supposed to be funny.

Throughout Afro-America, black bondsmen used satiric songs and mimicry just as they had done traditionally in Africa. In nineteenth-century Jamaica, James Phillippo observed that "white men have frequently seen themselves exhibited by black imitators as subjects of amusement to the whole fraternity of a Negro village." A century earlier Père Labat had noted a similar tradition of satire in the French West Indies: The blacks, he said, are "satirical to excess, and few people apply themselves with greater success to knowing the defects of people, and above all of the whites, to mock among themselves."[30]

While such satire usually furnished the subject matter of humorous Afro-American ballads, the satire also gave rise to ridiculous physical imitations during the farcical "plays" so common to Africa and Afro-America. Thus Captain Hugh Clapperton found a white "devil" the object of Yoruba satire in 1826:

[It] went through the motions of taking snuff, and rubbing its hands; when it walked, it was with the most awkward gait, treading as the most tender-footed white man would do in walking barefoot, for the first time over new frozen ground. The spectators often appealed to us, as to the excellence of the performance. . . . I pretended to be fully as pleased with this caricature of a white man as they could be, and certainly the actor burlesqued the part to admiration.[31]

Similarly, the *South Carolina Gazette* noted in 1772 that a local black entertainment was opened "by men copying (or *taking off*) the manners of their masters, and the women their mistresses, and relating some highly curious anecdotes, to the inexpressible diversion of that company." A young black woman from Beaufort, South Carolina, describing a similar situation, explained, "Us slaves watch the white folk's parties when the guests danced a minuet and then paraded in a grand march. Then we'd do it too, but we used to mock 'em every step. Sometimes the white folks noticed it but they seemed to like it. I guess they thought we couldn't dance any better."[32]

Much of the humor of New England's black elections and trainings probably came from such satiric gestures. Certainly such satire was used against Yankee masters in Lynn, Massachusetts. During election there it was reported, "The masters did not interfere until the utmost verge of decency had been reached, good-naturedly submitting to the hard hits leveled against themselves, and possibly profiting a little by some shrewd allusion."[33]

In Afro-America such satire was also often self-directed, and that, too, was probably the case in New England. In awkwardly imitating the stiffness, pretensions, and authority of white New England, blacks were lampooning a society about which they had conflicting feelings; they were also mocking their own attempts to assimilate into that society.

The election holidays were a time when, freed of restraints, black New Englanders could gather and celebrate their own unity. On such days the African heritage was remembered by the old immigrants and passed on to younger Afro-Americans. Commenting on what he called "the still bewitching influence" of these black elections, William Bentley observed in 1817 that "such [blacks] as have no eccentricities at any other time have them in these."[34] By eccentricities he meant an African style still persistent in the black holiday activities of early nineteenth-century New England.

This African style affected white New England as well as black. While in mid-eighteenth-century New England musters were both a social occasion and a day for drill, the exercises were always preceded by prayers and psalms; frivolous amusements were severely censored. By the turn of the century muster had become a day of festive merriment, and the trainings themselves had become farcical displays.[35] Perhaps this only reflected America's new independence and security; but a similar deterioration had struck the militia company that escorted the governor of Connecticut years before. In 1768 the Hartford militia escort, appearing in fantastic dress, turned the election day parade of Connecticut's white governor into a spectacle described as "antique and horrible."[36] Given the model of black election day drilling in Hartford, it would not be surprising if the white militia was simply imitating black fun; similar mimicry may have been going on in the 1859 Newport, Rhode Island, parade of "Antiques and Horribles," a carnivallike procession which included blackface marchers.[37]

By the mid-nineteenth century, New England whites were consciously adopting a black satirical style like that utilized in black elections and trainings. Walter Burnham recalled an 1844 example from the Gunn Academy in Connecticut, where the cadets formed a satirical drilling corps. This was a sort of burlesque, "Coon Militia," a military organization regularly officered, corporals, sergeants, lieutenants, captains, etc., just a take-off making everything as ridiculous as possible. They sized up the state militia that way— everything to put it in as ridiculous a light as could be, so instead of putting the men who corresponded in height, for instance, by the side of Orville [Platt, who became a major interpreter of Negro Election Day] they put a little short fellow . . . and they had a "General Training Day."[38]

In the exchange of cultures in eighteenth-century New England, the predominant transformation was the assimilation of African immigrants into black Yankees. But there were also other effects, and one of them may well have been a mellowing of the Puritan spirit of the whites. The evidence suggests that the manner of celebrating holidays saw a blending of the joyful and humorous African style into the traditions of white New England. That case should not be overstated, but it is clear that the African style animated the holidays and life-styles of the black Yankees at the very least, and that black New England cannot be understood without reference to both African and Afro-American cultures.

Part 5

On Resistance:
A Summary Conclusion

Chapter 12

A Resistant Accommodation

BLACK New Englanders had become part of the wider Yankee culture, but at the same time maintained an identity of their own. They had never been willing to be assimilated totally into the way of life white New Englanders had chosen for them. Indeed, as the historian Lorenzo J. Greene has demonstrated, individual slaves in New England commonly rejected oppressions of racism and bondage by escapist behaviors such as heavy drinking or running away; others struck back directly through acts of physical violence, arson, and theft. As runaway notices in colonial newspapers suggest, slaves also resisted by feigning illness ("can pretend sickness" as a notice explained), prevaricating ("a great lyer" complained one notice, "a crafty, subtle, sly fellow" noted another), and talking back (like the slaves described as "very surly" and "very saucy").[1] But common as such individual acts of resistance were, they remained for the most part individual acts.

This chapter focuses on something else. It reexamines many of the arguments presented thus far from the perspective of cultural resistance and accommodation in order to understand how the region's blacks, both free and slave, adjusted themselves to the realities of New England while at the same time attempting to persuade white New Englanders to adjust to the realities of Afro-American life.

There was nothing about the ethnic makeup or attitudes of the Africans who came to New England to suggest they would endure enslavement better than their countrymen who were proving so rebellious in the West Indies and lower Americas. Indeed, at the beginning of the eighteenth century, as we have seen, African slaves were often sold to the northern colonies precisely because they were "refractory," "turbulent," and prone to run away. On the other hand, we should not assume that Yankee slaves would find their new situation intolerable, or even worse than their recent pasts. Whether the new slaves had been captured in war, kidnapped, or sold, the journey they had begun in Africa was a soul-testing experience.

First there was a brutal march to the sea under callous local slavers who regarded their human merchandise as cargo to be moved as quickly and cheaply as possible. Driven to exhaustion, emaciated by meager rations, those who survived the coffles found themselves sold to coastal traders who threw them into pestilent barracoons near the sea. Then things became worse. The frightened captives were brought out like human livestock to be prodded, poked, and then purchased by hairy, "red" aliens who looked like veritable devils. Armed to the teeth, vile-smelling, and rumored to be cannibals, these horrible foreigners were as pasty under their shirts as if they had crawled out from beneath rocks; they quickly chained the new slaves into the dark, fetid bowels of monstrous craft. Little could ever be worse than the stench-filled holds where, during storms at sea, vomit and other vile excreta sloshed across decks already reeking of filth. And always there were the barked commands of the fierce and ugly crew, with their fevered, hollow eyes and unrelenting distemper.

It is from this obscene context that we must understand the slaves' reaction to arrival in the Americas and New England. The rolling of the sea had finally ceased. Chains were struck from chafed and cramped limbs as the hatches were thrown back in an explosion of blinding light. A fresh shore air replaced the horrid, miasmic stench from below. The new life, even in slavery, could not help but be better than those vile preceding days. Most Africans could imagine an endurable form of bondage because such unfree labor had existed in their own motherlands. Judged by eighteenth-century standards, enslavement entailed an unfortunate loss of status, but it was not considered the remarkably cruel and unusual fate we judge it today.

Most Africans accepted the lawfulness of servitude, but not the barbarous oppressions and abuses of the commercial slave trade or American bondage. Slaves in the Americas often rebelled against cruel masters and tried to escape by running away; when the numbers were right they sometimes even struggled for black political dominance, but until the late eighteenth century they never organized social revolutions against the institution of bondage itself. This helps explain the anomaly of freedom-fighting maroons in Brazil and elsewhere sometimes continuing to hold slaves of their own. The targeting of slavery as an institution depended on the development of an Afro-American consciousness that combined traditional resistance to abuse with new philosophies about the "universal" rights of man.[2]

So terrible was the experience of the middle passage that most black new-comers were in a state of psychological shock. It was at that moment, when the new slaves were most thoroughly shaken by the horrors of the Atlantic crossing, that they arrived in the Americas. The result was that once they learned they would not be eaten but, instead, put to work, the new slaves saw their release from the cramped and stinking holds of the slave ships as an escape. Police forces have long known that a process of alternating cruelty and relative kindness—"the bad and good policeman technique" in which a small gesture of friendliness by a new questioner after a long and vicious interrogation by a more brutal inquisitor—can be used to break down the resistance of terrified and desperate suspects. When the slave ships finally reached New England, it was figuratively the "good" police-man's turn, for the worst of the fears and the most brutal of the treatment were over. The "new negroes," as they were called, were usually very young and, by the time they were sold to Yankee masters, totally separated from their former shipmates. In their terrible loneliness and dislocation, most of these slave immigrants were eager to reestablish human contacts and reconnect to social order. That the new country had impressive mate-rial wealth and a mysterious but powerful technology only added to the potential attraction of assimilation.

Thus, we must not suppose that the only, or even the most common, result of the brutality of the middle passage was a total rejection of Amer-ican culture, such as that which marked the fictional Kunta Kinte's reaction to his new life in Virginia.[3] Ironically, the trauma of the middle passage often predisposed many among the unwilling immigrants to accept what-ever positive features this return to human life offered.

Most of those newly arrived on the New England coast found themselves sold into white households where their days and nights would be filled with bicultural and biracial contacts. To survive and carry on normal social interchange, the immigrants had to adapt, for to Africans from a communal world an isolated life was unthinkably inhuman. Equally to the point, the

New England experience did not give many choices, since new slaves lived so close within their masters' families. In the quiet grey of New England dawns, whites and blacks must have heard each other's waking noises as the households shuffled into life, and when the sun had risen higher, many were the noons that must have found them working side by side. Even late in the evenings, master and man shared final yawns before retiring to dream their separate but related dreams.

Still, even bondsmen were allowed their own time now and again, and since the Afro-American population of New England was concentrated near the coasts in the towns and cities, most Yankee blacks lived close enough together to enjoy friends and acquaintances of their own race. These leisure time social contacts created an Afro-American community that continued throughout the century to reinforce African values and attitudes. This continuity of shared traditions gave black New Englanders a double identity, a sense of themselves as a special folk within the larger Yankee community.

The Afro-American subculture they created became a reservoir of stability, helping black New Englanders resist the constant onslaught of demeaning Euro-American prejudices. At the same time, the effect of having many more men than women in the black community during these formative years reinforced the conservatism natural to any folk culture, since many of these first generation Afro-Americans lacked the children who would have connected them to the New World. Conservation of African values was not unusual among Africans in the Americas, but it is crucial that we understand why black New Englanders, too, maintained African approaches to life so long in a region where both the power and the population were always over 95 percent white.

In day-to-day life, the dominance of the whites was less daunting than statistics might suggest, since most Yankee masters and their slaves shared a common residence and daily activities. This led to a necessary intimacy, fostering both a relatively mild form of servitude and a kind of household kinship. In its paternalism, Yankee bondage followed an already established regional pattern of treating white servants as part of their masters' patriarchal families. New England masters reinforced this sense of near kinship by purchasing very young slaves who could learn from infancy what was expected of live-in family servants.

Black children and young Africans raised by white families theoretically could have become as assimilated as their masters permitted. Nonetheless, few bondspeople reached the high level of assimilation epitomized by black poet Phillis Wheatley. Masters as a rule discouraged a cultural polish in their bondsmen that might imply too unseemly an equality, and black bondsmen also rejected full assimilation, preferring to maintain a biculturalism which reinforced their sense of self-worth and moral superiority.

If the paternalism of family slavery led many Yankee masters to think of their servants almost as poor relations, the real testing of these bonds came in old age, when decrepit slaves became burdensome obligations rather than profitable assets. Often elderly slaves, especially the men, let their masters off the hook by choosing freedom in poor black neighborhoods rather than subservience in the back rooms or attics of their masters' homes. But other bondsmen saw their retirement housing and board as entitlements which they had earned through years of loyal service. When masters tried to shirk these obligations by offering to "free" themselves and their servants from the legal ties of ownership, the slaves often refused, citing the Afro-American folk proverb that established their own rights as collateral members of their masters' households: "Massa eat the meat; he now pick the bone."

Since West Africans traditionally used proverbs both in legal argument and as a rhetorical device in resolving family and village controversies, we should understand the use of proverbial wisdom by black bondsmen before the bar of New England public opinion to be a continuation of an African form of resistance to injustice.[4] This tradition of arguing the "legality" of an issue with proverbs coincided with the use of the American court system late in the century by a small elite of black Americans. Both were strategies of "legal" resistance, but the former was an Afro-American product out of African culture, the latter was an act of blacks acculturated enough to adopt a European strategy. The African approach was more direct and until, after the American Revolution, more effective, but it had a serious weakness. Individualistic New England, with its voluminous court records, was not communal Africa, with its proverbial long memory; nor were artificial kin real kin. Hence a stubborn and antisocial master could prove immune to even such a subtle and civilized form of persuasion.

Because they so often shared the same household with their bondsmen, Yankee masters were serious about their obligations to train their new servants and thereby "Americanize" them. For the first few weeks such training was probably nearly a full-time job. Because of the great versatility in job roles required of New England slaves, the new immigrants had to learn some basic English quickly, although they did not need to know the new language perfectly. Most spoke a form of black English which sounded "broken" to their masters but was sufficiently functional on the job and was especially well suited to the cultural mixture of Afro-American society. Additionally, the relatively high skill levels common to the black work force of New England meant a rapid acculturation into the Yankee working class.

But that was where Americanization stalled. The public education, economic freedom, and opportunity for upward mobility commonly seen as benchmarks of the American way of life were seldom offered either to slaves or to black freedmen. Even in New England, racial prejudice denied most black Yankees more than the rudiments of literacy. Northern whites might treat black laborers more like help than like slaves, but when the blacks aspired to more, no credit or aid was forthcoming. Without funds, legal protection, or even good wishes, black entrepreneurs were crippled by warnings out of town and by requirements to post bond which became self-fulfilling prophecies of business failure. White servants who served well went forward to freedom and upward to lower middle-class mobility. Black slaves, on the other hand, were worked past their primes and then, if they dared be more than loyal "poor relations," cut off from the protective association of their masters. Slavery in New England was able to clothe the region's black immigrants in the figurative outer garments of American culture while denying them the economic heartbeat that gave that culture life. Like scarecrows in the American garden, the black Yankees worked constantly, but someone else always reaped the harvest.

Masters might tell themselves that economic enterprise was their own cultural heritage, but when it came to Christianity they felt bound to try to share both the laws and the promise with their slaves. They did not expect all Afro-Americans would take up the new faith; they didn't even expect that of their own people. But it was a duty to preach the gospel, and most masters seem to have offered their servants at least some instruction in the Christian religion.

Churches in New England commonly baptized slave children under their masters' covenants. This was in line with the theory that bondsmen were members of their masters' Christian households and therefore in the most basic religious sense belonged more to their masters' families than to their natural parents outside the covenant. Older slaves were more difficult to bring into the church since they had to demonstrate both Christian character and a solid knowledge of scripture before baptism.

What the whites preached to the bondsmen was a rather self-serving and expurgated Christianity. As the masters explained it to slaves, the Protestant ethic meant poverty, humility, a deference to "betters," and an end to disobedience, lying, theft, drunkenness, fornication, and the sheltering of runaways. It should not be surprising that most of the African immigrants and the vast majority of Afro-Americans found this preached gospel to be hypocrisy designed to make the humiliations of bondage sound honorable and the acts of day-to-day resistance seem shameful. How could they take such a faith seriously?

The minority of assimilated blacks who knew enough English to listen closely, however, heard a very different message. For the bondspeople the good news that God brought salvation out of evil helped explain their plight. Slavery and the slave trade were great sins of the white man and his pagan African allies, which God was turning to the advantage of his Afro-American children. When God promised to bring down the exalted sinner and raise up the poor and humble Christian, the symbolism was clear to black New Englanders. The odd thing was that the masters were so caught up in preaching against sex, rum, and relaxation that they seemed to miss the point.

Only a tiny elite of black Yankees became practicing Christians; but those who did used their faith as a philosophy of resistance that promised an end to slavery and a reordering of society in line with the principles of justice. Moreover, they used their special status as a Christian upper class to win white approval for their "religious" organizations. These "African societies," as they were commonly called, were social and religious organizations designed to lift black New Englanders up from urban poverty. In this they were typical of the Afro-American communal self-help enterprises found throughout the Americas. However, because of their elitist nature, these organizations made no significant impact on the lives of the majority of the bondsmen. Indeed, after a number of years of heart-bruising encounters with continuing white racism, these basically assimilationist organizations were slowly and ironically transformed into separatist churches more in line with the feelings of the wider black community.

More Africans would doubtless have become Christian if the white master class had altered their rigid, literalist, and dogmatic approach to religion to better accommodate the African immigrants' participatory religious aesthetic of possession, music, and dance. White ministers across the Americas were quick to note that Afro-Americans were attracted to the music and singing that sometimes accompanied church services and that they were exceptional judges of the verbal and emotional qualities of preaching. Nonetheless, in New England puritanical attitudes and the need for order, decorum, and control predominated over any purely missionary impulse. Too often efforts at conversion remained chained to leaden catechisms and dull homilies which never let the spirit take flight above the world of pain and toil.

Yankee ministers had cause to worry about the effect of taking too many newcomers into the faith. Elsewhere in the Americas, slave Christianity was often a syncretic blending of African and European beliefs and worship. Even in New England the Africans and Afro-Americans who attended local church services began to influence the style of religious celebration. The African newcomers seldom affected the intellectual substance of the faith, since they rarely understood even its most basic tenets. But they could affect the emotional expression of the religious impulse, and they did so in the early eighteenth century.

The revival of the Christian faith in New England during the 1730s and 1740s began as ministers discovered that by adjusting their sermons to the responses of their audiences, they could increase the effectiveness of their preaching. The extemporaneous style the New Light preachers developed was far better suited than the old "plain" style to reach the illiterate members of the congregation who, like the new slaves, were seldom able to appreciate fine-honed, scriptural-based reasoning but who could enjoy the emotional release of a rousing sermon. Was it New England's African immigrants, with their heritage of emotional expression during religious celebration, who first writhed in their pews, groaning and crying out in response to the preacher's call, or did these black Yankees simply reinforce the emotionalism of awakening whites? Whatever the origins, clearly a series of subliminal feedback mechanisms was creating a dynamic new style of preaching, and anyone who has read the descriptions of the emotionalism that marked early Afro-American Christianity can see how ideally suited the black Yankees were to this new approach.

As intellectuals, the preachers never really wanted to understand that it was the style of their sermons much more than the substance that was reawakening the Christian spirit. There were suspicions, of course. In 1740 James Davenport complained in frustration that his newly imported African slave girl, Flora, could be moved by Eleazer Wheelock's preaching but could only give a "broken account" of why.[5] The explanation is that her animated response was part of her African taste for a participatory and emotional religious experience. Perhaps it was not Wheelock's preaching that moved her so much as it was she and others like her who were moving Wheelock.

Because Yankee ministers feared they might be affecting hearts more than minds, they guarded against what they considered excesses of enthusiasm, emphasizing the highly intellectual requirements of their faith. For black church membership this was unfortunate, since few of the blacks who were moved by the emotionalism of the Awakening had the education to master scripture well enough to be brought into the church. This was a lost opportunity for conversion, but it helps explain why so much of the African religious impulse remained outside the Protestant churches and within the folk beliefs of the black community.

New arrivals from Africa used their old faiths to resist the oppressions of their new lives. Thus, suicides by new slaves, although not as common in New England as elsewhere, were usually acts of religious martyrdom by Africans who were convinced that death would return them to the land of their birth. Many other Afro-Americans who never attempted suicide still retained a similar belief in transmigration, some even saving up wealth to carry home with them. While they were in no hurry to end their lives, this belief in a return to Africa after death continued to signify their ultimate identification with the land and culture of their forefathers.

The same kind of idea transposed into Christian terminology appeared among the second and third generations of black New Englanders; among these more acculturated Afro-Americans, "heaven" replaced Africa as the true home to which black Yankees would return after their sojourn in the oppressive country of their white masters. Thus in New England as elsewhere in the New World, after the burial ceremony Afro-American funerals became occasions of joyous festivity; African "mourners" believed their old friends were bound to the land of their ancestors where, despite what their masters said, there would be no punishments, only reunions. The more assimilated Afro-Americans believed that the dead were on their way to heaven, where they would finally find justice.

Other African religious ideas survived as well. The wandering funeral processions that the Boston selectmen banned in 1741 were the product of an African belief that most deaths were caused by evil forces, and that persons who killed through sorcery could be discovered by a mysterious tipping and shaking of the coffin as it passed the malefactor's house. Certainly black Yankees and many of their white "converts" accepted the African belief that seers and mediums among the immigrants could find lost or stolen property, bewitch thieves into returning their loot, and even see into the future. Many old black women were known as expert herbalists, and others were suspected to have practiced witchcraft.

Yankee ministers noted that among their African slaves were those who prayed to "devils," that is African gods, and one cleric reported seeing a rough stone "idol" his slave had carved. In Africa people most commonly prayed to the ancestral spirits of their recently departed kinsmen, but in New England the living dead were to be avoided with the help of such protective stratagems as sacred circles, clothes turned inside out, and fetishes. Most of the region's blacks also used their charms for protection from disease, accident, and sorcery. Since these magic amulets additionally gave the wearers power and protection from human enemies, they doubtless were used to protect bondsmen from the oppressions of slavery as well.

We normally play down magic as a mode of resistance because it does not fit into our world view. Nonetheless, the power of charms and witchcraft were important tools of political power and rebellion in Africa, and it is logical that they should have carried such meanings across to the New World. While magical talismans may not have destroyed the power of the white master class, they probably did reduce the anxieties of the slaves. By protecting bondsmen from fears of mistreatment, charms made their lives more comfortable. The whites were rarely aware of this counterforce, which made the covert use of magic far safer than more open acts of rebellion.

Many of us find our refuge from the buffeting squalls of everyday life within the safe harbor of our families, but the slave trade had cut New England's black immigrants off from the large extended unilineages of Africa. At best the newcomers might build new nuclear family units, but even this was difficult under the limitations of bondage and poverty.

On the face of it, all they needed to begin new families was to get married and have children; but slaves lacked the autonomy to make such decisions on their own. Moreover, the severe demographic imbalance within the region's black population left far too many men without available women; there was also the difficulty of reestablishing an institution with so many of its foundation stones missing. Was kinship within the new families to be patrilineal, matrilineal, or bilateral as it was among the whites? Could the African ideal of polygyny be reconciled with Christianity? Would women maintain the relative economic independence they usually had in Africa? So much was uncertain or unclear.

In Africa conjugal life had been defined in initiation rites and placed within the context of extended lineages. But in New England there was no way the early unions among slaves could replace these supporting institutions. In addition, since the slave immigrants were from a variety of African societies and ethnic groups, most black marriages were "mixed" marriages lacking a single set of traditional standards. All of this made slave marriages potentially unstable. Since most Yankee masters looked upon slave marriages as an expense for themselves and a distraction for their servants, those who had male slaves tended to overlook their premarital and extramarital sexual activities. For their part, the men wished to form relationships with several women if possible, in line with the polygamous African pattern. Black women, therefore, found their favors much desired, and doubtless enjoyed the power and excitement love brought to lives otherwise stunted by the impositions of bondage. The owners of the women, however, did not approve of such freedom since "illegitimate" children would reflect on the morality of their households.

The result of this welter of conflicting interests was an institutional breakdown. The bridewealth payments that had legitimized African marriage and tied the interests of two families to its success could not be replaced by new Christian sanctions since so few of the Yankee blacks had large families or were Christian. Thus, men and women commonly "married" each other informally in what the masters called "negro marriages," but since these unions were not recognized by law, the slave spouses could neither establish households nor avoid possible penalties for fornication or bastardy. These informal unions also seem to have had little stability, probably in part because they had so little institutional and family support. Even those slaves who were able to marry legally, and many did, faced serious challenges since they were often unable to share homes with their spouses or to form a single economic unit.

African morality and marriage customs had been overridden by Christian mores and kinship support systems by the international slave trade, and yet the Christian marriages which the laws and folkways of New England required simply could not be made stable under the insecurities and separations of bondage. Most of those black New Englanders who did build sound marriages had to first work their way to freedom and then purchase their spouses and families. It was more than a double burden.

Despite these problems, black parents who raised families loved their offspring all the more fiercely for having to be separated from them so much during the working day. Doubtless, they resented competing with white masters and mistresses for the affection and admiration of their own small children—whom the masters often pampered. Slave mothers had to both love their children and teach them that the world would soon betray them; it was a hard message to ask any parent to deliver. To make matters even more difficult, adolescent members of even stable black households were often sent away to enter service elsewhere since the region's economy could not support the luxury of black young people staying with their parents until marriage. Through it all, the children developed a pride in their parents and a positive sense of themselves. But the weakened black families were struggling against powerful tides of Euro-American culture; and after the American Revolution the chaotic effects of membership in the region's lowest economic class waxed stronger than the waning influence of the aging African immigrants who had previously held New England's Afro-American subculture together.

The African immigrants who came to New England had used their cultural heritage not only to set the tone of black society but at times as a valuable source of personal income. Elderly slaves and others with free time helped support themselves by using old African ways to spin yarn, to build toy drums as well as traps and snares for small game, to make baskets and recane chairs, to dispense herbal medicine, and to cook. Additionally, both old slaves and runaways found a good fiddler with an African ability to energize white music could always bring in a little extra cash.

Black bondspeople also retained the African aesthetic for personal adornment. Their use of gold hoop earrings and gaudy, colorful clothes with jarring contrasts of color and pattern marked not only a retention of African style but a blatant rejection of their master's tastes. In their free hours the black Yankees chose a mode of dress and a pattern of speech that expressed their positive self-image as Afro-Americans and their joy in the life which was theirs alone.

In Boston and probably elsewhere, they continued as well to enjoy their Sunday markets—even though these activities were obviously discouraged by the government as a scandal to a Christian commonwealth. Poor whites, however, seem to have enjoyed the music, dancing, joking, gambling, and drinking that were part of most black recreation, and occasionally they took up some of the black folkways themselves. Thus, the region's most popular game of chance—"paw paw" or "props"—was based on a West African divination technique. In the same manner, and much to the annoyance of the local elite, lower-class whites enlivened the region's Training Day and election day traditions with some of the extravagance and satirical humor which had made Negro election days so much fun. Likewise, black fiddlers and dance callers quickly came to dominate New England's less formal entertainments because of their African talent for creating exciting jigs and reels and their wonderful way of spicing improvised dance calls with humorous topical lyrics.

Folk arts are usually examined as documenting the internal values of a folk culture; in the experience of black Yankees they should also be considered as a mode of overt resistance. When black nannies sang to their charges or old African storytellers entertained a circle of enchanted children, they followed the African tradition of using such entertainments both as topical commentary against abuses of power and as a mode of imparting ethical standards to the young. The whites as well as the blacks who heard these stories and songs remembered years later the horror they felt over the stealing of African children by slave traders. The tactic seems to have been effective. The abolitionist Henry B. Stanton dated his concern for the oppressed races back to a black woman's hauntingly sung lament decrying the death of Chief Miantonomo of the Narragansetts at the hands of white treachery. It should not be forgotten that Harriet Beecher Stowe too grew up under the occasional tutelage of old black slaves.

It was not just Yankee children who felt the stinging barbs of black criticism. Much of the region's white folk humor, as recorded in nineteenth-century town histories, was based on long-relished retellings of the satirical observations of local slaves. Like their African forefathers who had used humorous topical songs as the common man's "constitutional" check against the abuses of headmen, Yankee blacks used satire to deflate the pomposities and hypocrisies of their white masters. Open rebellion would bring swift physical punishment, and running away was chancy at best. A pointed joke, on the other hand, was a wonderful revenge that could last for years and even grow in the retelling. Moreover, there was no defense that the victim of such wit could attempt without making himself appear even more ridiculous.

Satirical anecdotes from town histories are the best remaining evidence of the black folk culture's own perspective on the religious hypocrisy and class prejudices of white society. Yet only those humorous observations that passed into the white anecdotal repertoire have survived in print, and these were the anecdotes that depended on a high level of assimilation, because for the jokes to work the slaves had to communicate the foolishness of the white position by using the master class's own logic against it. Thus, when a slave rejects his master's offer of a pass to the family burial vault on the grounds that the devil might take the slave by mistake, the humor depends upon the slave understanding the Christian message better than his master. If the philosophy behind the criticism was American, the satiric vehicle and the approach were clearly out of the African tradition of political resistance.

Americans tend to emphasize political force and economically motivated violence in analyzing ethnic and class struggles, but among the region's slaves, who were outnumbered more than fifty to one, brute force simply could not be an effective strategy. Acts of revenge against masters were motivated far more often by personal grievances than by class or cultural attitudes. In fact, once a new slave felt part of the new society, his understanding of social obligations would have discouraged violence.

African cultures traditionally emphasized communal harmony and therefore disfavored internal violence as immoral and politically illegitimate. They much preferred to defuse interpersonal and group conflicts by bringing them into the open for community judgment. This was often done through rites of healing, but it could also be accomplished by airing grievances in public discourse and song. Ironically, we have no difficulty understanding the critical role of colonial pamphleteers in resisting British authority, but we too often miss African and Afro-American critical commentaries because they were delivered orally: thus the evidence is lost. These satirical assessments of white society were probably the strongest mode of social control that the region's enslaved minority could have effectively adopted, and such satire was consistent with the first line of legitimate political defense in Africa. We seldom think of illiterate slaves explicitly attacking the philosophical underpinnings of their oppressors' ideology. Yet that was precisely what the African satirical style emphasized. By condensing an opponent's argument to its essentials and then illustrating the flaws publicly with an apt proverb, tale, or joke, African resistance to oppression tended to counteract the brute force of authority with the subtleties of wit. Ironically, this style of resistance was so civilized that it has often been mistakenly characterized as the childish foolery of a "Sambo-like" personality.

Probably the most interesting institution with overtones of resistance developed by Afro-American New England was the grand celebration known as Negro election day. White New Englanders mistakenly thought such activities were awkward imitations of their own elections, but the commonness of royal celebrations by Afro-Americans across the New World points to other meanings for the institution. For example, Afro-Americans were not copying Euro-American culture in electing their rulers; in the eighteenth century the election of kings was common in Africa at a time when western Europeans and their colonial subjects still recognized the eldest son (whatever his competence) of a deceased ruler as the legitimate heir. To understand the significance of New England's black election days, we must examine them in the context of Afro-American culture.

It is a reflection of the strength of the Afro-American subculture of New England that Yankee blacks were able to win their masters' approval for the elections, and then cajole them into contributing money for the entertainment and expensive clothes and horses for the inaugural parade. If all that were not peculiar enough for a slave society, the bondsmen were also allowed to parade their new ruler through the streets with flags flying, bands playing, and a military honor guard riding escort and firing occasional salutes. Moreover, the festivities lasted the better part of a week, during which the slaves offered little if any work.

The office of black governor or king carried high honor among the region's blacks, and the men holding these positions were consistently remembered as proud and dignified rulers who enforced order within the Afro-American community and won the respect of white society as well.

Many of the first kings and governors were the scions of African royal families; later, as the immigrant generations began to die off, American-born men of high personal achievement took power. These latter men commonly were (or had been) slaves to some of the region's richest and most politically active masters—which gave them greater status as well as greater opportunities to demonstrate their competence and leadership. Moreover, their abilities to tap their masters' wealth gave their candidacies the superior economic resources needed to carry out the duties of office in proper style. It was not until several decades into the nineteenth century, when white economic support and the political significance of the offices declined, that the caliber of the rulers began to fall off.

Like African royalty elsewhere in the Americas, New England's black rulers enforced a kind of indirect rule over Afro-American society and oversaw informal courts open to the small claims of both white and black petitioners. These offices were recognized by whites because they were useful and could affect everyday activities in the black community in a way the region's white courts could not. But the black Yankees saw the offices in a different light. For them the kings and governors represented a proud and royal heritage. They obeyed the black rulers not to make life easier for the whites but to recognize the legitimacy of their own political traditions.

Throughout the eighteenth and early nineteenth centuries, the election of black rulers remained a unifying symbol for the region's black population. These were celebrations of communal awareness that proudly proclaimed the dual cultural identity which today we capture in the term "Afro-American." But they served other more psychologically complex functions as well.

Both African and European cultures had celebrated days of masking and misrule when the lower orders could mimic their social betters and criticize authority. Throughout the Americas usually one major holiday, like Carnival in Brazil and the West Indies, became dominated by celebrations of black royalty which provided occasions for the free expression of the Afro-American satiric genius. So it was in New England. The staid election day of Yankee whites was soon eclipsed in popularity by the far more entertaining Negro election day celebrations, during which the Afro-American community adopted the clothing and titles of the region's white authorities and mimicked both black social aspirations and white behavior.

At the same time, the holidays honored the royal heritage of Africa and satirized the pomposities of the Euro-American and Afro-American elites. Although the revolutionary potential of gathering black bondsmen under their own king was occasionally feared elsewhere, such holidays were not revolutionary in intent. They were part of a more civilized African mode of resistance through which black slaves released themselves from the power-lessness of bondage by adopting "masks" of royal office that permitted their inner feeling to show while at the same time exposing the foibles of au-thority. The great royal parades of black America were thus a kind of informal folk theater. At the center were rulers unmatched in dignity and royal bearing, representing the African soul normally hidden beneath the cloak of bondage; circling them came rude court jesters whose mocking antics ridiculed the New World pretensions of white and black alike; and surrounding them all was an incessant and frenzied music which seemed to possess the accompanying subjects and spectators. The ceremony attacked the oppressions of bondage from three fronts at the same time: revitalizing pride in Afro-American culture, ridiculing white authority, and providing a release from the pressures of servitude.

Today, except for Mardi Gras in New Orleans, such festivals have for the most part disappeared from North America. In New England, Negro election day began to decline after the abolition of slavery, and the festivals were eventually ended after lower-class whites screaming racial epithets began to assault black parades, sometimes even trying to drag the governors down off their horses.[6] The same exotic festivals which had so appealed to poorer and younger whites during the colonial era aroused furious racial anger during the first third of the nineteenth century. Apparently, colonial slaves who "pretended" to be kings and mocked local authority were funny to the white New Englanders in a way that black freedmen demonstrating ethnic pride and social criticism were not. At the same time, within black society the truly noble generations of African leadership had passed away, and the new self-made men coming to dominate black society were turning toward more direct political action with more assimilationist goals. Cul-turally speaking, the Afro-American years were ending with the last of the Africans, but the dual identity which they had helped engender in the region's black population would survive to shape the dual consciousness of Negro life in the nineteenth century.

The Africans who had come to New England as immigrants in chains had found themselves vastly outnumbered in a pervasive and ethnocentric

Euro-American society that meant to take the best of their lives and labor in exchange for a mere expurgated Christianity. But the Africans never agreed to such a one-sided bargain. They understood from the beginning that Americanization, even under slavery, was a process of give and take. Despite the overwhelming power of the region's master class, the slaves resisted being ground down in someone else's mill. Instead, they created a life-style of their own, taking from the cultures of Africa as well as from white America. Their choices gave their lives a definition that the oppressions of bondage could not obliterate; indeed, the abuses of slavery were a constant proof of the moral superiority of their own position. In their religious beliefs and their styles of worship, in their work habits and crafts, in their cooking and music, in their dance and dress, their medicine and gambling, their physical postures and sexual relations, and in the grand celebrations of their public holidays, the black New Englanders remained their own people—no longer Africans, but surely not second-class Europeans either. In creating their own way of life within the Yankee way of life, they became good citizens and good New Englanders. As they did, their choices influenced the lives of white Yankees as well, helping to mellow those rather puritanical people. The black Yankees, too, had come to build America.

Appendix

Table 1   *The Negro Population of Connecticut by County, 1756–1790*

Counties	1756	1774	1782[a]	1790[a]
Hartford	854	1053	1320	693
New Haven	226	852	885	858
New London	829	1194	1920	1315
Fairfield	711	1153	1134	1122
Windham	345	476	485	524
Litchfield	54	331	529	556
Tolland				141
Middlesex				360
TOTAL	3019	5059	6273	5569

SOURCE: Evarts B. Greene and Virginia Harrington, *American Population Before the Federal Census of 1790* (Gloucester, 1966), 58–61; and for 1774, United States Department of Commerce, Bureau of the Census, W. S. Rossiter, ed., *A Century of Population Growth, 1790–1909*.

[a]Includes Indians.

Table 2   The Negro Population of Massachusetts by County, 1754–1790

Counties	1754	1764	1776	1790
Suffolk	1215	1351	682	1056
Middlesex	339	860	702	597
Essex	362	1070	1049	880
Worcester	62	252	432	409
Hampshire	74	194	245	451
Plymouth	121	462	487	503
Bristol	61	293	585	729
Barnstable	66	231	171	372
Dukes	7	46	59	33
York[a]	116	225	241	153
Cumberland[a]		95	162	156
Lincoln[a]		24	85	151
Nantucket		44	133	110
Berkshire		88	216	323
Hancock[a]				38
Washington[a]				20
TOTAL	2423	5235	5249	5983

SOURCE: Population of 1754 is found in "Number of Negro Slaves in the Province of the Massachusetts Bay, Sixteen years Old and Upward," *MHSC* 3, 2nd series (1815), 95–97. Population of 1764 is in Rossiter, *Population Growth*, 161–62; other years are in Greene and Harrington, *American Population*, 30, 46.

[a]Maine counties

Table 3   The Negro Population of New Hampshire by County, 1773–1790

Counties	1773	1775	1786	1790
Rockingham	466	435	206	389
Strafford	111	103	17	85
Hillsborough	77	87	57	176
Cheshire	9	7	61	88
Grafton	20	24	56	49
TOTAL	683	656	397	787

SOURCE: Greene and Harrington, *American Population*, 73–74, 85.

Table 4   The Negro Population of Rhode Island by County, 1708–1790

Counties	1708	1748	1755	1783	1790
Newport	298	611[a]	2152	947	1180
Providence	7	283	455	536	860
Kent	16	261	412	246	414
Kings (Washington)	105	749	1446	920	1711
Bristol		178	232	183	190
TOTAL	426	2082	4697	2832	4355

SOURCE: Greene and Harrington, *American Population*, 65–67, 69–70.

[a]This number seems far too low to be credible.

Table 5 The Population of New England, 1690–1740, Including Percentage of Negro Population

Population	Massachusetts	Connecticut	Rhode Island	New Hampshire	New England
1690					
Negro	400	200	250	100	950
White	49,104	21,445	3,974	4,064	78,587
Total	49,504	21,645	4,224	4,164	79,537
Percentage Negro	1	1	6	2	1
1700					
Negro	800	450	300	130	1,680
White	55,141	25,520	5,594	4,828	91,083
Total	55,941	25,970	5,894	4,958	92,763
Percentage Negro	1	2	5	3	2
1710					
Negro	1,310	750	375	150	2,585
White	61,080	38,700	7,198	5,531	112,509
Total	62,390	39,450	7,573	5,681	115,094
Percentage Negro	2	2	5	3	2

1720					
Negro	2,150	1,093	543	170	3,956
White	88,858	57,737	11,137	9,205	166,937
Total	91,008	58,830	11,680	9,375	170,893
Percentage Negro	2	2	5	2	2
1730					
Negro	2,780	1,490	1,648	200	6,118
White	111,336	74,040	15,302	10,555	211,233
Total	114,116	75,530	16,950	10,755	217,351
Percentage Negro	2	2	10	2	3
1740					
Negro	3,035	2,598	2,408	500	8,541
White	148,596	86,982	22,847	22,756	281,181
Total	151,631	89,580	25,255	23,256	289,722
Percentage Negro	2	3	10	2	3

SOURCE: United States Department of Commerce, Bureau of the Census, *Historical Statistics of the United States* (Washington, 1961), series Z 1–19, series A 128–180, 13, 756.

Table 6 The Population of New England, 1750–1800, Including Percentage of Negro Population

Population	Massachusetts	Connecticut	Rhode Island	New Hampshire	New England
1750					
Negro	4,075	3,010	3,347	550	10,982
White	183,925	108,270	29,879	26,955	349,029
Total	188,000	111,280	33,226	27,505	360,011
Percentage Negro	2	3	10	2	3
1760					
Negro	4,866	3,783	3,468	600	12,717
White	257,734	138,687	42,003	38,493	476,917
Total	262,600	142,470	45,471	39,093	489,634
Percentage Negro	2	3	8	2	3
1770					
Negro	5,229	5,698	3,761	654	15,342
White	261,336	178,183	54,435	61,742	555,696
Total	266,565	183,881	58,196	62,396	571,038
Percentage Negro	2	3	6	1	3

1780

Negro	5,280	5,885	2,671	541	14,377
White	312,480	200,816	50,275	87,261	650,832
Total	317,760	206,701	52,946	87,802	665,209
Percentage Negro	2	3	5	1	2

1790

Negro	5,882	5,473	4,336	851	16,542
White	469,445	232,473	64,489	141,034	907,441
Total	475,327	237,946	68,825	141,885	923,983
Percentage Negro	1	2	6	1	2

1800

Negro	7,101	6,275	3,663	919	17,958
White	567,463	244,727	65,459	182,937	1,060,586
Total	574,564	251,002	69,122	183,856	1,078,544
Percentage Negro	1	2	6	1	2

SOURCE: Bureau of the Census, *Historical Statistics*, 13, 756; Negro data for 1790 and 1800 is from Bureau of the Census, *Negro Population of the United States* (Washington, 1918), 51.

Table 7   The Increase in New England Population 1690–1750, with Percentage of Increase by Race

Population Change	Massachusetts	Connecticut	Rhode Island	New Hampshire	New England
1690–1700					
Negro Increase	400	250	50	30	730
White Increase	6,037	4,075	1,620	764	12,496
Negro Increase	100%	125%	20%	30%	77%
White Increase	12%	19%	41%	19%	16%
1700–1710					
Negro Increase	510	300	75	20	905
White Increase	5,939	13,180	1,604	703	21,426
Negro Increase	64%	67%	25%	15%	54%
White Increase	11%	52%	29%	15%	24%
1710–1720					
Negro Increase	840	343	168	20	1,371
White Increase	27,778	19,037	3,939	3,674	54,428
Negro Increase	64%	46%	45%	13%	53%
White Increase	45%	49%	55%	66%	48%

SOURCE: My figures are based on tables 5 and 6 above.

1720–1730

Negro Increase	630	397	1,105	30	2,162
White Increase	22,478	16,303	4,165	1,350	44,296
Negro Increase	29%	36%	203%	18%	55%
White Increase	25%	28%	37%	15%	27%

1730–1740

Negro Increase	255	1,108	760	300	2,423
White Increase	37,260	12,942	7,545	12,201	69,948
Negro Increase	9%	74%	46%	150%	40%
White Increase	33%	17%	49%	116%	33%

1740–1750

Negro Increase	1,040	412	939	50	2,441
White Increase	35,329	21,288	7,032	4,199	67,848
Negro Increase	34%	16%	39%	10%	29%
White Increase	24%	24%	31%	18%	24%

Table 8 The Increase in New England Population 1750–1800, with Percentage of Increase* by Race

Population Change	Massachusetts	Connecticut	Rhode Island	New Hampshire	New England
1750–1760					
Negro Increase	791	773	121	50	1,735
White Increase	73,809	30,417	12,124	11,538	127,888
Negro Increase	19%	26%	4%	9%	16%
White Increase	40%	28%	41%	43%	37%
1760–1770					
Negro Increase	363	1,915	293	54	2,625
White Increase	3,602	34,496	12,432	23,249	73,779
Negro Increase	7%	51%	8%	9%	21%
White Increase	1%	28%	30%	60%	15%
1770–1780					
Negro Increase	51	187	(1,090)	(113)	(965)

White Increase	51,144	22,633	(4,160)	25,519	95,136
Negro Increase	1%	3%	(29%)	(17%)	(6%)
White Increase	20%	13%	(8%)	41%	17%
1780–1790					
Negro Increase	602	(412)	1,665	310	2,165
White Increase	156,942	31,711	14,108	53,837	256,598
Negro Increase	11%	(7%)	62%	57%	15%
White Increase	50%	16%	28%	62%	39%
1790–1800					
Negro Increase	1,219	802	(673)	68	1,416
White Increase	98,018	12,254	970	41,903	153,145
Negro Increase	21%	15%	(16%)	8%	9%
White Increase	21%	5%	2%	30%	17%

SOURCE: My figures are based on tables 5 and 6 above.

*Figures in parentheses represent a decrease.

Table 9   Black Rulers of New England by Location

Ruler	Location	Approximate Date
	Connecticut	
Quash Freeman	Derby	1810
Tobia	Derby	1815
Roswell Quash (Freeman?)	Derby	1830–1835
Eben Tobias	Derby	1840–1845
Caesar	Durham	1800
Peter Freeman	Farmington	1780
London	Hartford	1755
Quaw	Hartford	1760
Cuff	Hartford	1766–1776
John Anderson	Hartford	1776
Peleg Nott	Hartford	1780
Boston	Hartford	1800
William Lanson	New Haven	1825
Quash Piere	New Haven	1832
Thomas Johnson	New Haven	1833–1837
Boston Trowtrow	Norwich	1770
Sam Huntington	Norwich	1772–1800
Jubal Weston	Seymour	1825
Nelson Weston	Seymour	1850
Wilson Weston	Seymour	1855
London	Wethersfield	1760
Cuff	Woodbridge	1840
	Massachusetts	
King Pompey	Lynn	1740s
King Ring[a]	North Bridgewater	1800
King Mumford	Salem	1790
	New Hampshire	
King Nero Brewster	Portsmouth	1770
	Rhode Island	
Prince Robinson	South Kingston	1700s
Guy Watson	South Kingston	1790
John	South Kingston	1800
Aaron Potter	South Kingston	1815
George Eldridge	Warwick Neck	1801–1804

[a]King Ring is assumed to have been a black ruler on the basis of his title.

Table 10   Sites of Black Election Day Celebrations

	Approximate Date
Connecticut	
Hartford	1755–1800
Wethersfield	1760
Norwich	1770–1800
Farmington	1780
Derby	1800–1850
Durham	<1800
Middletown	<1800
Oxford	<1800
Wallingford	<1800
Waterbury	<1800
New Haven	1825–1837
Seymour	1825–1855
Woodbridge	1840
Massachusetts	
Lynn	1740s(?)
Salem	1760–1790
Danvers	<1800
North Bridgewater[a]	<1800
New Hampshire	
Portsmouth	1770s
Rhode Island	
Newport	1750s
South Kingston	<1790–1815
Warwick Neck	1801–1804

[a]Presumed to have had a celebration since King Ring resided there.

Notes

Abbreviations Used in the Notes

CSMP   Colonial Society of Massachusetts, *Publications*
EIHC   Essex Institute, *Historical Collections*
JNH   *Journal of Negro History*
MHSC   Massachusetts Historical Society, *Collections*
MHSP   Massachusetts Historical Society, *Publications*
NEHGR   *New England Historical and Genealogical Register*
NYHSC   New York Historical Society, *Collections*
RIHSC   Rhode Island Historical Society, *Collections*
WMQ   *William and Mary Quarterly*

Introduction

1   Lorenzo J. Greene, *The Negro in Colonial New England* (New York, 1942).

2   William D. Piersen, "Colonizing a New Society," in Richard M. Dorson, ed., *Handbook of American Folklore* (Bloomington, 1983), 4–10.

Chapter 1   New Slaves in a New World

1   J. Hammond Trumbull, ed., *Public Records of the Colony of Connecticut*, 15 vols. (Hartford, 1859), 3:298.

2   Elizabeth Donnan, *Documents Illustrative of the History of the Slave Trade to America*, 4 vols. (New York, 1965), 2:106.

3   Jeremy Belknap, "Queries Respecting Slavery," *MHSC*, 5th ser., 3 (1877): 399.

4   Browne's letter is quoted in Gertrude S. Kimball, *Providence in Colonial Times*

(Boston, 1912), 247. Captain Nathaniel Jarvis advertised in the *Boston Gazette*, 29 September 1726, "A likely Negro Girl, lately Arrived from the West Indies," suggesting that he had disposed of all his cargo but one before he reached New England. Isaac Elizer of Newport wrote to Christopher Champlin, 10 March 1763, in the West Indies ordering him to "dispatch the Vessel and the Slaves that won't Sell, Immediately home to this port." Quoted in Darold D. Wax, "Preferences for Slaves in Colonial America," *JNH* 63 (1973): 375.

5   Edmund Morgan, *The Gentle Puritan* (New Haven, 1962), 125; and Donnan, *Documents*, 3:139.

6   Governor George Burrington of North Carolina commented scathingly in 1733 that since his colony did not buy directly from Africa, they had to purchase "the refuse, refractory and distempered Negroes brought from other governments." William Laurence Saunders, ed., *Colonial Records of North Carolina*, 10 vols. (Raleigh, 1886–90), 3:430; 4:172. In the same vein, Council President Rip Van Dam of New York reported to the Board of Trade, 2 November 1731, that the slaves imported from the West Indies were "refuse and very bad." Quoted in Donnan, *Documents*, 3:447.

Governor Dudley of Massachusetts is quoted in Donnan, *Documents*, 3:23–25; Rhode Island's problems are discussed in Sidney V. James, *Colonial Rhode Island* (New York, 1975), 163. On the general topic of refuse slaves see Wax, "Preferences for Slaves," 374–89; and James A. Rawley, *The Transatlantic Slave Trade* (New York, 1981), 333–34.

7   Lowell J. Ragatz, *The Fall of the Planter Class in the English Caribbean 1763–1853* (New York, 1963), 87; Lewis C. Gray, *History of Agriculture in the Southern United States to 1860*, 2 vols. (Gloucester, 1958), 1:363; and Stanley L. Engerman and Eugene D. Genovese, eds., *Race and Slavery in the Western Hemisphere: Quantitative Studies* (Princeton, 1975), 76 n.

8   Joseph Williamson, "Slavery in Maine," *Maine Historical Society Collections* 7 (1876): 213; "Deaths in Newport, R.I., 1760–1764," *NEHGR* 62:290; and George H. Moore, *Notes on the History of Slavery in Massachusetts* (1866; repr. New York, 1968), 60.

9   Justin Winsor, ed., *The Memorial History of Boston*, 4 vols. (Boston, 1881), 2:262. Smallpox immunity increased the value of a slave: see Edgar J. McManus, *Black Bondage in the North* (Syracuse, 1973), 37.

10   *NYHSC* 61 (1928): 31.

11   *Boston Gazette*, 13 July 1761; and *Connecticut Courant*, 22 September 1766.

12   McManus, *Black Bondage*, 36; and J. Harry Bennett, Jr., *Bondsmen and Bishops* (Berkeley, 1958), 48.

13   This seems to have been generally true of northern masters. See Wax, "Preferences for Slaves," 398. On the New World view of various African nationali-

ties, see William Dillon Piersen, "Afro-American Culture in Eighteenth Century New England: A Comparative Examination" (Ph.D. diss., Indiana University, 1975), 20 n.

14 Lorenzo J. Greene, *The Negro in Colonial New England* (New York, 1942), 34–36.

15 Donnan, *Documents*, 3:455.

16 Ibid. See also Philip D. Curtin, *The Atlantic Slave Trade: A Census* (Madison, 1969), 143; McManus, *Black Bondage*, 21; William B. Weeden, *Economic and Social History of New England*, 2 vols. (Boston, 1891), 2:456; and Winthrop D. Jordan, "The Influence of the West Indies on the Origins of New England Slavery," *WMQ*, 3rd ser. 18 (April 1961): 143–251.

17 Harriet Forbes, ed., *The Diary of Ebenezer Parkmen* (Westborough, 1899), vi. See also Piersen, "Afro-American Culture," 22.

18 Donnan, *Documents*, 3:33–35.

19 Lorenzo Greene's work suggests a minimum figure of nearly 60 percent of New England's black immigrants were of African origin, but many of those imported from the West Indies had been born in Africa, suggesting a figure nearer 80 percent African-born. This estimate closely corresponds to evidence from the Boston Overseers of the Poor report, "Persons Warned Out of Boston 1745–1792" (ms. Massachusetts Historical Society, Boston), which indicates that 78 percent of the blacks warned out of Boston in 1791 were African-born.

20 Not all slaves shipped from the Gold Coast were originally from the immediate area; an African coastal trade brought slaves from Lagos, Gabon, and Benin to Anambo for sale. See Rawley, *Transatlantic Slave Trade*, 362.

On origins of the slaves see Curtin, *Atlantic Slave Trade*, 167; Tommy T. Hamm, "The American Slave Trade With Africa, 1620–1807" (Ph.D. diss., Indiana University, 1975), 273; and Piersen, "Afro-American Culture," 23.

21 The Gold Coast tie is also suggested in the prominence with which "Gold Coast Negroes" are mentioned in slave advertisements in New England; see Greene, *Negro in New England*, 36.

On day names, see John Atkins, *A Voyage to Guinea* (London, 1735), 99; Edward Long, *History of Jamaica*, 3 vols. (London, 1774), 3:427; and Melville J. Herskovits, *The New World Negro* (Bloomington, 1969), 97.

22 The best statistical breakdown on the entry of Africans into slavery comes from the nineteenth-century informants of S. W. Koelle, recaptives interviewed in Sierra Leone in 1850. Of a sample of 141 persons, 34 percent were taken in war, 30 percent were kidnapped (often by fellow tribesmen), 11 percent were sold for their own or relatives' crimes (most commonly adultery), 7 percent were sold by relatives, 7 percent were sold to satisfy debts, and the other 11 percent were apparently

slaves from birth. Interestingly, 16 percent of the recaptives had been held as slaves in Africa for a period after their original loss of freedom; see P. E. H. Hair, "The Enslavement of Koelle's Informants," *JNH* 6 (1965): 193–203. However, Koelle's sample was not necessarily typical, since it was 99 percent male, skewed for breadth of linguistic coverage, and considerably influenced by the dislocations of the Fulbe wars.

For the eighteenth century, statistical evidence is available from a sample of twenty-five slaves carefully interviewed by the historian Bryan Edwards in Jamaica. Of these, 20 percent were taken in war, 20 percent were kidnap victims, and 60 percent were born into slavery and sold by owners to satisfy debts or for profit. Edwards states that acculturated slaves would rarely admit to less than a free birth in Africa, and suggests that slaves did not like to admit to having been sold because of the imputation that such action implied misconduct. Edwards believes other observers overestimated the protections from sale given domestic slaves in African society; Bryan Edwards, *The History, Civil and Commercial, of the British West Indies*, 2 vols. (London, 1819), 2:124–27. Other accounts from the period vary, but suggest that kidnapping and slave raids were the principal sources of new slaves. See *Abridgement of the Evidence Taken Before a Committee of the Whole House, . . . To Consider the Slave-Trade*, 4 vols. (London, 1789–91); and Piersen, "Afro-American Culture," 24 n.

23   See, for example, John Adams, *Sketches Taken During Ten Voyages to Africa Between the Years 1786–1800* (London, 1822), 9; J. G. F. Wurdemann, *Notes on Cuba* (Boston, 1844), 257; and Charles Leslie, *A New History of Jamaica* (London, 1740).

24   Heinrich Barth, *Travels and Discoveries in North and Central Africa . . . 1849–1855* (1857–58; repr. New York, 1957), 48; Mungo Park, *Travels in the Interior Districts of Africa* (London, 1799), 353–406; and William Bosman, *A New Accurate Description of the Coast of Guinea* (London, 1705), 304. For firsthand narratives from the slave's viewpoint see "Narrative of Samuel Ajayi Crowther," in Philip D. Curtin, ed., *Africa Remembered* (Madison, 1968), 310; Venture Smith, *A Narrative of the Life and Adventures of Venture Smith* (New London, 1798), 10–13; and Paul Edwards, ed., *Equiano's Travels* (Crawley, Sussex, 1967), 15–24.

Contemporary observers believed that between the executions of original seizure and the illnesses of the coastal barracoons, the number of captives was reduced by nearly half; Alexander Falconbridge, *An Account of the Slave Trade on the Coast of Africa* (London, 1788), 12–19; Thomas F. Buxton, *The African Slave Trade and Its Remedy* (London, 1839), 113; Adams, *Sketches Taken During Ten Voyages to Africa*, 9. Park, *Travels in the Interior*, 353, relates that in his coffle 10 percent died in travel and 20 percent more died on the coast. Melville J. Herskovits, working with much later evidence, believes there was a loss of only about 6 percent on the trip to the coast; see

New World Negro, 91–93. Patrick Manning, "Contours of Slavery and Social Change in Africa," *American Historical Review* 88, no. 4 (October 1983): 850, using computer simulation, estimates about 15 percent of those entering slavery (domestic and foreign) on the western coast died in the process.

25   Edwards, *History of the West Indies*, 2:127; Buxton, *The African Slave Trade*, 117; and for Angola, *Abridgement of the Evidence*, 2:5. On the funeral sacrifices and plantation labor, *Abridgement*, 3:61; and 4:9.

26   William D. Piersen, "White Cannibals, Black Martyrs: Fear, Depression, and Religious Faith as Causes of Suicide Among New Slaves," *JNH* 62, no. 2 (April 1977): 147–59.

27   Edwards, *Equiano's Travels*, 27. Often an interpreter aboard ship explained both the crossing and destination to new slaves; see, for example, William Snelgrave, *A New Account of Some Parts of Guinea and the Slave Trade* (London, 1734), 162–63.

28   Edwards, *History of the West Indies*, 2:152–53; and Henry Koster, *Travels in Brazil*, 2 vols. (London, 1817), 2:252.

29   Hugh Crow, *Memoirs of the Late Captain H. Crow of Liverpool* (1830; repr. 1850), 129, 137. A similar expression of such belief from Whydah is found noted in Thomas Phillips, *A Journal of a Voyage Made in the "Hannibal" of London 1693–1694*, in Awnsham and John Churchill, eds., *A Collection of Voyages and Travels*, 6 vols. (London, 1732), 6:242. Similarly, Karfa Taura, the Slatte slave trader and friend of Mungo Park, told Park that "black men are nothing" when he compared them to Europeans with their mastery of material culture and technology; Park, *Travels in the Interior*, 403–6.

30   Benjamin Colman, *Some Observations on the New Method of Receiving the Small Pox by Ingrafting or Inoculation* (Boston, 1721), 16; and James Stewart, *A New View of the Past and Present State of the Island of Jamaica* (Edinburgh, 1823), 258.

31   Bosman, *Description of the Coast of Guinea*, 146–47.

32   Thomas E. Bowdich, *Mission from Cape Coast Castle to Ashantee* (London, 1819), 261–62. Note a similar story told by Jamaican blacks in the nineteenth century as recorded in J. M. Phillippo, *Jamaica: Its Past and Present State* (London, 1843), 188–89; for the story in the United States see Richard M. Dorson, *American Negro Folktales* (Greenwich, 1967), 172–73.

33   Edwards, *Equiano's Travels*, 43. Stewart, *New View of the Island of Jamaica*, 258, notes that "the Negroes are astonished at the ingenuity of the Europeans, and there are some articles of their manufacture which appear quite unaccountable to them, as watches, telescopes, looking-glasses, gunpowder, &c." This is undoubtedly an over-statement, as mirrors and gunpowder would have been familiar to many Africans, yet the basic point has validity. Stewart once amazed a party of slaves with a magic lantern which they assumed to be an example of witchcraft. Similarly, Mrs. Car-

michael, *The Domestic Manners and Social Conditions of the West Indies*, 2 vols. (London, 1833), 2:150, reports that a new Negro believed that "jumbee" (spirit) was the explanation for the thermometer.

34   Theodore Canot, *Captain Canot or Twenty Years of an African Slaver*, ed. Brantz Mayer (New York, 1854), 108; and Carmichael, *Domestic Manners of the West Indies*, 1:311. On the African custom of finger-snapping, see John M'Leod, *A Voyage to Africa* (London, 1820), 98 and 104.

35   Esther B. Carpenter, *South County Studies* (1887; repr. Boston, 1924), 223.

36   Ottabah Cugoano, *Thoughts and Sentiments on the Evil of Slavery* (1787; repr. London, 1969), 26; see also Park, *Travels in the Interior*, 403–4.

37   Crow, *Memoirs of the Late Captain Crow*, 220. Crow includes another example of this African predisposition observed by a Captain Adams on the more southern coast. Similarly, Joseph Hawkins, *A Voyage to the Coast of Africa* (Philadelphia, 1797), 89, explains European dress and ornaments were "uniformly the signs of riches and respect" in the Ibo area; and for Central Africa see Georges Balandier, *Daily Life in the Kingdom of the Kongo* (New York, 1969), 10, 82, 166.

38   See, for example, Bosman, *Description of the Coast of Guinea*, in John Pinkerton, ed., *A General Collection of the Best and Most Interesting Voyages and Travels*, 17 vols. (London, 1808–1814), 16:510; and John Atkins, *A Voyage to Guinea, Brazil, & the West Indies* (London, 1735), 198–99.

39   On the African love of European liquor and American tobacco and rum, see Samuel Ajayi Crowther as quoted in Curtin, *Africa Remembered*, 308; John Barbot, *A Description of the Coasts of North and South Guinea*, in Awnsham and John Churchill, eds., *A Collection of Voyages and Travels*, 6 vols. (London, 1746), 5:138; and Bosman, *Description of the Coast of Guinea*, 107, 268–70, 286. Crow, *Memoirs of the Late Captain Crow*, 273, gives an interesting description of the house that Duke Ephraim of Bonny had built in Liverpool and shipped to the coast, furnished with European prestige items such as clocks, beds, tables, and pictures. Philip Quaque lived in much the same manner on the Cape Coast; see Curtin, *Africa Remembered*, 111.

40   Edwards, *Equiano's Travels*, 43. Stewart, *New View of the Island of Jamaica*, 261, reported that blacks "are of the opinion, in unison with the African habits, that we should, on most occasions, bow to superior power, and be influenced and directed in great measure by favor, affection, and interests." While Stewart is prone to overstatement, this observation is in general agreement with the anthropological opinion of Melville J. Herskovits, *Myth of the Negro Past* (Boston, 1941), 141.

Chapter 2   *A Clustered Minority*

1   For the percentage of white population by nationality in 1790, see the United States Bureau of the Census, *Historical Statistics of the United States, Colonial Times to 1957* (Washington, 1961), series Z, 20:756.

In Boston, the Overseers of the Poor recorded the birthplaces of those warned out of town in 1791; of those from foreign areas the African-born followed in order those from England, Ireland, and Scotland. Twelve percent of those warned were of African birth (compared to 3 percent from the West Indies). The Africans were almost 3 percent of those warned at a time when the entire Negro population of Massachusetts, including the native-born, was less than 1 percent of the state's total population. The manuscript is available at the Massachusetts Historical Society, but the totals can be found in Allan Kulikoff, "Progress of Inequality in Revolutionary Boston," *WMQ*, 3rd ser., 28 (July 1971): 401.

2   Estimates of the Negro population of New England vary widely in totals and in the years covered. The most useful estimates for extrapolation are in the Bureau of the Census, *Historical Statistics*, series Z, 1–19:756.

Estimates of the Negro population for 1790 and 1800 can be taken from the United States Bureau of the Census, *Negro Population in the United States 1790–1915* (Washington, 1918), 51; white data for the same years is available in the Bureau of the Census, *Historical Statistics*, series A, 128–180:13. See this volume, 473–74, on the considerable problem of underestimation and reliability of Negro population estimates; see also Lorenzo J. Greene, *The Negro in Colonial New England* (New York, 1942), 72–73.

3   Greene, *Negro in New England*, 78; for the Negro population by sex see Charles Brewster, *Rambles About Portsmouth* (Portsmouth, 1859), 208.

4   W. S. Rossiter, ed., *A Century of Population Growth in the United States 1790–1900* (Washington, 1909), 158–62; and Evarts B. Greene and Virginia Harrington, *American Population Before the Federal Census of 1790* (New York, 1932), 31.

5   Greene and Harrington, *American Population*, 67.

6   J. H. Trumbull and C. J. Hoadly, eds., *Public Records of the Colony of Connecticut*, 15 vols. (Hartford, 1887), 14:483–92.

7   See Table 7 in the Appendix.

8   If we extrapolate a natural increase of 15 percent a decade for New England's Negroes, slightly lower than the 18 percent James A. Henretta, *Evolution of American Society 1700–1815* (Lexington, 1973), 58, estimates for the eighteenth-century southern colonies, the importation of 1,200 blacks a decade seems likely. However, the low level of increases in the late eighteenth-century Negro population of New England suggests that a natural increase of 15 percent a decade may be too high an

estimate. Either way, the largest importation came between 1720 and 1740. See Tables 7 and 8 in the Appendix.

9   See Table 8 in the Appendix.

10   These estimates are, at best, extremely rough extrapolations estimated by working out the likely survival rates of immigrants for each decade according to a formula suggested by Robert W. Fogel and Stanley L. Engerman, *Time on the Cross: Evidence and Methods*, 2 vols. (Boston, 1974), 1:31–32. A table is not given here because it would suggest a reality about these figures which is not warranted. This guess probably underestimates the percentages of foreign-born New England blacks in the eighteenth century by underestimating the original importation.

11   Amateur demographers like Benjamin Franklin and Edward Wigglesworth, professor of divinity at Harvard, commented in the late eighteenth century on the low fertility rate of northern slave women when they maintained Negro population could only be maintained through importation; see Gary B. Nash, "Slaves and Slaveowners in Colonial Philadelphia," *WMQ*, 3rd ser., 30 (April 1973): 239. On the other hand, J. P. Brissot de Warville, *New Travels in the United States of America, 1788* (Cambridge, 1964), 238n, argues that married blacks in the North had at least as many children as whites, but that more of them died. For comparative data on this subject, see Robert V. Wells, *The Population of the British Colonies in America Before 1776* (Princeton, 1975), 279.

12   *Connecticut Courant*, 23 February 1773, 33; Greene, *Negro in New England*, 213–16; Edgar J. McManus, *Black Bondage in the North* (Syracuse, 1973), 37–38; and, comparatively, Fogel and Engerman, *Time on the Cross*, 1:78–86.

13   Greene and Harrington, *American Population*, 67; and Rossiter, *Century of Population Growth*, 166–69.

14   Greene, *Negro in New England*, 212, 216, estimates that many slave women were mothers at eighteen. Inspection of the advertisements in the *Connecticut Courant* would suggest that in the last half of the eighteenth century black women became mothers at about twenty-one on average. For comparative white data see Robert V. Wells, "Quaker Marriage Patterns in Colonial Perspective," *WMQ*, 3rd ser., 29 (July 1972): 420, 429; and Maris Vinovskis, *Fertility in Massachusetts from the Revolution to the Civil War* (New York, 1981), 45. Comparative evidence examined by Fogel and Engerman, *Time on the Cross*, 1:137, suggests that the age at first birth for black women in the nineteenth-century American South was 22.5. Working with nineteenth-century South Carolina evidence, Herbert Gutman, *The Black Family in Slavery and Freedom 1750–1925* (New York, 1976), 50, suggests age at first birth as 19.6.

15   The sex ratios for Massachusetts of 1.64 and 1.36 for 1754 and 1764 might have been lower if children under sixteen had been included. For the census of 1754, see "Number of Negro Slaves in the Province of the Massachusetts Bay, Sixteen

Years Old and Upward," *MHSC*, 2nd ser., 3 (1815): 95–97; for 1764 see Rossiter, *Century of Population Growth*, 158–62. All my Massachusetts figures include Maine in their total.

The Connecticut census of 1774 suggests a sex ratio of 1.30; *Public Records of Connecticut*, 14:483–92. The New Hampshire data for 1773 suggests a sex ratio of 1.28; Rossiter, *Century of Population Growth*, 150. The white New England data is available in Herbert Moller, "Sex Composition and Correlated Culture Patterns of Colonial America," *WMQ*, 3rd ser., 2 (April 1945): 124.

Comparative data on sex ratios from New York suggest the adult sex ratio correlates strongly to slave importation. New York's sex ratio among blacks rose from 1.01 in 1703 to 1.60 in 1731 (counting those over ten as adults). The rate then fell from 1.42 in 1746 (for those over sixteen) to 1.20 in 1771. See Greene and Harrington, *American Population*, 95–104; for wider comparison see Wells, *Population of British Colonies*, 271–73. The sex ratio for slaves imported into the Americas from Africa was about 2.00; Patrick Manning, "Contours of Slavery and Social Change in Africa," *American Historical Review* 88, no. 4 (October 1983): 839.

16   Rossiter, *Century of Population Growth*, 162; *Public Records of Connecticut*, 14:483–92; on the general topic of Indian-Negro marriage in New England, see Greene, *Negro in New England*, 198–200.

17   William J. Brown, *The Life of William J. Brown of Providence, R.I.* (Providence, 1883), 10–11.

18   For the Boston data see *MHSC*, 2nd ser., 3 (1815): 95. For the 1765 data counting "Negroes and Molattoes," see Boston Registry, *Reports of the Record Commissioners*, "Selectmen's Minutes from 1764–1768," 170; for comparative Boston white data see Kulikoff, "Progress of Inequality," 378; and for comparative Massachusetts data see Rossiter, *Century of Population Growth*, 158–62.

19   Rossiter, *Century of Population Growth*, 149–50.

20   Greene and Harrington, *American Population*, 67.

21   Ibid.; and Rossiter, *Century of Population Growth*, 166–69.

22   A normal sex ratio for children under sixteen is 1.03 to 1.04. See Moller, "Sex Composition," 124n.

23   For a list of Boston burials from 1701 to 1752 taken from the *Boston Gazette and Weekly Advertiser*, see Greene, *Negro in New England*, Appendix, 348–49; for burials from 1759 to 1778, see John Boyle, "Journal of Occurrences in Boston, 1759–1778," *NEHGR* 84 (1930) and 85 (1931).

24   John B. Blake, *Public Health in the Town of Boston 1630–1822* (Cambridge, 1959), 250.

25   Greene, *Negro in New England*, 84–85 and 348–49; Greene and Harrington, *American Population*, 22n; and Boyle, "Journal."

26   Boston Registry, Selectmen's Minutes from 1764–1768," 80; for the treat-

ment of slave illness in New England, see Greene, *Negro in New England*, 227–30.

27   Newport's rates, like Boston's, include those lost at sea. For the Newport data taken from Ezra Stiles's manuscripts, see "Deaths in Newport, R.I., 1760–1764," *NEHGR* 62 (1908): 287, 290, 358; and 63 (1909): 56. Working from limited data from the *Newport Mercury*, Greene, *Negro in New England*, 229, estimates an average of thirty-eight blacks died each year between 1760 and 1772—about 19 percent of Newport's total deaths.

Comparative data from Philadelphia suggests a mortality rate of about sixty-eight per thousand between 1765 and 1769; Nash, "Slaves and Slaveowners," 241. In the West Indies the mortality rate was even higher, with six blacks dying for each born; see Patricia A. Molen, "Population Patterns in Barbados in the Early Eighteenth Century," *WMQ*, 3rd ser., 28 (1971): 289–90.

28   "Deaths in Newport," *NEHGR* 62 (1908): 209, 290; and 63 (1909): 56. On seasoning in the New World, see above, chapter 1.

29   Wells, *Population of the British Colonies*, 82, 101. Boston was also simply unhealthy; see Vinovskis, *Fertility in Massachusetts*, 37.

30   See, for example, the letter of Samuel Hopkins of Newport to Grenville Sharpe, 15 January 1789, as quoted in Edwards A. Park, ed., *Memoir of the Life and Character of Samuel Hopkins* (Boston, 1854), 140–41; Jeremy Belknap, "Queries Relating to Slavery in Massachusetts," *MHSC*, 5th ser., 3 (1877): 400; William Bentley, *Diary of William Bentley, D.D.*, 4 vols. (Gloucester, 1962), 9 March 1818, 4:506; William Grimes, *The Life of William Grimes the Runaway Slave* (New Haven, 1855), 81–82; and Robert S. Rantoul, "Negro Slavery in Massachusetts," *EIHC* 24 (1887): 99.

31   Jeremy Belknap, "Belknap Papers," *Liberator* 1 (12 March 1831): 4, as quoted in Donald Martin Jacobs, "A History of the Boston Negro From the Revolution to the Civil War" (Ph.D. diss., Boston University, 1968), 40.

Chapter 3   Family Slavery

1   Edmund Morgan, *The Puritan Family* (New York, 1966), 144–45.

2   Cotton Mather, *The Negro Christianized* (Boston, 1706): 6; and Elihu Coleman, *Testimony Against That Antichristian Practice of Making Slaves of Men* (Boston, 1733), 6.

3   William Bentley, *The Diary of William Bentley, D.D.*, 4 vols. (Gloucester, 1962), 4:507; Samuel F. Batchelder, *Notes on Colonel Henry Vassall* (Cambridge, 1917), 74n; and Sarah A. Emery, *Reminiscences of a Nonagenarian* (Newburyport, 1879), 101.

4   Adin Ballou, *History of the Town of Milford* (Boston, 1882), 550; and George Sheldon, *History of Deerfield Massachusetts 1636–1886*, 2 vols. (Deerfield, 1896), 2:896.

5   Bentley, *Diary*, 4:506–7. On the close ties between masters and slaves who grew up together, see George C. Mason, *Reminiscences of Newport* (Newport, 1884),

106; and William D. Johnston, *Slavery in Rhode Island 1755–1776* (Providence, 1894), 139.

6   Quoted in Ulrich B. Phillips, *Life and Labor in the Old South* (Boston, 1929), 195. Both Protestant and Catholic missionaries in the Americas believed that a large-scale conversion of new slaves was only possible with children; see Frank J. Klingberg, *An Appraisal of the Negro in Colonial South Carolina; A Study of Americanization* (Washington, 1941), 32; Darold D. Wax, "The Demand for Slave Labor in Colonial Pennsylvania," *Pennsylvania History* 34 (1967): 337; and John Atkins, *A Voyage to Guinea, Brazil, and the West Indies* (1735; repr. Holland, 1970), 177n.

7   Phillis Wheatley, *Memoirs and Poems of Phillis Wheatley* (Boston, 1823), 12; and Esteban Montejo, *The Autobiography of a Runaway Slave*, ed. Miguel Barnet (New York, 1968), 34–35.

8   Clarence W. Bowen, *The History of Woodstock Connecticut* (Norwood, Mass., 1926), 202; Of eighteen sales of slaves recorded in Beverly, Massachusetts, ten were of children; see Charles L. Hill, "Slavery and Its Aftermath in Beverly, Massachusetts: Juno Larcom and her Family," *EIHC* 116, no. 2 (April 1980): 118; see also Jeremy Belknap, "Queries Respecting Slavery," *MHSC*, 5th ser., 3:383; George H. Moore, *Slavery in Massachusetts* (New York, 1866), 27; Lorenzo J. Greene, *The Negro in Colonial New England* (Boston, 1942), 213; Batchelder, *Notes on Colonel Vassall*, 74n; Lawrence W. Towner, "A Good Master Well Served: A Social History of Servitude in Massachusetts 1620–1750" (Ph.D. diss., Northwestern University, 1955), 440; Jane de Forest Shelton, "The New England Negro: A Remnant," *Harpers New Monthly Magazine* 88 (March 1894), 538; Nathaniel Bouton, *History of Concord New Hampshire 1725–1853* (Concord, 1856), 252; for two interesting narratives, Ballou, *History of Milford*, 549–50.

The desire to avoid the expense of a child often led to the sale of a slave woman for becoming pregnant; such sales were common throughout the North; Edgar J. McManus, *Black Bondage in the North* (Syracuse, 1973), 37–38. This also meant that slave women would try to avoid having children if they were afraid of such a sale—one more reason for the low fertility rate among northern Negro slaves.

9   For separation and binding out in general, see Morgan, *The Puritan Family*, 38; John Demos, "Notes on Life in Plymouth Colony," *WMQ*, 3rd ser., 22 (1965): 284–86; Richard B. Morris, *Government and Labor in Early America* (New York, 1965), 385. For the Townsend case, see Delorain P. Corey, *The History of Malden, Massachusetts 1633–1785* (Malden, 1899), 421.

10   Shelton, "The New England Negro," 538; see also Nancy Prince, *A Narrative of the Life and Travels of Miss Nancy Prince* (Boston, 1850), 6–7. Poor or orphaned black children were often placed in white families, who were given a small compensation until the child was seven and then received the child's labor as remuneration for board until the child was twenty-one. Then a gift was in order for the young

adult: Bernard Greene gave his Negro ward $110 and two suits; see Corey, *History of Malden*, 423n; and Emery, *Reminiscences of a Nonagenarian*, 101. Poor whites received the same kind of indentures; see Jeremy Belknap, "Queries Respecting the Slavery and Emancipation of Negroes in Massachusetts," *MHSC*, 1st ser., 4:207.

11   Margaretta M. Odell, "Memoir of Phillis Wheatley," in Phillis Wheatley Peters, *Poems* (Boston, 1835), 12.

12   Harriet S. Tapley, *Chronicles of Danvers (Old Salem Village), Massachusetts 1632–1923* (Danvers, 1923), 53.

13   Hagar Merriman, *The Autobiography of Aunt Hagar Merriman of New Haven Connecticut* (New Haven, 1861), 3–4, 8.

14   J. P. Brissot de Warville, *New Travels in the United States of America 1788* (Cambridge, 1964), 134.

15   Samuel Stringer's letter of 1770 is quoted in Winthrop D. Jordan, *White Over Black* (Baltimore, 1969), 105. Something of the same kind was often found in the American South; see Eugene D. Genovese, *Roll, Jordan, Roll* (New York, 1974).

16   John Langdon Sibley and Clifford Kenyon Shipton, *Sibley's Harvard Graduates*, 14 vols. (Boston, 1873–1968), 8:245.

17   Harriet Beecher Stowe, *Oldtown Fireside Stories* (New York, 1900), 331; Thomas R. Hazard, *The Jonny-Cake Papers of "Shepard Tom"* (Boston, 1915), 68; and Theophilus Parsons, *Memoirs* (Boston, 1859), 17.

18   *MHSP* 1st ser., 15:389; and Elizabeth Donnan, *Documents Illustrative of the History of the Slave Trade*, 4 vols. (New York, 1965), 3:67.

19   Daniel Huntoon, *History of the Town of Canton* (Cambridge, 1893), 503–4; for similar sales at Hartford, see Chauncey E. Peck, *The History of Wilbraham, Massachusetts* (Wilbraham, 1913), 310.

20   Tapley, *Chronicles of Danvers*, 51.

21   Sarah Knight, *The Journal of Madam Sarah Knight* (New York, 1825), 38; J. Hector St. Crèvecour, *Letters From an American Farmer* (London, 1782), 249; and Sheldon, *History of Deerfield*, 2:905. See also Belknap, "Queries Respecting Slavery," *MHSC* 1st ser., 4:200; *MHSC* 5th ser., 3:302, 399; and Greene, *Negro in New England*, 22.

22   Abner C. Goodell, Jr., "John Saffin and His Slave Adam," *CSMP* 1 (March 1893): 85–113; Sheldon, *History of Deerfield*, 2:905; Odell, "Memoir of Phillis Wheatley," 15; and Sheldon H. Harris, *Paul Cuffee: Black America and the African Return* (New York, 1972), 24. Seating distinctions were found among the Ibo in Africa, where slaves were not permitted to eat with the free citizens; see Paul Edwards, ed., *Equiano's Travels* (London, 1967), 10.

23   From the *Diary of Ebenezer Bridge*, 2:265, as quoted in Sibley, *Sibley's Harvard Graduates*, 10:20. Many southern slave owners adopted similar patriarchal stances, referring to their slaves as family members; see Genovese, *Roll, Jordan, Roll*.

24   The quotations are from the diaries of Ebenezer Parkman, John Winthrop, and David Hall, as quoted in Sibley, *Sibley's Harvard Graduates*, 6:518; 9:246; and 7:352.

25   Charles Brewster, *Rambles About Portsmouth* (Portsmouth, 1859), 208–9; see also Alice M. Earle, *Customs and Fashions in Old New England* (New York, 1893), 94.

26   Bouton, *The History of Concord*, 253.

27   Anne Grant, *Memoirs of an American Lady, with Sketches of Manners and Scenery in America, . . . Previous to the Revolution* (1809; repr. New York, 1903), 80. When such relationships existed in the South, the too easy acculturation of black children destroyed social distance and led to such practices being discouraged; see E. Franklin Frazier, *The Free Negro Family* (Nashville, 1932), 27.

28   Bouton, *The History of Concord*, 253.

29   Ibid.

30   J. H. Temple, *The History of Framingham, Massachusetts* (Framingham, 1887), 237; William J. Brown, *The Life of William J. Brown of Providence* (Providence, 1883), 47; and Sibley, *Sibley's Harvard Graduates*, 5:57.

31   See, for example, Brewster, *Rambles About Portsmouth*, 211; Benjamin Hobart, *History of the Town of Abington* (Boston, 1866), 252; and Ballou, *History of Milford*, 550n.

32   Batchelder, *Notes on Colonel Henry Vassal*, 73, 76. For similar descriptions of slaves as the bards of their "families" see Benjamin F. Browne, "Some Notes Upon Mr. Rantoul's Reminiscences," in *EIHC* 5 (August 1863): 199; and Temple, *History of Framingham*, 326. Stowe, *Oldtown Fireside Stories*, 389, offers an excellent description of the strong identification which a slave had in regard to his master and his family.

33   "The Will of a Negro Slave in 1733," printed in *Connecticut Magazine* 10, no. 4 (1906): 693; and "Will of a Boston Slave, 1743," *PCSM* 25 (April 1923): 253–54. *Connecticut Courant*, 19 October 1795, 34.

34   Lyman Beecher, *Autobiography*, 2 vols. (Cambridge, 1961), 1:14. For slave money lending, see Johnston, *Slavery in Rhode Island*, 139; for an example of problems, see Venture Smith, *A Narrative of the Life and Adventures of Venture, a Native of Africa* (New London, 1798), 21.

35   William D. Piersen, "Afro-American Culture in Eighteenth Century New England: A Comparative Examination" (Ph.D. diss., Indiana University, 1975), 94. Herbert Gutman, *The Black Family in Slavery and Freedom, 1750–1925* (New York, 1976), 232, notes surnames often symbolized the ties between a slave family and its family of origin, not between a family and its last owner. Blacks sometimes also took the titles of their former owners as well; see Belknap, "Queries," *MHSC* 1st ser., 4 (1795): 208.

36   Bentley, *Diary of William Bentley*, 4:361.

37 Benjamin Quarles, *The Negro in the American Revolution* (Chapel Hill, 1961), 51–52. Similarly, see Jedediah Dwelley and John F. Simmons, *History of the Town of Hanover, Massachusetts* (Hanover, 1910), 184.

38 Abiel Brown, *Genealogical History of the Settlers of West Simsbury* (Hartford, 1856), 140; and Sylvester Judd, *History of Hadley* (Springfield, 1905), 313.

39 Harris, *Paul Cuffee*, 264.

40 Henry Koster, *Travels in Brazil*, 2 vols. (London, 1817), 2:286–87; and Piersen, "Afro-American Culture," 110. On the effect of slave-to-master ratio, see also H. Hoetiak, "Surinam and Curacao," in David W. Cohen and Jack P. Greene, eds., *Neither Slave Nor Free* (Baltimore, 1972), 157.

41 "Negro Petition for Freedom," *MHSC*, 5th ser., 3 (1877): 433.

Chapter 4   The Training of Servants

1 Van Rensselaer is quoted in Edgar J. McManus, *A History of Negro Slavery in New York* (Syracuse, 1966), 5. See also John Brickell, *The Natural History of North Carolina* (1737; repr. Murfreesboro, 1968), 272; Carl Bridenbaugh, *Cities in the Wilderness* (New York, 1971), 201; and Eugene D. Genovese's essay in Ann J. Lane, ed., *The Debate Over Slavery* (Urbana, 1971), 64.

2 Richard S. Dunn, *Sugar and Slaves* (Chapel Hill, 1972), 232; see also S. W. Koelle, *African Native Literature* (Graz, Austria, 1963), 21; Philip D. Curtin, ed., *Africa Remembered* (Madison, 1968), 41; Hugh Crow, *Memoirs of the Late Captain H. Crow of Liverpool* (London, 1830), 199; and Charles Ball, *Slavery in the United States* (1836; repr. New York, 1969), 126.

3 John G. Stedman, *Narrative of a Five Year's Expedition Against the Revolted Negroes of Surinam* (1796; repr. Barre, Mass., 1971), 2:369; see also the testimony of Dr. Harrison, *Abridgement of the Evidence Taken Before a Committee of the Whole House, . . . To Consider the Slave-Trade*, 4 vols. (London, 1791), 4:50; and of Dr. Thomas Trotter and Sir George Young, 3:81, 212.

4 Testimony of the Reverend Rob. Boucher Nicholls, *Abridgement of Evidence*, 3:331.

5 John Josselyn, *An Account of Two Voyages to New England* (1674; repr. Boston, 1865), 26; and George Sheldon, *A History of Deerfield, Massachusetts 1636–1886*, 2 vols. (Deerfield, 1896), 2:897.

6 See, for example, Mungo Park, *Travels in the Interior Districts of Africa* (London, 1799), 287–98; and Douglas Grant, *The Fortunate Slave* (New York, 1968), 81.

7 Hugh Jones, *The Present State of Virginia* (1724; repr. New York, 1865), 38; and Henry Koster, *Travels in Brazil*, 2 vols. (London, 1817), 2:252.

8 *Memoir of Mrs. Chloe Spear, A Native of Africa, Who was Enslaved in Childhood, and Died in Boston, January 3, 1815 . . . Aged 65 Years* (Boston, 1832), 17.

9   Paul Edwards, ed., *Equiano's Travels* (Crawley, Sussex, 1967), 33; see also the testimony of Ecrocide Claxton, *Abridgement of Evidence*, 4:36; and William F. Gray, *From Virginia to Texas, 1835: Diary of Col. Wm. F. Gray* (1909; repr. Houston, 1965), 159.

10   J. Harry Bennett, Jr., *Bondsmen and Bishops: Slavery and Apprenticeship on the Codrington Plantations of Barbados 1710–1838* (Berkeley, 1958), 33; Edwards, *Equiano's Travels*, 31; Peter H. Wood, *Black Majority* (New York, 1974), 169; and George P. Rawick, ed., *The American Slave: A Composite Autobiography*, 19 vols. (Westport, 1972), 2:30.

11   Abiel Brown, *Genealogical History of the Settlers of West Simsbury* (Hartford, 1856), 141.

12   Thomas Weston, *History of the Town of Middleboro, Massachusetts* (Boston, 1906), 101–2. On the African belief in white cannibalism, see William D. Piersen, "White Cannibals, Black Martyrs: Fear, Depression, and Religious Faith as Causes of Suicide Among New Slaves," *JNH* 62, no. 2 (April 1977): 147–50.

13   Cotton Mather, "A Letter to a Friend," as quoted in George L. Kittredge, "Some Lost Works of Cotton Mather," *MHSP* 45 (February 1912): 430.

14   Cotton Mather, *The Angel of Bethesda*, as quoted in Kittredge, "Some Lost Works of Cotton Mather," 431.

15   Lorenzo J. Greene, *The Negro in Colonial New England* (New York, 1942), 38; and Lorenzo J. Greene, "The New England Negro as Seen in Advertisements for Runaway Slaves," *JNH* 29 (April 1944): 125–44. Of the fifty-two advertisements, forty-five made no mention of language ability, seventeen mentioned that the slaves could speak English, and of these thirteen spoke "good English," two spoke "broken English," and one spoke Spanish. In the South the situation was quite different; there slaves were much slower to pick up English; see, for example, Winthrop D. Jordan, *White Over Black* (Baltimore, 1969), 184n; and Gerald W. Mullin, *Flight and Rebellion* (New York, 1972), 40, 89.

16   *Connecticut Courant*, 14 October 1776, 33; and 2 July 1771, 32. "Country-born" Negroes were not necessarily New Englanders from birth; they might have been imported from the West Indies or from some other colony. See Marcus W. Jernegan, *Laboring and Dependent Classes in Colonial America 1607–1783* (New York, 1960), 8.

17   *Connecticut Courant*, 16 September 1776. See also the ad for thirty-five-year-old Dick "of the Eboe country . . . speaks good English," who was carried off by the British from New Charleston near Boston; *South Carolina Gazette and Advertiser*, 24 July 1784, as quoted in *JNH* 1 (April 1916): 200.

18   Boston *News Letter*, 18 October 1759, as quoted in Elizabeth Donnan, ed., *Documents Illustrative of the History of the Slave Trade to America*, 4 vols. (New York, 1965), 3:67; *Connecticut Courant*, 6 November 1766, 33; and 18 March 1776, 33.

Mullin, *Flight and Rebellion*, 46, believes it only took two or three years for Africans in eighteenth-century Virginia to become conversant in English, but John W. Blassingame, *The Slave Community* (New York, 1972), 22, suggests it often took several years for adult Africans to add just a few English words to their vocabulary.

19   *Connecticut Courant*, 30 June 1794, 33; 30 October 1774, 33; and 19 September 1796, 34; and William C. Nell, *The Colored Patriots of the American Revolution* (Boston, 1855), 135. Many slave runaways in the American South seem to have spoken two European languages, adding either French or Spanish to English. See *JNH* 1 (April 1916): 191–94.

20   Falconer is quoted in Lawrence A. Cremin, *American Education: The Colonial Experience* (New York, 1970), 533; for a comparison to Brazil, see Koster, *Travels in Brazil*, 2:288.

21   Brown, *Genealogical History of West Simsbury*, 141; and *Memoir of Mrs. Chloe Spear*, 73.

22   Edwards Amasa Park, *Memoir of the Life and Character of Samuel Hopkins* (Boston, 1854), 131, 366.

23   Ferguson, *Memoir of Hopkins*, as quoted in Park, *Memoir of Hopkins*, 154.

24   Fanny Saltar, "Fanny Saltar's Reminiscences of Colonial Days in Philadelphia," *Pennsylvania Magazine of History and Biography* 40 (1916): 189; for a similar description of an old slave in New Jersey, see Andrew D. Mellick, Jr., *Lesser Crossroads* (New Jersey, 1948), 372.

25   H. R. McIlwaine, ed., *Journals of the House of Burgesses of Virginia, 1695–1702* (Richmond, 1905–15), 174. The Bray Associates of Charles Town were of the same opinion in 1740 when they entered only "homeborn" Negro children into their free schools under black masters; "this good work must not be attempted in the gross or inclusive of the whole body of slaves of so many various ages, nations, and languages." Quoted in Carl Bridenbaugh, *Cities in Revolt* (New York, 1971), 175. See also Lefroy, comp., *Memorials of Bermuda*, 2:569, as quoted in Jordan, *White Over Black*, 184.

26   Cotton Mather, *The Negro Christianized* (Boston, 1706), 25; see also Elihu Coleman, *A Testimony Against That Antichristian Practice of Making Slaves of Men* (Boston, 1733), 10.

27   Ka-Le to John Quincy Adams, New Haven, 4 January 1841, as quoted in John W. Blassingame, *Slave Testimony* (Baton Rouge, 1977), 33.

28   Sarah L. Bailey, *Historical Sketches of Andover, Massachusetts* (Boston, 1880), 598.

29   *Connecticut Courant*, 3 March 1766, 31.

30   The most useful listings of slave occupations are found in Lawrence W. Towner, "A Good Master Well Served: A Social History of Servitude in Massachu-

setts 1620–1750" (Ph.D. diss., Northwestern University, 1955), Appendix M, 441; and Greene, *Negro in New England*, 100–23.

A wide variety of labor skills among slaves was typical in the more urban North; see Edgar J. McManus, *Black Bondage in the North* (Syracuse, 1973), 42; and Gary B. Nash, "Slaves and Slaveholders in Colonial Philadelphia," *WMQ*, 3rd ser., 30 (April 1973): 250–52, who estimates that 50 percent of Philadelphia's slaves worked for artisan masters and that around 60 percent of the city's masters held slaves to work in their crafts or small-scale industries.

31   Stephen B. Luce, "Some Old Papers Relating to the Newport Slave Trade," Newport Historical Society, *Bulletin*, no. 62 (July 1927), 34.

32   Mather, *The Negro Christianized*, 29; testimony of Wm. Dove, *Abridgement of Evidence*, 3:107; Sheldon, *History of Deerfield*, 2:183; and Greene, *Negro in New England*, 104.

33   Francis G. Walett, ed., *The Diary of Ebenezer Parkman* (Worcester, 1974), 27 August 1728, 33; and Clifford K. Shipton, *Sibley's Harvard Graduates* 4:128.

34   Mather, *Negro Christianized*, 29.

35   On the African history of black English, see David Dalby, *Black Through White: Patterns of Communication in Africa and the New World*, Hans Wolff Memorial Lecture, Indiana University (Bloomington, 1969). A good New World discussion is found in Wood, *Black Majority*, 167–94.

36   Greene, *Negro in New England*, 236–41.

37   *Memoir of Chloe Spear*, 26. Despite the opposition of his master, Prince Richards of East Bridgewater, Massachusetts, learned to write by using a charred stick; Nell, *Colored Patriots of the American Revolution*, 35.

38   William J. Brown, *The Life of William J. Brown of Providence, R.I.* (Providence, 1883), 11.

39   Cremin, *American Education: The Colonial Experience*, 194–95. Cotton Mather had a night charity school for Negroes and Indians in Boston in 1717; see Greene, *Negro in New England*, 238. Alice Morse Earle, *Customs and Fashions in Old New England* (New York, 1898), 90, also notes a Negro school in Boston in 1728. But more typical was New Haven, which set up its first "colored school" in 1811; see Rollin G. Osterweis, *Three Centuries of New Haven* (New Haven, 1953), 229.

40   Jeremy Belknap, "Correspondence Between Jeremy Belknap and Ebenezer Hazard: Part II," *MHSC*, 5th ser., 3 (1877): 12.

41   Park, *Memoir of Samuel Hopkins*, 154; and George C. Mason, *Reminiscences of Newport* (Newport, 1884), 159.

42   Phillis Wheatley, *Memoirs and Poems of Phillis Wheatley* (Boston, 1823), 16.

43   Alexis de Tocqueville, *Democracy in America* (1835; repr. New York, 1966), 315–16, 322–23.

44   J. P. Brissot de Warville, *New Travels in the United States of America 1788* (Cambridge, 1964), 239.

45   William Grimes, *The Life of William Grimes* (New Haven, 1855), 71–82, passim; compare with Venture Smith, *A Narrative of the Life and Adventures of Venture, a Native of Africa But Resident above Sixty Years in the United States of America* (New London, 1798), 30; and Greene, *Negro in New England,* 304.

46   See the Boston Overseers of the Poor report, "Persons Warned Out of Boston 1745–1792" (ms., Massachusetts Historical Society, Boston).

47   Alfred M. Bingham, "Squatter Settlements of Freed Slaves in New England," Connecticut Historical Society, *Bulletin* 41, no. 3 (July 1976): 65–80.

48   In 1742 there were 110 Negroes in the almshouse and thirty-six in the workhouse out of a total black population of 1,520. See Boston Registry Department, *A Report of the Record Commissioners,* "Selectmen's Minutes 1736–1742," 369. For whites in the poorhouse in 1742 and a general discussion of the poor in Boston, see Allan Kulikoff, "The Progress of Inequality in Revolutionary Boston," *WMQ,* 3rd ser. 28 (June 1971): 383, 394.

49   Francis M. Caulkins, *History of New London, Connecticut* (New London, 1860), 382; and Greene, *Negro in New England,* 312–13.

50   Jeremy Belknap, "Belknap Papers," *Liberator* 1 (12 March 1831): 4, as quoted in Donald Martin Jacobs, "A History of the Boston Negro From the Revolution to the Civil War" (Ph.D. diss., Boston University, 1968), 40.

Chapter 5   *A Christianity for Slaves*

1   John Winthrop, "History of New England," 13 April 1641, *Winthrop's Journal,* 2 vols. (1853; repr. 1959), 2:26.

2   Lorenzo J. Greene, *The Negro in Colonial New England* (New York, 1942), 289; and Delorain P. Cory, *The History of Malden Massachusetts* (Malden, 1899), 417.

3   J. H. Trumbull and C. J. Hoadly, eds., *Public Records of the Colony of Connecticut,* 5 vols. (Hartford, 1859), 3:298; Francis Hawks and William Perry, eds., *Documentary History of the Protestant Episcopal Church in Connecticut 1704–1789* (New York, 1863), 199; Ezra Stiles, *Literary Diary of Ezra Stiles,* ed. F. B. Dexter, 3 vols. (New York, 1901), 24 February 1772, 1:214. See also the report of the Reverend John Usher who noted three black communicants out of nearly thirty blacks who attended his services, cited in John L. Sibley, *Sibley's Harvard Graduates,* 6:347.

The condition seems to have been the same in nearby New York. Elias Neau complained in 1711 that "there are not one in ten that comes to the catechism. They are naturally libertines and those to whom they belong do not bother themselves much about their welfare as long as they serve well." Quoted in Frank J. Klingberg, *Anglican Humanitarianism in New York* (Philadelphia, 1940), 131.

4   Quoted in Winthrop D. Jordan, *White Over Black* (Chapel Hill, 1968), 184.

5   Wilfred H. Munro, *The History of Bristol Rhode Island* (Providence, 1880), 147; Cotton Mather, *The Negro Christianized* (Boston, 1706), 11; Cotton Mather, *Magnalia Christi Americana*, vol. 1, book 3 (Hartford, 1855), 581; Cotton Mather, *Small Offers Towards the Tabernacle in the Wilderness* (Boston, 1689), 58; George H. Moore, *Notes on the History of Slavery in Massachusetts* (New York, 1866), 37; Wilkins Updike, *The History of the Episcopal Church in Narragansetts Rhode Island* (New York, 1847), 212–13; and Greene, *Negro in New England*, 259–60. Comparatively, see Jordan, *White Over Black*, 92–93; and A. J. R. Russell Wood, "Iberian Expansion and the Issue of Black Slavery: Changing Portuguese Attitudes, 1440–1770," *American Hispanic Review* 83, no. 1 (1978): 37.

6   Cotton Mather, *Diary*, 23 August 1702, in *MHSC* 8 (1912): 462; Daniel Wadsworth, *The Diary of Rev. Daniel Wadsworth 1737–1747* (Hartford, 1894), 100; and *Connecticut Courant*, 12 September 1774, 11. Paul Cuffe noted this prejudice from a black point of view in a letter to Samuel Mills quoted in Sheldon H. Harris, *Paul Cuffe* (New York, 1972), 202.

7   *MHSP* 45 (1912): 587; Clarence W. Bowen, *The History of Woodstock Connecticut* (Norwood, Mass., 1926), 88; George K. Clarke, *History of Needham Massachusetts* (Cambridge, 1912), 213; Sylvester Judd, *History of Hadley* (Springfield, 1905), 313; Leonard A. Morrison, *The History of Windham in New Hampshire* (Boston, 1883), 238; Bradford Kingman, *History of North Bridgewater* (Boston, 1886), 95–96; Samuel Orcutt, *History of the Old Town of Derby Connecticut* (Springfield, 1880), 128; J. H. Temple, *History of Framingham Massachusetts* (Framingham, 1887), 288; William Bentley, *Diary of William Bentley, D.D.*, 4 vols. (Gloucester, 1962), 31 September 1804, 3:108; Henry B. Stanton, *Random Recollections* (New York, 1887), 11; Bernard C. Steiner, *History of Slavery in Connecticut* (Baltimore, 1893), 20; and Greene, *Negro in New England*, 283–84, who points out that seating in New England's churches was based upon class as well as race. On blacks taking communion last, see Samuel F. Batchelder, *Notes on Colonel Henry Vassal* (Cambridge, 1917), 77; and, for a broader view, Leon F. Litwack, *North of Slavery* (Chicago, 1961), 196.

8   *Memoir of Mrs. Chloe Spear, A Native of Africa, Who was Enslaved in Childhood, and Died in Boston, January 3, 1815 . . . Aged 65 Years* (Boston, 1832), 21.

9   Winthrop S. Hudson, *Religion in America* (New York, 1965), 129; Franklin H. Littel, *From State Church to Pluralism* (Chicago, 1962), 32; and William W. Sweet, *The Story of Religion in America* (New York, 1950), 5.

10   Greene, *Negro in New England*, 263–67, 274; and Marcus W. Jernegan, *Laboring and Dependent Classes in Colonial America* (New York, 1960), 30.

11   William B. Sprague, *Annals of the American Pulpit*, 9 vols. (New York, 1859), 1:326; Greene, *Negro in New England*, 62–63; for the Saffin-Sewall controversy, see Abner C. Goodell, Jr., "John Saffin and His Slave Adam," *CSMP* 1 (March 1893):

85–113; see also "A Forensic Dispute on the Legality of Enslaving the Africans, Held at the Public Commencement in Cambridge New England, July 21st, 1773," quoted in Louis Ruchames, ed., *Racial Thought in America* (Amherst, 1969), 153–55. Some blacks seem to have accepted this doctrine; see Jupiter Hammon, *An Address to the Negroes in the State of New York* (New York, 1787), 19; or Phillis Wheatley's poem, "On Being Brought From Africa to America."

12   *Memoir of Chloe Spear*, 51.

13   See, for example, Sibley, *Sibley's Harvard Graduates*, vols. 4–10, which note some 118 Harvard-educated New England ministers who together held more than 200 slaves between 1717 and 1783; see also Greene, *Negro in New England*, 62, 350–59.

14   On collections for purchasing a slave for the minister, see Sibley, *Sibley's Harvard Graduates*, 4:195; Francis M. Caulkins, *History of Norwich Connecticut* (Hartford, 1866), 328; or J. Hammond Trumbull, ed., *The Memorial History of Hartford* (Boston, 1866), 2:406. For Andrew Eliot's refusal of such an offer see Sprague, *Annals of the American Pulpit*, 1:420.

15   Mather, *Diary*, 21 October 1718, 2:562.

16   George Curtis, *A Century of Meriden Connecticut* (Meriden, 1906), 248–49; Martha McD. Frizzell, *A History of Walpole New Hampshire*, 2 vols. (Walpole, 1963), 1:623; *Massachusetts Archives*, 9:448–49. In New England masters usually made provisions so that freed slaves would not become town charges; see Greene, *Negro in New England*, 228.

17   Mather, *Diary*, 6 June 1721, 2:624; *Memoir of Chloe Spear*, 33. Missionaries in the West Indies used "the seasons of sickness" to their best advantage in the same manner to convert worried slaves; see, for example, *Instructions for Missionaries to the West Indies*, Instruction No. 14 (London, 1800), as quoted in Elsa V. Goveia, *Slave Society in the British Leeward Islands* (New Haven, 1965), 279.

18   Sibley, *Sibley's Harvard Graduates*, 9:292; Martin Smith, "When the Bugle of the Stage Echoed Through the Village," *Connecticut Magazine* 8 (1904): 207; Francis M. Caulkins, ed., "Memoir of the Reverend Eliphant Adams," *MHSC*, 4th ser., 1 (1852): 36–37; Stiles, *Literary Diary*, 1:525; see also Cotton Mather's wrestlings with instruction and preparation for conversion of his slaves as noted in his *Diary*. Even hard work would not guarantee success. The Reverend Solomon Williams of Lebanon, Connecticut, bought two African children and taught them to read the Bible, but only the boy gave strong evidence of sincere belief; see Sprague, *Annals of the American Pulpit*, 1:326.

19   Mather, *Diary*, 24 February 1722, 2:683.

20   *Records of the General Association of Connecticut*, 1:2, as quoted in Greene, *Negro in New England*, 267; William S. Tilden, *The History of the Town of Medfield Massachusetts* (Boston, 1887), 134; Stiles, *Literary Diary*, 1:240; for other examples see the

church records of Meriden, Connecticut, 1 March 1741, as quoted in G. W. Perkins, *History of Meriden, Connecticut* (West Meriden, 1849), 87; Sibley, *Sibley's Harvard Graduates*, 10:172; and the case of Esther noted in Henry Wheatland, ed., "Records of the First Church of Salem," *EIHC*, 8, no. 3, 15. New Englanders were following a traditional seventeenth-century line of thought whereby infant servants or other servants were considered under the household covenant; see Edmund Morgan, *The Puritan Family* (New York, 1966), 135–36. Society for the Propagation of the Gospel ministers like Robert Jenny of Rye, New York, followed a similar plan for infant baptism; see Klingberg, *Anglican Humanitarianism*, 156. However, in the Leeward Islands English masters would not baptize children of unconverted slaves, "there being no hope that such will be educated in the Fear and Admonition of the Lord." Quoted in Goveia, *Slave Society*, 279.

21   See, for example, Jernegan, *Laboring and Dependent Classes*, 42; and Frank J. Klingberg, *An Appraisal of the Negro in Colonial South Carolina* (Washington, 1941), 17.

22   Mather, *Negro Christianized*. Slaves might also learn from the New England Catechism or Assemblies Catechism. See Mather, "Diary," *MHSC*, 7th ser., 7 (1911): 177; John Usher's report to the Society for the Propagation of the Gospel (1730) as quoted in Munro, *History of Bristol*, 147; and more generally, Klingberg, *An Appraisal of the Negro*, 28; and Jordan, *White Over Black*, 211.

23   Thomas Weston, *History of the Town of Middleboro Massachusetts* (Boston, 1906), 104; Harriet S. Tapley, *Chronicles of Danvers* (Danvers, 1923), 53; Cotton Mather, *Rules for the Society of Negroes* (Boston, 1888), 5–6; William Chauncey Fowler, "The Historical Status of the Negro in Connecticut," in *Local Law in Massachusetts and Connecticut Historically Considered* (Albany, 1872), 128; Frederick Calvin Norton, "Negro Slavery in Connecticut," *Connecticut Magazine* 5 (June 1899): 321–22; Mather, *Negro Christianized*, 6. For the Sharpener case see letter of William Burton to Nicholas Brown & Co., 20 November 1767, quoted in James Hedges, *The Browns of Providence Plantations* (Cambridge, 1952), 142. It was an old English custom to read the Bible and catechize servants and children together. See Carl Bridenbaugh, *Vexed and Troubled Englishmen, 1590–1642* (New York, 1968), 86; Sunday was about the only time even a committed slave had for Bible reading; see Stiles, *Liberary Diary*, 1:366. For New World comparisons see Jupiter Hammond, *A Winter Piece* (Hartford, 1782), 5; Anne Grant, *Memoirs of an American Lady* (New York, 1903), 80; and E. Franklin Frazier, *The Negro Church in America* (New York, 1963), 9.

24   Charles Edward Stowe, *The Life of Harriet Beecher Stowe* (Boston, 1889), 6–7.

25   Munro, *History of Bristol*, 147; and Mather, *Diary*, 5 May 1718, 2:532.

26   Tapley, *Chronicles of Danvers*, 53; for prohibitions against night entertainments and socializing among slaves see Greene, *Negro in New England*, 136–37. Bentley, *Diary*, 4:582, felt that even the evening lectures favored the "bad habits" of the slave population. For Samuel Hopkins's remarks see his letter to Dr. West,

23 June 1780, as quoted in Edwards Amasa Park, *Memoir of the Life and Character of Samuel Hopkins* (Boston, 1854), 166.

27   Greene, *Negro in New England*, 330–31; Updike, *History of the Church in Narragansett*, 177; and David Brion Davis, *The Problem of Slavery in Western Civilization* (Ithaca, 1966), 218.

28   Mather, *Negro Christianized*, 22.

29   Mather, *Diary*, 1:177. For the general acculturative effect of such Christianity, see Lawrence A. Cremin, *American Education: The Colonial Experience* (New York, 1970), 360; but this should be tempered with a comparison to the more militant Christianity discussed by Eugene D. Genovese, *Roll, Jordan, Roll* (New York, 1974), 166, 659.

30   Mather, *Negro Christianized*, 39.

31   Ashley is quoted in George Sheldon, *A History of Deerfield Massachusetts*, 2 vols. (Deerfield, 1896), 2:901. For other examples of typical evening or catechism lectures by Ezra Stiles, Cotton Mather, Samuel Hopkins, James McSparran, the Reverend Thurston, Andrew Eliot, William Bentley, and Daniel Wadsworth, see Stiles, *Liberary Diary*, 1:204; Mather, *Diary*, 1:176, and 2:364, 532; Park, *Memoir of Samuel Hopkins*, 166; James MacSparran, *A Letter Book* (Boston, 1899), 85; William Rogers, "Journal of My Visit to the Eastward Commencing in August, 1781," in *RIHSC* 33 (January 1940): 43; Eleazer Wheelock, "Diary of Eleazer Wheelock," *Historical Magazine*, 2nd ser., 5 (1869): 238; Lawrence W. Towner, "A Good Master Well Served: A Social History of Servitude in Massachusetts" (Ph.D. diss., Northwestern University, 1955), 235; Bentley, *Diary of William Bentley*, vol. 4, 582; Greene, *Negro in New England*, 287; and Alice Morse Earle, *Customs and Fashions in Old New England* (New York, 1898), 90.

Among the texts used by New England ministers for special lectures to the blacks were Luke 14:16–24, Ephesians 1:5–7, Psalms 68:31, Romans 5:12, Jeremiah 5:4, Job 27:8, and Hosea 13:13. Lorenzo Greene contends that prominent among the themes was emphasis upon faithful service and abstention from theft and fornication; but conversion is the most important theme in the texts noted above. Comparatively, the favorite text of sermons to slaves in the Old South was Ephesians 5:5–8, "Servants obey in all things your masters." See Genovese, *Roll, Jordan, Roll*, 208.

32   *Memoir of Chloe Spear*, 27, 51, 74; and Thomas Bicknell, *A History of Barrington, Rhode Island* (Providence, 1898), 404.

33   Phillis Wheatley to Obour Tanner of Newport, 19 May 1772, quoted in *MHSP* 7 (1863): 273; Stiles, *Literary Diary*, 9 March 1773, 1:355. Zingo was probably Zingo Stevens; see Park, *Memoir of Samuel Hopkins*, 166.

34   Stiles, *Literary Diary*, 1:366, and 2:378; and Park, *Memoir of Samuel Hopkins*, 130–35.

35   Mather, *Diary*, 1 December 1693, 1:176.

36   *Boston Gazette*, 10–17 June 1734, quoted in Towner, "A Good Master Well Served," 236; and Bentley, *Diary*, 11 June 1801, 2:379.

37   Thomas Prince, Jr., ed., *The Christian History Containing Accounts of the Revival and Propagation of Religion in Great Britain & America*, (Boston, 1744), 1:44.

38   Greene, *Negro in New England*, 315; John Eliot, "Slavery in Massachusetts," *MHSC*, 5th ser., 3 (1877): 383; and Julian Rammelkamp, "The Providence Negro Community 1820–1842," *Rhode Island History* 7 (January 1948): 27.

39   Robert G. Sheree, Jr., "Negro Churches in Rhode Island Before 1860," *Rhode Island History* 25 (January 1966): 10; J. Earl Clauson, "These Plantations," *Providence Evening Bulletin*, 1 February 1935, 23; Park, *Memoir of Samuel Hopkins*, 1:140–41; Hollis R. Lynch, "Pan-Negro Nationalism in the New World Before 1862," in *Boston University Papers on Africa* (Boston, 1966), 2:150–51; and Donald Martin Jacobs, "A History of the Boston Negro From the Revolution to the Civil War" (Ph.D. diss., Boston University, 1968), 40.

40   George E. Brooks, Jr., "The Providence African Society's Sierra Leone Emigration Scheme, 1784–1795: Prologue to the African Colonization Movement," *International Journal of African Historical Studies* 7, no. 2 (1974): 183–202; Bentley, *Diary*, 16 July 1807, 3:309; Jeremy Belknap, "Queries Respecting the Slavery and Emancipation of Negroes in Massachusetts," *MHSC*, 5th ser., 3 (1877): 12; and Litwack, *North of Slavery*, 187–213.

41   Even at the turn of the century William Bentley hoped to revive the catechism to solve the problem of a lack of literacy among the blacks; see Bentley, *Diary*, 8 January 1798, 2:252.

42   George Mason, *Reminiscences of Newport* (Newport, 1884), 158.

43   *The Appendix: Or, Some Observations on the Expediency of the Petition of the Africans* (Boston, 1773), 10. See also Elihu Coleman, *Testimony Against That Unchristian Practice of Making Slaves of Men* (Boston, 1729), 18.

Chapter 6   The Great Awakening

1   Jupiter Hammon, *An Address to the Negroes in the State of New York* (New York, 1787), 12.

2   Ezra Stiles, *Literary Diary of Ezra Stiles*, ed. E. B. Dexter, 3 vols. (New York, 1901), 1:213; see also Cotton Mather, *Rules for the Society of Negroes* (Boston, 1888), 5; and Jeremy Belknap, "Queries Respecting the Slavery and Emancipation of Negroes in Massachusetts," *MHSC*, 5th ser., 3 (1877): 12.

3   Davies is quoted in Richard Morton, *Colonial Virginia*, 2 vols. (Chapel Hill, 1960), 2:595; see also John Leland, *The Virginia Chronicle* (Norfolk, 1790), 13; and Edmond Botsford to John Rippon in John Rippon, ed., *The Baptist Annual Register, 1790–1793* (London, 1793), 105. Slaves often found the musical activities at church

the most attractive feature of Christianity; see Eileen Southern, *The Music of Black Americans: A History* (New York, 1971), 58–59.

4   Samuel Davies, *Letters From the Rev. Samuel Davies* (London, 1759), 14, as quoted in Dena J. Epstein, *Sinful Tunes and Spirituals* (Urbana, 1977), 104.

5   Melville J. Herskovits, "African Gods and Catholic Saints in New World Negro Belief," *American Anthropologist* 39, no. 4 (1937): 635–36; and Neal Salisbury, "Red Puritans: The 'Praying Indians' of Massachusetts Bay and John Eliot," *WMQ*, 3rd ser., 31 (January 1974): 51.

6   Elias Neau to John Chamberlayne, as quoted in Frank J. Klingberg, *Anglican Humanitarianism in New York* (Philadelphia, 1940), 128; see also 129, 146.

7   George Wilson Bridges, *Annals of Jamaica*, 2 vols. (London, 1827), 2:442–43. In Louisiana the editor of the *Planter's Banner* observed that blacks responded more to intonation, gesture, and emotional cues than they did to the content of a sermon; see Eugene D. Genovese, *Roll, Jordan, Roll* (New York, 1974), 206; similarly, see George W. Moore, *The Gospel Among Slaves*, ed. W. P. Harrison (Nashville, 1893), 151–52.

For the Jesuits' use of music and ceremony to attract black converts in colonial Peru, see Frederick P. Bowser, *The African Slave in Colonial Peru* (Palo Alto, 1974), 246.

8   Blacks were said to wander about Boston on Sundays "with neglect of attending on the public worship of God . . . and bringing . . . corn, apples and other fruit of the earth to the great disturbance of the public peace and scandal of our Christian profession." See Boston Registry Department, *A Report of the Record Commissioners*, "Selectmen's Minutes 1743–1753," 21 August 1751, 268 and 285; see also "Minutes 1716–1736," 223, and "Minutes 1736–1742," 2. This was a general New World problem. As Abel Alleyne of the Codrington Plantation, Barbados, complained, nothing could keep the blacks from their markets short of locking them up; J. Harry Bennett, Jr., *Bondsmen and Bishops* (Berkeley, 1958), 24; and Elsa V. Goveia, *Slave Society in the British Leeward Islands* (New Haven, 1965), 238.

9   Letter of Ebenezer Punderson of North Groton, Connecticut, to the Bishop of London, 12 December 1741, as quoted in Francis L. Hawks and William S. Perry, eds., *Documentary History of the Protestant Episcopal Church in Connecticut 1704–1789* (New York, 1863), 174–75; see also Edwin Scott Gaustad, *The Great Awakening in New England* (Chicago, 1968), 39.

10   E. Franklin Frazier, *The Negro Church in America* (New York, 1963); Melville Herskovits, *The Myth of the Negro Past* (Boston, 1941), chapter 7; and, especially, Alfloyd Butler, "The Blacks' Contribution of Elements of African Religion to Christianity in America: A Case Study of the Great Awakening in South Carolina," (Ph.D. diss., Northwestern University, 1975), 189–91.

11   Jonathan Edwards, *Thoughts on the Revival of Religion in New England*, in *Works of Jonathan Edwards*, 8 vols. (New York, 1881), 3:209; George Whitefield, *Journals*

(London, 1965), 422; the Tennent letter is quoted in Gaustad, *Great Awakening*, 35; Henry B. Parkes, *Jonathan Edwards* (New York, 1930), 154; Moorhead is quoted in *MHSP* 53:212; on the Awakening and Boston's blacks, see also Joseph Tracy, *The Great Awakening* (Boston, 1842), 117.

Especially susceptible to the Awakening were the young, blacks, and women; see, for example, William Cooper, *"One Shall be Taken, and Another Left," A Sermon Preached to the Old South Church in Boston, 22 March 1740–1741* (Boston, 1741), 13; Parkes, *Jonathan Edwards*, 149; and Tracy, *The Great Awakening*, 222. The Reverend Samuel McCorkle came to the same conclusion regarding revivalism in the South in 1802; see Guion G. Johnson, *Ante-Bellum North Carolina* (Chapel Hill, 1937), 404.

12   Note, for example, the success of the New Light Reverend Nathaniel Leonard of Plymouth with blacks; John L. Sibley, *Sibley's Harvard Graduates*, 6:325. The New Lights were equally successful in the South; see, for example, Jack P. Greene, ed., *The Diary of Landon Carter of Sabine Hall, 1752–1778* (Charlottesville, 1965), 31 March 1770, 1:378; Frazier, *Negro Church*, 8; and Winthrop D. Jordan, *White Over Black* (Chapel Hill, 1972), 213.

13   Phillis Wheatley, "On the Death of the Rev. George Whitefield—1770," in *The Poems of Phillis Wheatley* (Chapel Hill, 1966). For Whitefield's own reference to his work among New England blacks see his *Journals*, 3 January 1745, 539.

14   Hezekiah Prince, "Twelve Hundred Miles on Horseback One Hundred Years Ago," from the diary of Hezekiah Prince, ed. George Prince, *New England Magazine* 9 (1893): 733; Leland, *The Virginia Chronicle*, 13; for a general overview see Albert J. Raboteau, *Slave Religion* (Oxford, 1978), 55–75.

15   Quoted in Thomas Weston, *History of the Town of Middleboro Massachusetts* (Boston, 1906), 102–3; for a similar reaction noted by George Whitefield in Philadelphia, see Whitefield, *Journals*, 8 May 1740, 419–20.

16   Whitefield, *Journals*, 422; Eleazer Wheelock, "Diary of Eleazer Wheelock, D. D., During His Visit to Boston," *Historical Magazine*, 2nd ser., 5 (1869): 238; the Williams quotation is noted in Jacob Eliot, "Diary of Jacob Eliot," ibid., 33.

17   Cedric B. Cowing, "Sex and Preaching in the Great Awakening," *American Quarterly* 20 (1968): 640; Herskovits, *Myth of the Negro Past*, 225–31; and F. M. Davenport, *Primitive Traits in Religious Revivals* (New York, 1905), 92. On the general topic of Afro-American possession see Johnnetta B. Betsch, "The Possession Pattern in Traditional West African and New World Negro Culture" (Master's thesis, Northwestern University, 1959).

18   Isaac Browne to Philip Bearcroft, 25 March 1743, as quoted in Klingberg, *Anglican Humanitarianism*, 178.

19   Travis is quoted in C. F. Deems, ed., *Annals of Southern Methodism* (New York, 1856); and in Johnson, *Ante-Bellum North Carolina*, 545–46.

20   Quoted in William S. Perry, ed., *Historical Collections Relating to the American*

Colonial Church, 5 vols. (Hartford, 1870), 3:357. The Awakening seems to have accelerated an already present trend; a black slave in Rye, New York, baptized by John Bartow used his knowledge of English and his religious status to marry fellow slaves with the Office of Common Prayer until his master found out and forbade the practice as a desecration. See John Bartow to David Humphreys, 15 November 1725, as quoted in Klingberg, *Anglican Humanitarianism*, 155.

21   Charles Chauncy, *Seasonal Thoughts on the State of Religion in New England* (Boston, 1743), 226. There is an interesting description of a young white child preaching to blacks in Somers, Connecticut, taken from a letter of the Reverend Samuel Allis to William Cooper, quoted in Thomas Prince, Jr., ed., *The Christian History Containing Accounts of the Revival and Propagation of Religion in Great Britain & America*, 2 vols. (Boston, 1744), 1:409–11; see also Jacob Eliot, "Diary," 5 June 1742, 34.

22   *Boston Weekly News-Letter*, 1 July 1742, quoted in Gaustad, *Great Awakening in New England*, 128.

23   Eliot, "Diary of Jacob Eliot," 5 June 1742, 34.

24   *Boston Gazette*, 29 April 1765; Lorenzo Dow was from Guilford, Connecticut; see Lorenzo Dow, *Travels and Labors of Lorenzo Dow*, 15 June 1802 (Rochester, 1842), 108; Lorenzo J. Greene, *The Negro in Colonial New England* (New York, 1942), 277; and Edward Amasa Park, *Memoir of the Life of Samuel Hopkins* (Boston, 1854), 131, 136, 154.

25   William Bentley, *The Diary of William Bentley, D. D.*, 4 vols. (Gloucester, 1962), 3:313.

26   James Davenport to Eleazor Wheelock, 9 July 1740, as quoted in Jon Butler, "Enthusiasm Described and Decried: The Great Awakening as Interpretative Fiction," *Journal of American History* 69, no. 2 (September 1982): 319.

27   Alan Heimart, *Religion and the American Mind from the Great Awakening to the Revolution* (Cambridge, 1966), 206–17; and Moore, *The Gospel Among Slaves*, 169.

Chapter 7   An Afro-American Folk Religion

1   Griffith Hughes, *The Natural History of Barbados* (London, 1750), 15.

2   Zaphaniah Swift, *Oration on Domestic Slavery* (Hartford, 1791), 15; for a general discussion of this topic see William D. Piersen, "White Cannibals, Black Martyrs: Fear, Depression, and Religious Faith as Causes of Suicide Among New Slaves," *JNH* 62, no. 2 (April 1977): 147–59.

3   *Boston Gazette*, 21–28 May 1733.

4   Sibley, *Sibley's Harvard Graduates*, 6:31.

5   *Memoir of Mrs. Chloe Spear, A Native of Africa, Who was Enslaved in Childhood, and*

Died in Boston, January 3, 1815 . . . Aged 65 Years (Boston, 1832), 17. Compare, for example, with Alfred Burdon Ellis, *The Yoruba-Speaking Peoples of the Slave Coast of West Africa* (1894; repr. Oosterhout, 1970), 128–29.

6   Henry David Thoreau, *The Writings of Henry David Thoreau*, ed. Bradford Torrey (Boston, 1906), "Journal, X," 285. On the West African belief in a dream soul see Alfred Burdon Ellis, *The Tshi-Speaking Peoples of the Gold Coast of West Africa* (London, 1887), 15–16; and Mary H. Kingsley, *West African Studies* (New York, 1899), 200.

7   George Sheldon, *A History of Deerfield, Massachusetts*, 2 vols. (Deerfield, 1896), 2:897–98.

8   Ibid., 898. 6 vols. On the use of cowrie shell currency in Africa see John Barbot, *A Description of the Coast of North and South Guinea*, in John and Awnsham Churchill, eds., *A Collection of Voyages and Travels*, 6 vols. (London, 1746), 5:328; and Hughes, *Natural History of Barbados*, 16.

9   William C. Fowler, *The Historical Status of the Negro in Connecticut* (Albany, 1872), 131. Similarly, see the beliefs of Old Caesar, a New York slave, reported in Washington Irving, *Salmagundi* (New York, 1931), 1:ix–x. Compare such visions of heaven with Richard Burton's report that in the Dahomean afterlife "the earthly King is a King, the slave a slave forever and ever." Richard Francis Burton, *A Mission to Gelele King of Dahome* (1864; repr. New York, 1966), 302.

10   Thomas Weston, *History of the Town of Middleboro, Massachusetts* (Boston, 1906), 104. Similarly, see the final wishes of Darby, a slave of the Vassal family; Samuel F. Batchelder, *Notes on Colonel Henry Vassal* (Cambridge, 1917), 76. For burial near the house as an African survival see Jerome S. Handler, Frederick W. Lange, and Robert Riorden, *Plantation Slavery in Barbados* (Cambridge, 1978), 310.

11   Hagar Merriman, *The Autobiography of Aunt Hagar Merriman* (New Haven, 1861), 20–23; and Jupiter Hammon, *An Address to the Negroes in the State of New York* (New York, 1787), 12.

12   *Memoir of Mrs. Chloe Spear*, 74.

13   John Sharpe, "Proposals for Erecting a . . . Chapel at New York," in New York Historical Society, *Collections* 13 (1880): 355. See also John Watson, *Annals of Philadelphia*, 2 vols. (Philadelphia, 1884), 1:406.

14   See, for example, Hugh Crow, *Memoirs of the Late Captain Hugh Crow of Liverpool* (London, 1830), 241; and John Mathews, *A Voyage to the River Sierra Leone* (London, 1788), 101.

15   Swift, *Oration on Domestic Slavery*, 15. Nicholas Cresswell, *Journal of Nicholas Cresswell* (New York, 1924), 39, 40, noticed the same thing in eighteenth-century Barbados; at funerals, Cresswell reported, the blacks "instead of weeping and wailing . . . dance and sing and appear to be the happiest mortals on earth." For a gen-

eral discussion of the African essence in New World Afro-American funerals see John W. Blassingame, *Slave Community* (New York, 1972), 33–37; and Roger Bastide, *African Civilizations in the New World* (New York, 1971), 161–62.

16   William Bentley, *The Diary of William Bentley, D. D.*, 4 vols. (Gloucester, 1962), 28 August 1797, 2:235; for other black funerals described by Bentley, see 25 July 1793, 2:36; and 24 June 1806, 3:237. The 1806 event was the first funeral at which members of the African Society appeared with their music.

17   *Boston Records*, 8:176–77, as quoted in Lawrence W. Towner, "A Good Master Well Served: A Social History of Servitude in Massachusetts 1620–1750" (Ph.D. diss., Northwestern University, 1955), 236. Slave funerals were commonly legislated against in the New World; see, for example, Edwin Olson, "The Slave Code in Colonial New York," *JNH* 29 (April 1944), 153; Richard L. Morton, *Colonial Virginia*, 2 vols. (Chapel Hill, 1960), 1:302; Claude Levy, "Slavery and the Emancipation Movement in Barbados 1650–1833," *JNH* 55 (January 1970): 11; Bryan Edwards, *The History of the British Colonies in the West Indies*, 3 vols. (London, 1801), 2:202; and Herbert I. Priestley, *The Coming of the White Man* (New York, 1929), 89.

18   The "interrogation of the corpse" about the cause of death was a widespread West African custom. See, for example, Olaudah Equiano, "The Early Travels of Olaudah Equiano," in Philip D. Curtin, ed., *Africa Remembered* (Madison, 1968), 80; Barbot, *A Description of the Coast*, 281; Thomas Winterbottom, *An Account of the Native Africans in the Neighborhood of Sierra Leone*, 2 vols. (London, 1803), 1:236; Mathews, *A Voyage to Sierra Leone*, 122–24. For a modern study see Geoffrey Parrinder, *West African Religion* (London, 1961), 118, 166–67. For a continuation of the custom in the West Indies see Vere L. Oliver, *The History of the Island of Antigua* (London, 1894), 1:134; Thomas Atwood, *The History of the Island of Dominica* (London, 1791), 268; Charles Leslie, *A New and Exact Account of Jamaica* (Edinburgh, 1739), 325; Matthew Gregory Lewis, *Journal of a West India Proprietor* (London, 1834), 97–98; and Alexander Barclay, *A Practical View of the State of Slavery in the West Indies* (London, 1826), 134–35.

19   Hughes, *Natural History of Barbados*, 15n.

20   Boston Registry Department, *A Report of the Record Commissioners*, "Selectmen's Minutes 1717–1736," 24 December 1735 (Boston, 1881–1909), 283.

21   Bentley, *Diary*, 1 June 1809, 3:437.

22   Cotton Mather, *Negro Christianized* (Boston, 1706), 15.

23   Charles Eliot, *New England History*, 2 vols. (New York, 1857), 2:180. Coastal Georgia blacks often made small clay images; see Savannah Unit of the Georgia Writers Project of the Works Progress Administration, *Drums and Shadows* (Athens, 1940), 106. So did blacks in Saint-Domingue as described in E. Louis-Elie Moreau de Saint-Méry, *Description Topographique, Physique, Civile, Politique et Historique de la partie françoise de l'Isle Saint-Domingue*, 2 vols. (Philadelphia, 1797), 1:36. For African

precedents for such clay or wood figures see Barbot, *A Description of Guinea*, 240.

24   Cotton Mather, *Magnalia Christi Americana* (1702; repr. Hartford, 1853), 2:362; on this belief as preached to black children see Merriman, *The Autobiography of Aunt Hagar Merriman*, 23. For the Afro-American examples see Daniel Horsmanden, *The New York Conspiracy* (1810; repr. Boston, 1971), 297; Henry R. Stiles, *The History and Genealogies of Ancient Windsor Connecticut 1635–1891* (Hartford, 1891), 1:436; Judge Martin Smith, "Old Slave Days in Connecticut," *Connecticut Magazine* 10 (1906): 322; and Robert Ferris Thompson, *Flash of the Spirit* (New York, 1984), 84–97.

25   Smith, "Old Slave Days in Connecticut," 116–17, 330–31. On the general topic of protective fetishes see Newbell Niles Puckett, *Folk Beliefs of the Southern Negro* (Chapel Hill, 1926), 259–61; Maurice Delafosse, *The Negroes of Africa* (Washington, 1931), 326–27; and John Adkins, *A Voyage to Guinea, Brazil, and the West Indies* (London, 1735), 56.

26   African and European witchcraft beliefs had many similarities. See, for example, Geoffrey Parrinder, *Religion in Africa* (Baltimore, 1969), 65; and, for elsewhere in the New World, Georgia Writers Project, *Drums and Shadows*, 95, 121. For the New England examples of witchcraft see Samuel G. Drake, *Annals of Witchcraft in New England* (New York, 1869), 107, 205; Marion L. Starkey, *The Devil in Massachusetts* (Garden City, 1950), 110. For the examination of Tituba see Samuel G. Drake, *Witchcraft Delusion in New England* (Roxbury, 1866), 3:187–95; and George L. Burr, ed., *Narrative of the Witchcraft Cases, 1648–1706* (New York, 1914), 414. On the role of Tituba see also Starkey, *Devil in Massachusetts*, 49–61; and Chadwick Hansen, *Witchcraft at Salem* (New York, 1969), 31, who believes along with Drake that Tituba was a Carib Indian and not Negro.

27   *Massachusetts Archives* 85:18, discussed in Lorenzo J. Greene, *The Negro in Colonial New England* (New York, 1942), 153; and Hansen, *Witchcraft at Salem*, 70–72. Note the similarity of Candy's charm to typical African and Afro-American *nkisi* discussed in Thompson, *Flash of the Spirit*, 130.

28   *Essex County Records* (Boston, 1678–80), 7:329–30; and Delorain P. Corey, *The History of Malden, Massachusetts* (Malden, 1899), 331.

29   Quoted in Esther B. Carpenter, *South County Studies* (Boston, 1924), 161.

30   Alice Morse Earle, *In Old Narragansett: Romances and Realities* (New York, 1898), 72; Thomas Hazard, *Recollections of Olden Times* (Newport, 1879), 22; Caroline Hazard, *College Tom* (Boston, 1893), 45; and William B. Weeden, *Early Rhode Island* (New York, 1910), 302.

31   Earle, *In Old Narragansett*, 70–74. The "moonack" monster has strong resemblances to the "rolling calf" feared by the blacks of Guiana and Jamaica; see Roger D. Abrahams and John F. Szwed, eds., *After Africa* (Binghamton, 1983), 149, 159.

Tuggie's project was said to include sprigs of southernwood from the victim's dooryard, rusty nails, the tail of a herring, a scrap of red flannel, grave dirt, and a rabbit's foot—all typical conjuring articles. For comparative examples of Afro-American boiling conjuring see Stewart Culin, "Notes and Queries," *Journal of American Folklore* 2, no. 6 (1889): 233; for an Igbo example, see Elechi Amadi, *The Great Ponds* (Nairobi, 1970), 128.

32   Peter Kalm, *Peter Kalm's Travels in North America*, 2 vols. (New York, 1937), 1:210. For a description similar to Kalm's see Charles C. Jones, *Negro Myths From the Georgia Coast* (Boston, 1888), 152.

33   Hughes, *Natural History of Barbados*, 16. On this subject generally see Walter B. Cannon, "Voodoo Death," *American Anthropologist* 44 (April 1942): 169–81; and John S. Mbiti, *African Religions and Philosophy* (New York, 1970), 253–65.

34   *Newport Mercury*, 7 December 1742, as noted in Greene, *Negro in New England*, 157; *New England Weekly Journal*, 4 August 1735, in *CSMP* 20 (March 1883): 123. Denmark Vesey also checked his Bible for justification in planning his slave revolt; see Joseph C. Carroll, *Slave Insurrections in the United States 1800–1865* (New York, 1938), 86–87.

35   *Bristol Sessions* (1709), 2:158, as quoted in Towner, "A Good Master," 243; Bathsheba H. Crane, *Life, Letter and Wayside Gleanings, for the Folks at Home* (Boston, 1880), 49–50; Paul Coffin, "Journal of a Tour from Boston to Hanover, N. H. 1795," in Maine Historical Society, *Collections* 4 (1856): 294. For the African antecedents for such beliefs see Mbiti, *African Religions*, 224–25: "through a medium . . . a person may be directed to find a lost article or to know who stole his goods." For comparative New World examples see Colin A. Palmer, *Slaves of the White God* (Cambridge, 1976), 164–65; and "Concerning Negro Sorcery in the United States," *Journal of American Folklore* 3 (1890): 281.

36   Bentley, *Diary*, 8 May 1799, 2:302; Hazard, *Recollections of Olden Times*, 47–48; and Hazard, *Jonny-Cake Papers*, 161, 247; Carpenter, *South County Studies*, 216–17. On women mediums in Africa see Atkins, *Voyage to Guinea*, 104; and Parrinder, *Religion in Africa*, 75.

Tituba was the most famous of New England's fortune-tellers; see John Fiske, *Witchcraft in Salem Village* (Boston, 1902), 24. But many second-generation Afro-Americans pursued the calling; see Andrew Ford, *History of the Origin of the Town of Clinton Massachusetts* (Clinton, 1896), 123; Carpenter, *South County Studies*, 217; Corey, *History of Malden*, 413; and Charles L. Hill, "Slavery and Its Aftermath in Beverly, Massachusetts: Juno Larcom and Her Family," *EIHC* 116, no. 2 (1980): 128.

37   For black women as herb sellers see Bentley, *Diary*, 7 January 1804, 3:68; Corey, *History of Malden*, 413, 778; Alfred M. Bingham, "Squatter Settlements of Freed Slaves in New England," Connecticut Historical Society, *Bulletin* 41, no. 3

(July 1976); 76; and Thomas F. Devoe, *The Market Book*, 2 vols. (New York, 1861), 1:370.

38   Elbridge H. Goss, *The History of Melrose* (Melrose, 1902), 86. Note somewhat similar interrogatory techniques used by South Carolina slaves in the 1850s described in Jacob Stroyer, *Sketches of my Life in the South* (Salem, 1879), 42–45; and see George P. Rawick, ed., *The American Slave: A Composite Autobiography*, vol. 9, Arkansas Narratives, vol. 2, part 4 (Westport, 1971), 120.

Mande diviners in Africa used patterns traced in the sand for their insights. See D. T. Niane, *Sundiatta: An Epic of Old Mali* (London, 1965), 12, 89. In the Americas cards were often cut to determine a thief or find a witch; see Lewis, *Journal of a West India Proprietor*, 318; and James L. Smith, *Autobiography of James L. Smith* (Norwich, 1881), 5–6.

39   Francis Varnod to David Humphreys, 1 April 1724, as quoted in Frank J. Klingberg, *An Appraisal of the Negro in Colonial South Carolina* (Washington, 1941), 56. On black ghost beliefs in general see Puckett, *Folk Beliefs of the Southern Negro*, 78–167.

40   Earle, *In Old Narragansett*, 184–89; see also Rawick, *The American Slave*, 2:15; Georgia Writers Project, *Drums and Shadows*, 171; and Zora Neale Hurston, *Mules And Men* (1935; repr. Bloomington, 1978), 231. This may relate to Kongo inversion beliefs regarding the realm of the dead; see Thompson, *Flash of the Spirit*, 142.

41   Batchelder, *Notes on Colonel Henry Vassal*, 73; Gertrude S. Kimball, *Providence in Colonial Times* (Boston, 1912), 269; and George W. Chase, *The History of Haverhill Massachusetts* (Haverhill, 1861), 498. More generally see Smith, "Old Slave Days"; and Earle, *In Old Narragansett*, 184–89.

Chapter 8   To Build a Family

1   For general introductions to the African extended family see Alfred R. Radcliffe-Brown and Daryll Forde, eds., *African Systems of Kinship and Marriage* (London, 1950); and John S. Mbiti, *African Religions and Philosophy* (New York, 1970).

2   J. Harry Bennett, Jr., *Bondsmen and Bishops* (Berkeley, 1958), 35. Alleyne also reported that "those that have wives, only take them as they like them and so part with them at pleasure."

On polygyny among slaves in the New World see also John Atkins, *A Voyage to Guinea, Brazil, and the West Indies* (London, 1735), 208; and Richard S. Dunn, *Sugar and Slaves* (Chapel Hill, 1972), 251. Headmen on St. Vincent had many wives but only lived with one; Mrs. Carmichael, *Domestic Manners and Social Conditions of the West Indies*, 2 vols. (London, 1833), 1:182, 298. Polygyny was common as well in Jamaica; see Bryan Edwards, *The History of the British Colonies in the West Indies*, 3 vols. (London, 1801), 2:176; James M. Phillippo, *Jamaica* (Philadelphia, 1843), 85; and

J. Stewart, *A View of the Past and Present State of the Island of Jamaica* (Edinburgh, 1823), 284. On the British West Indies more generally see Frank W. Pitman, "Slavery in the British West India Plantations," *JNH* 11, no. 4 (1926): 638; and Elsa V. Goveia, *Slave Society in the British Leeward Islands at the End of the Eighteenth Century* (New Haven, 1965), 237. For the French West Indies see E. Louis-Elie Moreau de Saint-Méry, *Description Topographique, Physique, Civile, Politique et Historique de la partie françoise de l'Isle Saint-Domingue*, 2 vols. (Philadelphia, 1797), 1:57; and Lucien Peytraud, *L'Esclavage aux Antilles Françaises avant 1789* (Paris, 1897), 211. For similar arrangements in Brazil see Melville J. Herskovits, *The New World Negro* (Bloomington, 1969), 211. For the United States see Herbert G. Gutman, *The Black Family in Slavery and Freedom* (New York, 1976), 331.

3   William C. Fowler, *History of Durham, Connecticut* (Hartford, 1866), 161; and Lorenzo J. Greene, *The Negro in Colonial New England* (New York, 1942), 192–93.

4   Samuel Sewall, "The Selling of Joseph," in *MHSP* 7 (1864): 162. See also Lawrence W. Towner, "A Good Master Well Served" (Ph.D. diss., Northwestern University, 1955), 212–13; Arthur Calhoun, *A Social History of the American Family*, 3 vols. (Cleveland, 1917), 1:65; George H. Moore, *Notes on the History of Slavery in Massachusetts* (New York, 1866), 58; and Josiah Quincy, Jr., *Reports of Cases Argued and Adjudged in the Superior Court of Massachusetts Bay Between 1761 and 1772* (Boston, 1865), 30.

5   Cotton Mather, "Diary," vol. 1 (December 1693), in *MHSC*, 7th ser., 7 (1911): 177.

6   James MacSparran, *A Letter Book* (Boston, 1899), 15, notation for 24 October 1743; "Church Records of Milton, Massachusetts," *NEHGR* 23:254–56; and *NEHGR* 28:27; and Charles L. Hill, "Slavery and Its Aftermath in Beverly, Massachusetts: Juno Larcom and Her Family," *EIHC* 116, no. 2 (April 1980): 118.

7   Gutman, *The Black Family*, 63, points out that many southern slaves believed prenuptial intercourse and pregnancy compatible with settled marriage.

On African attitudes toward premarital sex see, for example, Denise Paulme, ed., *Women of Tropical Africa* (Berkeley, 1974), 9–10.

8   John Sharpe, "Proposals for Erecting a Chapel at New York," *NYHSC* 13 (1880): 355.

9   See, for example, Carmichael, *Domestic Manners*, 2:241–42; Fernando Ortiz, *Los negroes esclavos* (Havana, 1916), 349–50; and Herbert S. Klein, *Slavery in the Americas* (Chicago, 1967), 94–95. Sale of husbands or wives permitted a subsequent breach of monogamy in British America; see Goveia, *Slave Society*, 280; and Gutman, *The Black Family*, 419–25.

10   John Bartow to David Humphreys, quoted in Frank J. Klingberg, *An Appraisal of the Negro in Colonial South Carolina* (Washington, 1941), 14; see also John Bartow to David Humphreys, 15 November 1725; and Robert Jenny to David

Humphreys, 19 November 1725, both quoted in Frank J. Klingberg, *Anglican Humanitarianism in Colonial New York* (Philadelphia, 1940), 154, 57. This problem is also treated in Edgar J. McManus, *A History of Negro Slavery in New York* (Syracuse, 1966), 66.

11 Elihu Coleman, *A Testimony Against the Anti-Christian Practice of Making Slaves of Men* (Boston, 1733), 5–6.

12 George M. Curtis and C. Bancroft Gillespie, *A Century of Meriden, Connecticut* (Meriden, 1906), 245.

13 On the relative freedom of African divorce and separation see Melville J. Herskovits, *Myth of the Negro Past* (Boston, 1941), 173; and Mbiti, *African Religions*, 191.

14 This was especially true in the West Indies, where Phillippo, *Jamaica*, 85, reports marriage "was ridiculed by the Negroes and regarded as inimical to their happiness"; Alexander Barclay, *A Practical View of the State of Slavery in the West Indies* (London, 1827), 102, also noted, "The Negro declaims the master's rights to interfere with his matrimonial status. The blacks except for a few 'better informed' Negroes choose their mating arrangements." For a similar situation in St. Domingue see Père Pierre François Xavier de Charlevoix, *Historie de l'Isle espagnole ou St. Domingue* (Paris, 1731), 505, as quoted in Gwendolyn M. Hall, *Social Control in the Slave Plantation Societies* (Baltimore, 1971), 93.

15 *Memoir of Mrs. Chloe Spear, A Native of Africa, Who Was Enslaved in Childhood, and Died in Boston, January 3, 1815 . . . Aged 65 Years* (Boston, 1832), 17.

16 See, for example, Hugh Crow, *Memoirs of the Late Captain Hugh Crow of Liverpool* (London, 1830), 196, on eighteenth-century Bonny.

17 Edwards, *History of the British West Indies*, 2:176.

18 John Brickell, *The Natural History of North Carolina* (Murfreesboro, 1968), 274–75.

19 For an introduction to the status of women in African society see Paulme, *Women of Tropical Africa*, 4–9.

20 *MHSP* 7 (1863): 268; see also *Memoir of Chloe Spear*, 54–55.

21 Oliver P. Fuller, *The History of Warwick, Rhode Island* (Providence, 1875), 189.

22 Susan Snow is quoted in Norman R. Yetman, ed., *Life Under the "Peculiar Institution"* (New York, 1970), 290.

23 Bennett, *Bondsmen and Bishops*, 34; and William C. Nell, *The Colored Patriots of the American Revolution* (Boston, 1886), 134.

On African naming see Dilim Okafor-Omali, *A Nigerian Villager in Two Worlds* (London, 1965), 46; and Thomas Winterbottom, *An Account of the Native Africans in the Neighborhood of Sierra Leone* (1803; rev. ed. London, 1969), 1:151.

24 For the general New World situation see Philip D. Curtin, *Two Jamaicas* (New York, 1970), 25; Carmichael, *Domestic Manners*, 2:239; Hall, *Social Control*, 93;

Goveia, *Slave Society*, 236; and Yetman, *Life Under the "Peculiar Institution,"* 291.

25   Greene, *Negro in New England*, 204–8; see also Hall, *Social Control*, 142; Dunn, *Sugar and Slaves*, 254; and Orlando Patterson, *The Sociology of Slavery* (Rutherford, 1969), chapter 4.

26   Hill, "Slavery and Its Aftermath," 118.

27   "Slavery in Essex County," *EIHSC* 7 (1865); see also Greene, *Negro in New England*, 196; and Andrew Mellick, Jr., *Lesser Crossroads* (New Brunswick, 1948), 381.

28   Nathaniel Bouton, *History of Concord* (Concord, 1856), 252, estimates this labor at about forty dollars in wages. In patrilineal societies of West and Central Africa, children remained under the control of their mothers until the required bridewealth was paid, which may have predisposed the basic mother-child nucleus to assert itself in the New World; see Melville J. Herskovits, *Trinidad Village* (New York, 1964), 293.

29   Henry R. Stiles and Sherman W. Adams, *The History of Ancient Wethersfield, Connecticut*, 2 vols. (New York, 1904), 1:701; Adin Ballou, *The History of Milford* (Boston, 1882), 549–50; and George C. Mason, *Reminiscences of Newport* (Newport, 1884), 157.

30   Harriet Beecher Stowe, *Oldtown Folks* (New York, 1900), 55; see also Greene, *Negro in New England*, 197.

31   Abner Goodell, "The Murder of Captain Codman," *MHSP* 20 (1893): 127. For other accounts of separate residence see Thomas Bicknell, *History of Barrington, Rhode Island* (Providence, 1898), 404; and J. H. Temple, *History of Framingham, Massachusetts* (Framingham, 1887), 236. These separated families were often loosely tied; see Mather, "Diary," 24 February 1722, 683; Greene, *Negro in New England*, 211–12; Edgar J. McManus, *Black Bondage in the North* (Syracuse, 1973), 92; and Gary Nash, "Slaves and Slaveholders in Colonial Philadelphia," *WMQ* 30 (1973): 239.

32   Greene, *Negro in New England*, 196–97. There are many accounts of black men buying their wives and children. Two of the best are in Venture Smith, *A Narrative of the Life of Venture, A Native of Africa* (New London, 1798), 26–27; and Alonzo Lewis, *History of Lynn* (Boston, 1865), 345.

33   Hagar Merriman, *The Autobiography of Aunt Hagar Merriman* (New Haven, 1861), 3–4, 8, 20–23; and George Sheldon, *A History of Deerfield, Massachusetts*, 2 vols. (Deerfield, 1896), 2:897–98.

Chapter 9   Aspects of Black Folklife

1   *NEHGR* 6 (1852): 237–38.

2   Edward Kimber, "Observations in Several Voyages and Travels in America,"

London Magazine 15 (1746): 325, as quoted in Winthrop D. Jordan, *White Over Black* (Chapel Hill, 1968), 113.

3   The St. Kitts agent is quoted in Elsa V. Goveia, *Slave Society in the British Leeward Islands at the End of the Eighteenth Century* (New Haven, 1965), 119; on this subject see also William D. Piersen, "Afro-American Culture in Eighteenth Century New England: A Comparative Examination" (Ph.D. diss., Indiana University, 1975), 77–78.

4   Benjamin Browne, "Some Notes Upon Mr. Rantoul's Reminiscences," *EIHC* 5 (1863): 199; compare with the African practice illustrated in Alvin M. Josephy, Jr., ed., *The Horizon History of Africa*, 2 vols. (New York, 1971), 1:207.

5   Charles W. Brewster, *Rambles About Portsmouth* (Portsmouth, 1859), 210; Amos E. Jewett and Emily Jewett, *Rowley, Massachusetts* (Rowley, 1946), 220. On West African counting systems see Claudia Zaslavsky, *Africa Counts* (Boston, 1973), 47–48.

6   See Harry H. Johnson, *The Negro in the New World* (New York, 1910), 102; Gilberto Freyre, *The Masters and the Slaves* (London, 1956), 310; and Peter H. Wood, *Black Majority* (New York, 1974), 30–31.

7   James Hedges, *The Browns of Providence Plantations* (Cambridge, 1952), 142; George W. Schuyler, *Colonial New York*, 2 vols. (New York, 1855), 2:192; and Basil Davidson, *The African Slave Trade* (Boston, 1960), xx–xxi.

8   Harriet Beecher Stowe, *Oldtown Folks* (1869; repr. New York, 1900), 71; Washington Irving, *Salmagundi*, 2 vols. (1808; repr. New York, 1931), 2:45; Hagar Merriman, *The Autobiography of Aunt Hagar Merriman* (New Haven, 1861), 13; Martin Smith, "Old Slave Days in Connecticut," *Connecticut Magazine* 10 (1906): 326; Alain C. White, *The History of the Town of Litchfield, Connecticut 1720–1920* (Litchfield, 1920), 133; and Samuel Orcutt, *The History of the Old Town of Derby, Connecticut 1642–1880* (Springfield, 1880), 549.

9   Theron W. Crissley, *History of Norfolk, Litchfield County, Connecticut 1744–1900* (Everett, 1900), 273; and J. H. Temple, *History of Framingham, Massachusetts 1640–1880* (Framingham, 1887), 324.

10   Thomas Bicknell, *A History of Barrington, Rhode Island* (Providence, 1898), 404; and Piersen, "Afro-American Culture," 209.

11   For Mather see chapter 4; for the smallpox statistics see chapter 2.

12   "Colden's Letter," *American Museum* 3 (January 1784): 58; James Stewart, *A View of the Past and Present State of the Island of Jamaica* (1808; repr. Edinburgh, 1823), 303–4; and Bryan Edwards, *The History of the British Colonies in the West Indies*, 2 vols. (London, 1801), 2:81n. See also Le Page Du Pratz, *The History of Louisiana* (1758; repr. New Orleans, 1949), 360.

13   Vernon G. Baker, *Historical Archaeology at Black Lucy's Garden, Andover,*

Massachusetts, Papers of the Robert S. Peabody Foundation for Archaeology (Andover, 1978), 8:112–13; James Deetz, *In Small Things Forgotten* (Garden City, 1977), 149–52; John Vlach, "The Shotgun House: An African Architectural Legacy," *Pioneer America* 8, nos. 1 and 2 (1976): 47–70; Temple, *History of Framingham*, 324; Henry S. Nourse, *History of the Town of Harvard, Massachusetts 1732–1893* (Harvard, 1894), 403; and Esther B. Carpenter, *South Country Studies* (Boston, 1924), 218.

14 William Bentley, *The Diary of William Bentley, D. D.*, 4 vols. (Gloucester, 1962), 3:130; Browne, "Some Notes," 199; Carpenter, *South County Studies*, 220. Compare with African customs discussed in Richard Burton, *A Mission to Gelele King of Dahome* (1866; repr. New York, 1966), 138; and John S. Mbiti, *African Religions and Philosophy* (New York, 1970), 24.

15 Deetz, *In Small Things Forgotten*, 152–53.

16 Frances A. Kembell, *Journal of a Residence on a Georgia Plantation in 1838–1839* (1863; repr. New York, 1961), 236–37.

17 Ibid., 60.

18 William C. Fowler, *The Historical Status of the Negro in Connecticut* (Albany, 1872), 131; see also Anne Grant, *Memoirs of An American Lady* (1808; repr. New York, 1903), 265; Miguel Barnet, ed., *The Autobiography of a Runaway Slave* (New York, 1968), 158; and Mary Tolford Wilson, "Peaceful Integration: The Owner's Adoption of His Slave's Food," *JNH* 49, no. 2 (April 1964).

19 Vernon G. Baker, "Archaeological Visibility of Afro-American Culture: An Example from Black Lucy's Garden, Andover Massachusetts," in Robert L. Schuyler, ed., *Archaeological Perspectives on Ethnicity in America* (Farmingdale, N.Y., 1980), 34; Deetz, *In Small Things Forgotten*, 148; and *Memoirs of Mrs. Chloe Spear, A Native of Africa, Who Was Enslaved in Childhood, and Died in Boston, January 3, 1815 . . . Aged 65 Years* (Boston, 1832), 18–19.

20 Bentley, *Diary*, 2:374; 4:435–36; Thomas R. Hazard, *The Jonny-Cake Papers of "Shepard Tom"* (Providence, 1915), 68; Stowe, *Oldtown Folks*, 55, 331; Crissley, *History of Norfolk*, 371; William C. Nell, *The Colored Patriots of the American Revolution* (Boston, 1855), 54. See also Eugene D. Genovese, *Roll, Jordan, Roll* (New York, 1974), 548–49.

21 For typical observations on black dress from Nova Scotia, New York, the American South, and the West Indies see, for example, Isabella Bishop, *The Englishwoman in America* (1856; repr. Madison, 1966), 64; Edgar McManus, *A History of Negro Slavery in New York* (Syracuse, 1966), 64; Frances A. Kemble, *Journal of a Residence on a Georgia Plantation in 1838–1839* (1863; repr. New York, 1961), 64, 220, 326; and Bryan Edwards, *The History, Civil and Commercial, of the British West Indies*, 2 vols. (London, 1819), 1:165.

22 See, for example, the slave narratives in Norman R. Yetman, ed., *Life Under the "Peculiar Institution"* (New York, 1970), 192; George P. Rawick, ed., *The American*

Slave: A Composite Autobiography, vol. 2, *South Carolina Narratives*, (Westport, 1972), pt. 1, p. 122; and the analysis and examples in Eugene D. Genovese, *Roll, Jordan, Roll* (New York, 1974), 557–58.

23   Harriet Beecher Stowe, *Sam Lawson's Oldtown Fireside Stories* (Boston, 1872), 331; similarly, Thomas Weston, *History of the Town of Middleboro, Massachusetts* (Boston, 1906), 103; and Thomas Robinson Hazard, *The Jonny-Cake Papers of "Shepard Tom"* (1879; repr. Boston, 1915), 83.

24   *Connecticut Courant*, 9 June 1772, 33.

25   Boston Registry Department, *A Report of the Records Commissioners*, "Selectmen's Minutes 1743–1753," 21 August 1751, 268 and 285. See also "Minutes 1716–1736," 223, and "Minutes 1736–1742," 2. Abel Alleyne is quoted in J. Harry Bennett, Jr., *Bondsmen and Bishops* (Berkeley, 1958), 24; for similar complaints from the West Indies and South Carolina see Elsa V. Goveia, *Slave Society in the British Leeward Islands* (New Haven, 1965), 238; and Evarts B. Greene, *The Revolutionary Generation* (New York, 1943), 113.

26   Piersen, "Afro-American Culture," 230–31, 243–44; and Alice M. Earle, *Customs and Fashions in Old New England* (New York, 1898), 226.

27   Daniel Horsmanden, *The New-York Conspiracy* (1810; repr. New York, 1969), 180.

28   Zaslavsky, *Africa Counts*, 54; George Thomas Basden, *Niger Ibos* (repr. New York, 1969), 342–53; and Piersen, "Afro-American Culture," 244.

29   Isaac Norris is quoted in Edward R. Turner, *The Negro in Pennsylvania* (Washington, 1911), 42n; for Hamlet see Nell, *Colored Patriots*, 134–35; see also Washington Irving, *A History of New York* (1809; repr. New York, 1927), 138; and Harriet Martineau, *Retrospect of Western Travel*, 3 vols. (London, 1838), 1:183.

30   *Boston Evening Post*, 24 October 1743. On other black fifers see Samuel A. Green, *An Historical Sketch of Groton, Massachusetts 1655–1890* (Groton, 1894), 156; Harriet S. Tapley, *Chronicles of Danvers (Old Salem Village), Massachusetts, 1632–1923* (Danvers, 1923), 51; Fowler, *Historical Status of the Negro*, 130; and Hazard, *Jonny-Cake Papers*, 83. On the possible African provenience for these flutes see Dena J. Epstein, *Sinful Tunes and Spirituals* (Urbana, 1977), 55.

31   Irving Barlett, *From Slave to Citizen: The Story of the Negro in Rhode Island* (Providence, 1954), 92; and John F. Millar, "Newport's Early Composers," *Newport History* 53, part 2, no. 178 (Spring 1980): 72–73.

32   Delorain P. Corey, *The History of Malden, Massachusetts 1633–1785* (Malden, 1899), 418; Fowler, *Historical Status of the Negro*, 140; Charles H. Davis, *History of Wallingford, Connecticut 1670–1870* (Meriden, 1870), 341,344; George M. Curtis and C. Bancroft Gillespie, *A Century of Meriden, Connecticut* (Meriden, 1906), 248; Carpenter, *South County Studies*, 218; and Abiel Brown, *The Genealogical History of the Settlers of West Simsbury* (Hartford, 1856), 141.

33   Crissley, *History of Norfolk*, 370; Corey, *History of Malden*, 419; Carpenter, *South County Studies*, 218; Bentley, *Diary*, 2:8; and Lawrence E. Kander, ed., *The Northampton Book* (Northampton, 1954), 57.

34   On the black choice in Yankee music see Hazard, *Jonny-Cake Papers*, 83; and Stowe, *Oldtown Folks*, 400.

35   Nourse, *History of the Town of Harvard*, 403; Stowe, *Oldtown Folks*, 400; and Corey, *History of Malden*, 419n. See also Harold Courlander, *Negro Folk Music USA* (New York, 1963), 192; and Willis James, "The Romance of the Negro Folk Cry in America," *Phylon* 16, no. 1 (1955): 18.

36   William Grimes, *The Life of William Grimes the Runaway Slave* (New Haven, 1855), 67.

37   Stowe, *Oldtown Folks*, 54; see also Shelton, "The New England Negro," 537; and Robert C. Toll, *Blacking Up* (New York, 1974), 34.

38   Hazard, *Jonny-Cake Papers*, 84; Pierre C. de Laussat, *Mémoire sur ma Vie Pendant les Années 1803 et Suivantes . . . à la Louisianne . . .* (Pua, France, 1831), 395.

39   George Sheldon, *A History of Deerfield, Massachusetts 1636–1886*, 2 vols. (Deerfield, 1896), 2:897–98.

40   Henry B. Stanton, *Random Recollections* (New York, 1887), 5; see also Hazard, *Jonny-Cake Papers*, 83.

41   Crissley, *History of Norfolk*, 370.

42   Jedediah Dwelley and John F. Simmons, *History of the Town of Hanover, Massachusetts* (Hanover, 1910), 185; Sheldon, *History of Deerfield*, 2:896–97. See also Thomas F. Waters, *Ipswich in the Massachusetts Bay Colony*, 2 vols (Ipswich, 1917), 2:19; and Brewster, *Rambles About Portsmouth*, 152.

43   Jeremiah Asher, *Autobiography* (Philadelphia, 1862), 2; and Merriman, *Autobiography*, 3.

44   Browne, "Some Notes," 199; Sheldon, *History of Deerfield*, 2:899; Temple, *History of Framingham*, 326; Joseph O. Goodwin, *East Hartford Its History and Traditions* (Hartford, 1879), 236; Smith, "Old Slave Days," 326; Carpenter, *South County Studies*, 214; and Hazard, *Jonny-Cake Papers*, 85. See also Irving, *History of New York*, 254–55; Joseph B. Cobb, *Mississippi Scenes* (Philadelphia, 1851), 17; and George Rawick, ed., *The American Slave: A Composite Autobiography*, 31 vols. (Westport, 1973), 2:8.

45   Carpenter, *South County Studies*, 222–26.

46   See, for example, Philip D. Curtin, *Economic Change in Precolonial Africa* (Madison, 1975), 113–14.

47   Carpenter, *South County Studies*, 225. On "something goes around the house" riddles in the Afro-American tradition see J. Mason Brewer, *American Negro Folklore* (Chicago, 1968), 351.

48   See, for example, Robert Baird, *Impressions and Experiences of the West Indies and*

North America in 1849 (London, 1850), 81; M. Louis Elie Moreau de Saint-Méry, *Description . . . de la partie française de l'Isle Saint-Domingue,* 2 vols. (1797; repr. Paris, 1958), 1:56–57, 62; Clement Caines, *The History of the General Council and General Assembly of the Leeward Islands* (St. Christopher, 1804), 1:114; and William D. Piersen, "Puttin' Down Ole Massa: African Satire in the New World," *Research in African Literatures* 7, no. 2 (Fall 1976): 166–80. The Edwards quotation is from Bryan Edwards, *The History of the British Colonies in the West Indies,* 3 vols. (London, 1801), 2:100–101. For the Chloe Spear quotation see *Memoir of Chloe Spear,* 78.

49   Edmund Wheeler, *The History of Newport, New Hampshire* (Concord, 1879), 253; and Samuel A. Drake, *History of Middlesex County,* 2 vols. (Boston, 1880), 1:408.

50   William C. Fowler, *History of Durham, Connecticut* (Hartford, 1866), 164.

51   Wheeler, *History of Newport,* 253.

52   Henry R. Stiles, *The History and Genealogies of Ancient Windsor, Connecticut 1635–1891,* 2 vols. (Hartford, 1891), 1:586.

53   Fowler, *Historical Status,* 130–31. Note the similar tale among Kentucky slaves quoted in Lewis G. Clarke, "Narrative of Lewis Clarke," in *Interesting Memoirs and Documents Relating to American Slavery* (London, 1846), 91.

54   Benjamin Hobart, *History of the Town of Abington, Plymouth County Massachusetts* (Boston, 1866), 255. Like the Cato tale above, this tale is part of black folk tradition; see the similar example from East Texas quoted in J. Mason Brewer, *The Word on the Brazos* (1953; repr. Austin, 1976), 92–93.

55   Fowler, *History of Durham,* 164.

56   Ibid., 163; Paul Coffin, "Journal of a Tour From Boston to Hanover, N. H. 1795," Maine Historical Society, *Collections* 4 (1856): 294; and Temple, *History of Framingham,* 137. These are among the earliest known examples of "Master-John" tales where the slave proves superior to his master in a contest of wits; for the general context of this tale cycle see Roger D. Abrahams, ed., *Afro-American Folktales* (New York, 1985), 13, 265–66.

57   Thomas Weston, *History of the Town of Middleboro, Massachusetts* (Boston, 1906), 104. Parallels to Aaron's circle are found in the Kongo and Igbo areas of Africa; see, for example, Robert Ferris Thompson, *Flash of the Spirit* (New York; 1984), 110; and Rems Nna Umeasiegbo, *The Way We Lived* (London, 1977), 29. For a 1741 New York example see above, chapter 7.

58   Merriman, *Autobiography,* 14.

59   Nell, *Colored Patriots of the American Revolution,* 135.

60   Fowler, *Historical Status,* 129. See also John L. Sibley, *Sibley's Harvard Graduates,* 7:740; Weston, *History of Abington,* 104; Alfred M. Bingham, "Squatter Settlements of Freed Slaves in New England," Connecticut Historical Society, *Bulletin* 41, no. 3 (July 1976): 75; and Nathaniel Hawthorne, *Passages From the American Note-Books* (1865; repr. Boston 1892), 160–61.

61   Piersen, "Puttin' Down Ole Massa," 166–70.

62   Jewett and Jewett, *Rowley, Massachusetts*, 220.

63   James Fenimore Cooper, *Satanstoe* (1845; repr. Lincoln, 1962), 60.

Chapter 10   Black Kings and Governors

1   Alice Morse Earle, *Customs and Fashions in Old New England* (New York, 1898), 225; and J. Hammond Trumbull, ed., *The Memorial History of Hartford County Connecticut*, 2 vols. (Boston, 1886), 1:589.

2   William Dillon Piersen, "Afro-American Culture in Eighteenth Century New England: A Comparative Examination" (Ph.D. diss., Indiana University, 1975), 294–95, traces thirteen Yankee blacks who were recognized as being African royalty enslaved in New England.

3   Alonzo Lewis and James R. Newhall, *The History of Lynn* (Boston, 1865), 344; James R. Newhall, *The History of Lynn* (Lynn, 1883), 236; and Paul Faler, "Workingmen, Mechanics, and Social Change: Lynn Massachusetts, 1800–1860" (Ph.D. diss., University of Wisconsin, 1971), 258–60. For the Lynde quotation see *The Diaries of Benjamin Lynde and of Benjamin Lynde, Jr.* (Boston, 1880), 109.

4   Henry Bull, "Memoir of Rhode-Island," *Rhode-Island Republican* (Newport), 19 August 1837, 1; and Royal R. Hinman, *A Historical Collection from Official Records, Files, etc. of the Part Sustained by Connecticut During the War of the Revolution* (Hartford, 1842), 31–33.

5   Bull, "Memoir," 1. William J. Brown, *The Life of William J. Brown of Providence, R.I.* (Providence, 1883), 13, suggests the election holiday was used by the masters to insure their workmen would get the crops in by the proper season. Roger Bastide believes such institutions may have reflected both a deliberate policy by the governing classes to "divide and rule" their slaves and a spontaneous process of association among the blacks; see *African Civilizations in the New World* (New York, 1971), 9.

6   Piersen, "Afro-American Culture," 217.

7   Orville H. Platt, "Negro Governors," New Haven Colony Historical Society, *Papers* 6 (1900): 325.

8   Bull, "Memoir," 1; see also Jeremy Belknap, "Queries Respecting the Slavery and Emancipation of Negroes in Massachusetts," *MHSC*, 1st ser., 4 (1795): 200. The quotation is from William Bentley, *The Diary of William Bentley, D. D.*, 4 vols. (Gloucester, 1962), 4:457.

9   Piersen, "Afro-American Culture," 220.

10   Bull, "Memoir," 1; Sidney Perley, *The History of Salem Massachusetts*, ? vols. (Salem, 1926), 2:37; and Samuel Orcutt, *The History of the Old Town of Derby Connecticut* (Springfield, 1880), 55.

11   Samuel Blachley Webb, *Correspondence and Journals of Samuel Blachley Webb*, 3 vols. (New York, 1969), 1:142–43. See also Connecticut State Archives, *Revolutionary War Documents*, vol. 5, Document 391 (ms. in the Connecticut State Library, Hartford); a slightly abridged version can be found in Platt, "Negro Governors," 328–29.

12   Francis Manwaring Caulkins, *The History of Norwich Connecticut* (Hartford, 1866), 330–31; Charles W. Brewster, *Rambles About Portsmouth* (Portsmouth, 1859), 210; and Isaac W. Stuart, *Hartford in Olden Times* (Hartford, 1853, 38–40). The quotation is from Wilkins Updike, *The History of the Episcopal Church in Narragansett Rhode Island* (New York, 1847), 177–78.

Borrowing of the master's finery, horses, or carriages occasionally took place elsewhere in the New World during holidays and for dances, funerals, and weddings; see, for example, Charles William Day, *Five Years Residence in the West Indies*, 2 vols. (London, 1852), 1:295; 2:92; and Guion Johnson, *Ante-Bellum North Carolina* (Chapel Hill, 1937), 541.

13   Thomas Bailey Aldrich, *An Old Town by the Sea* (Boston, 1893), 78; Platt, "Negro Governors," 318; and Updike, *History of the Episcopal Church*, 177. This was also the case elsewhere in the New World; see, for example, Donald Pierson, *Negroes in Brazil* (Chicago, 1942), 77.

14   Telfer H. Mook, "Training Day in New England," *New England Quarterly* 11 (December 1938): 686.

15   Updike, *History of the Episcopal Church*, 178–79.

16   Jane de Forest Shelton, "New England Negro: A Remnant," *Harpers New Monthly Magazine* 88 (March 1894): 537; Joseph B. Felt, *Annals of Salem* (Salem, 1849), 2:419; and *Salem Town Records*, 16 May 1768, as quoted in James Duncan Phillips, *Salem in the Eighteenth Century* (Boston, 1937), 272; Platt, "Negro Governors," 332; and Orcutt, *History of the Old Town of Derby*, 550.

17   Piersen, "Afro-American Culture," 224.

18   Updike, *History of the Episcopal Church*, 177–78; Bull, "Memoir," 1; Felt, *Annals of Salem*, 2:419; Caulkins, *History of Norwich*, 330; and Shelton, "New England Negro," 537.

19   Updike, *History of the Episcopal Church*, 178; Bull, "Memoir," 1; and Platt, "Negro Governors," 332.

20   Bull, "Memoir," 1. Occasionally there was discord; see Caulkins, *History of Norwich*, 330; and Brown, *The Life of William J. Brown*, 13.

21   Bull, "Memoir," 1.

22   Caulkins, *History of Norwich*, 330–31. King Caesar of Durham wore a crown and sword among his "emblems of royalty"; see William C. Fowler, *The History of Durham Connecticut* (Hartford, 1866), 162; and Fowler, *Historical Status of the Negro*,

128. Governor Boston of Hartford was buried with honors, his cocked hat and sword on his coffin; see Stuart, *Hartford in Olden Times*, 40. King Pompey of Lynn was said to have been crowned with flowers; Lewis, *History of Lynn*, 344.

23   Stuart, *Hartford in Olden Times*, 38; Updike, *History of the Episcopal Church*, 177–78; Brewster, *Rambles About Portsmouth*, 210; Shelton, "New England Negro," 537; Platt, "Negro Governors," 332–33; and Phillips, *Salem in the Eighteenth Century*, 272.

24   Felt, *Annals of Salem* (Salem, 1827), 471; and *Salem Town Records*, 16 May 1768, as quoted in Phillips, *Salem in the Eighteenth Century*, 272.

25   Thomas W. Bicknell, *The History of the State of Rhode Island and Providence Plantations* (New York, 1920), 2:485; Fowler, *Negro in Connecticut*, 128; Shelton, "New England Negro," 537; Bull, "Memoir," 1; Stuart, *Hartford in Olden Times*, 38–39; George L. Clark, *A History of Connecticut, Its Peoples and Institutions* (New York, 1914), 159; and Platt, "Negro Governors," 332.

26   Updike, *History of the Episcopal Church*, 178; for an example of such an election toast see Henry R. Stiles, *The History and Genealogies of Ancient Windsor Connecticut*, 2 vols. (Hartford, 1891), 1:436–37.

27   Stuart, *Hartford in Olden Times*, 39. In the nineteenth century, when masters no longer treated the celebrants, the office of treasurer became important. One of the treasurer's duties was to persuade a local tavern owner to offer a free meal in exchange for the profits he could make on the drinking. See Brown, *The Life of William J. Brown*, 13.

28   Fitch E. Oliver, ed., *The Diary of William Pynchon of Salem* (Boston, 1890), 309.

29   Samuel E. Morison, "A Description of Election Day as Observed in Boston," Colonial Society of Massachusetts, *Transactions* 18 (February 1915): 60–61.

30   Bentley, *Diary*, 4:457; and Piersen, "Afro-American Culture," 230–31, 243–44.

31   The early observers all took this position; see Bull, "Memoir," 1; Felt, *Annals of Salem*, 2:419; Stuart, *Hartford in Olden Times*, 37; and Thomas R. Hazard, *The Jonny-Cake Papers of "Shepard Tom"* (Providence, 1915), 150. These set the standard interpretation adopted by later studies such as William Chauncey Fowler, *The Historical Status of the Negro in Connecticut* (Albany, 1872), 128; Shelton, "The New England Negro," 535; Platt, "Negro Governors," 318; and Lorenzo J. Greene, *The Negro in Colonial New England* (New York, 1942), 255.

Recently Joseph P. Reidy—in his master's thesis for Northern Illinois University (1974) and in " 'Negro Election Day' & Black Community Life in New England, 1750–1860," *Marxist Perspectives* 1, no. 3 (Fall 1978): 106–10—has followed the lead of Hubert H. S. Aimes, "African Institutions in America," *Journal of American Folk-*

lore 18 (1905): 15–32, and Piersen, "Afro-American Culture," 211–301, in seeing the New England institution in a wider African and Afro-American perspective.

32   Arthur Ramos, *The Negro in Brazil* (Washington, 1939), 96. Compare this to the British-styled court hierarchies followed by Carnival masqueraders in Tobago; Roger Abrahams, "Patterns of Performance," in Norman E. Witten and John F. Szwed, eds., *Afro-American Anthropology* (New York, 1970), 67.

33   Quoted in Pierson, *Negroes in Brazil*, 94; see also Gilberto Freyre, *The Masters and the Slaves* (London, 1956), 374.

34   Henry Koster, *Travels in Brazil*, 2 vols. (London, 1830), 2:340. There was also a black military regiment in the procession; see 218.

35   Lucien Peytraud, *L'Esclavage aux Antilles Françaises* (Paris, 1897), 182–83, 301. Masked balls and the carrying of weapons by the slaves were likewise banned in Guadeloupe in February 1765; see Shelby T. McCloy, *The Negro in the French West Indies* (Lexington, 1966), 36–37.

36   J. G. F. Wurdemann, *Notes on Cuba: Containing an Account of its Discovery and Early History* (Boston, 1844), 83; see also Fernando Ortiz, "La fiesta afro-cubana del 'dia de reyes'," *Revista Bimestre Cubana* 15 (1920): 5–26.

37   James M. Phillippo, *Jamaica: Its Past and Present State* (Philadelphia, 1843), 93.

38   Piersen, "Afro-American Culture," 291–92. See also David Barry Gaspar, "The Antigua Conspiracy of 1786: A Case Study of the Origins of Collective Resistance," *WMQ*, 3rd ser., 35, no. 2 (April 1978): 320 Thurlow Weed, *Letters from Europe and the West Indies* (Albany, 1866), 365; Angelina Pollak-Eltz, "The Devil Dances in Venezuela," *Caribbean Studies* 8, no. 2 (1968): 65–73; and Harold Courlander, *The Drum and the Hoe* (Berkeley, 1960), 105–9.

Chapter 11   The Functions and Character of Black Government

1   Alonzo Lewis, *The History of Lynn* (Boston, 1865), 344; and Eben D. Bassett, letter to Orville H. Platt, as quoted in Orville H. Platt, "Negro Governors," New Haven Historical Society, *Papers* 6 (1900): 331. The connection between New World black royalty and African royalty was also found elsewhere in the Americas; see Roger Bastide, *African Civilizations in the New World* (New York, 1971), 92.

2   Charles W. Brewster, *Rambles About Portsmouth* (Portsmouth, 1859), 210–11; Isaac W. Hammond, "Slavery in New Hampshire in the Olden Time," *The Granite Monthly* 4 (December 1880): 108–10; Isaac W. Stuart, *Hartford in Olden Times* (Hartford, 1853), 39–41; Jane de Forest Shelton, "The New England Negro: A Remnant," *Harpers New Monthly Magazine* 88 (March 1894): 536; Abiel Brown, *Genealogical History of the Settlers of West Simsbury* (Hartford, 1856), 140; Henry R.

Stiles and Sherman W. Adams, *The History of Ancient Wethersfield, Connecticut*, 2 vols. (New York, 1904), 1:702; and Francis M. Caulkins, *The History of Norwich, Connecticut* (Hartford, 1866), 330.

3 For a list of New England's black governors (as far as they are known) see William Dillon Piersen, "Afro-American Culture in Eighteenth Century New England: A Comparative Examination" (Ph.D. diss., Indiana University, 1975), 318.

4 Wilkins Updike, *History of the Episcopal Church in Narragansett Rhode-Island* (New York, 1847), 177; and Thomas B. Aldrich, *An Old Town by the Sea* (Boston, 1893), 78.

5 Piersen, "Afro-American Culture," 248–49, 261–62.

6 Samuel Orcutt, *Henry Tomlinson and His Descendants* (New Haven, 1891), 549. Orcutt also recalled an anecdotal feat of strength performed by Quosh's granddaughter.

7 Bradford Kingman, *The History of North Bridgewater, Plymouth County, Massachusetts* (Boston, 1866), 317; C. H. Webber, *Old Naumkeag* (Salem, 1877), 200. Mumford can be compared to "King Dick," the large and powerful Salem-born leader of the black American seamen imprisoned in England during the War of 1812; see William C. Nell, *The Colored Patriots of the American Revolution* (Boston, 1886), 27–28.

8 Stuart, *Hartford in Olden Time*, 39; Shelton, "New England Negro," 536; Alice M. Earle, *In Old Narragansett* (New York, 1898), 80–81; Updike, *History of the Episcopal Church*, 178; Thomas R. Hazard, *Recollections of Olden Times* (Newport, 1879), 121; and Sidney S. Rider, "An Historical Inquiry Concerning the Attempt to Raise a Regiment of Slaves by Rhode Island During the War of Rebellion," *Rhode Island Historical Tracts*, no. 10 (Providence, 1880), 62.

9 Stuart, *Hartford in Olden Time*, 39. See also Platt, "Negro Governors," 318; and Aldrich, *An Old Town by the Sea*, 78. The situation seems to have been the same elsewhere in the New World; see, for example, J. G. F. Wurdemann, *Notes on Cuba* (Boston, 1844), 83, who notes that the Cuban black kings "bore their honors with that dignity which the Negroes so much love to assume."

10 Caulkins, *History of Norwich, Connecticut*, 330–31.

11 Stuart, *Hartford in Olden Time*, 39–40.

12 Brewster, *Rambles About Portsmouth*, 210.

13 Stuart, *Hartford in Olden Time*, 40.

14 Shelton, "The New England Negro," 536.

15 Ibid., 536–37.

16 Platt, "Negro Governors," 331–32; Earle, *In Old Narragansett*, 81; and Henry M. Brooks, "Some Localities About Salem," *EIHC* 31 (1894): 115. The black leader

("King George") of the Carnival Court of Tobago achieves his rank primarily by his ability as a speaker; see Roger Abrahams, "Patterns of Performance in the British West Indies," in Norman E. Whitten, Jr., and John F. Szwed, eds., *Afro-American Anthropology* (New York, 1970), 167.

17   Henry Bull, "Memoir of Rhode Island," *Rhode-Island Republican* (Newport), 19 April 1837, 1.

18   Stuart, *Hartford in Olden Time*, 43–44; a similar court was held on the west side of Durham, Connecticut, under King Caesar; see William C. Fowler, *The History of Durham, Connecticut* (Hartford, 1866), 162.

19   Brewster, *Rambles About Portsmouth*, 210–11; and Aldrich, *An Old Town by the Sea*, 78–79.

20   Wurdemann, *Notes on Cuba*, 114; Gilberto Freyre, *The Masters and the Slaves* (London, 1956), 373; Robert R. Walsh, *Notices of Brazil in 1828–1829*, 2 vols. (London, 1830), 2:339–40; James Stewart, *A View of the Past and Present State of the Island of Jamaica* (1808; repr. Edinburgh, 1843), 75; Zora N. Hurston, "Cudjo's Own Story," *JNH* 12 (1927): 662; and Ulrich B. Phillips, *American Negro Slavery* (1918; repr. Baton Rouge, 1969), 296. Similarly, see Henry Hegart Breen, *St. Lucia: Historical, Statistical, and Descriptive* (London, 1844), 191; and Thomas Southy, *Chronological History of the West Indies* (London, 1827), 2:543.

21   Earle, *In Old Narragansett*, 81.

22   Stuart, *Hartford in Olden Time*, 38.

23   Quash Piere was a West Indian immigrant with an African day name; Platt, "Negro Governors," 334. On the symbolic African use of the gold-headed cane see Hugh Crow, *The Memoirs of the Late Captain Crow of Liverpool* (London, 1930), 217; for West Indian references to walking sticks, see, for example, Roger D. Abrahams and John F. Szwed, eds. *After Africa* (New Haven, 1983), 265, 306.

24   Telfer H. Mook, "Training Day in New England," *New England Quarterly* 11 (December 1938): 690.

25   Daniel Horsmanden, *The New York Conspiracy* (1744; repr. New York, 1969), 327. There was a general fear against training blacks in the martial arts throughout the North according to Edgar J. McManus, *Black Bondage in the North* (Syracuse, 1973), 69. Robert Dirks, "Slaves' Holidays," *Natural History* 84, no. 10 (December 1975): 82–84, 87–88, 90, suggests at least a third of the slave rebellions in the British West Indies were planned or executed in late December.

26   Stiles, *History of Windsor*, 437.

27   Ibid. For other references to black trainings in New England see Charles D. Warner, "Domestic and Social Life in Colonial Times," in J. Hammond Trumbull, ed., *The Memorial History of Hartford County Connecticut 1633–1884* (Boston, 1886), 1:358–59; and Caulkins, *History of Norwich*, 330.

28   See, for example, the anecdote centering on General Ti's inability to read the watch his master lent him for the occasion; Stiles, *History of Windsor*, 437; and above, chapter 11.

29   Shelton, "New England Negro," 536. These trainings have an interesting parallel in the *chaluska* Mardi Gras dance in Haiti, where the participants dressed as generals to heighten the effect of comic mimicry; see Harold Courlander, *The Drum and the Hoe* (Berkeley, 1960), 136.

30   Phillippo, *Jamaica*, 79; Jean Baptiste Labat, *Nouveau voyage aux Isles de l'Amerique* (Paris, 1724), 2:57–58. For a general overview of this kind of satire directed against whites see William D. Piersen, "Puttin' Down Ole Massa: African Satire in the New World," in Daniel J. Crowley, ed. *African Folklore in the New World* (Austin, 1977), 20–34.

31   Hugh Clapperton, *Journal of a Second Expedition into the Interior of Africa* (London, 1829), 55–56. For other examples see Piersen, "Puttin' Down Ole Massa," 23–24.

32   *South Carolina Gazette*, 17 September 1772, as quoted in Peter H. Wood, *Black Majority* (New York, 1974), 342; and Marshall Stearns and Jean Stearns, *Jazz Dance* (New York, 1968), 22.

33   William C. Fowler, *The Historical Status of the Negro in Connecticut* (Albany, 1872), 129.

34   William Bentley, *The Diary of William Bentley, D. D.*, 4 vols. (Gloucester, 1962), 4:457.

35   Mook, "Training Day in New England," 690.

36   Trumbull, *Memorial History of Hartford*, 1:189; and *Connecticut State Archives*, 12: Doc. 1099a (ms. in the Connecticut State Library, Hartford).

37   George C. Mason, *Re-Union of the Sons and Daughters of Newport, Rhode Island* (Newport, 1859), 156–57.

38   "Personal and Miscellaneous Subjects," *Orville H. Platt Collection*, 10:98–99 (ms. in Connecticut State Library, Hartford).

Chapter 12   A Resistant Accommodation

1   Lorenzo Johnston Greene, *The Negro in Colonial New England* (1940; repr. New York, 1968), chapters 6–7; Lorenzo J. Greene, "The New England Negro as Seen in Advertisements for Runaway Slaves," *Journal of Negro History* 29, no. 2 (1944): 125–44; and on feigned illness, *Connecticut Courant and Weekly Intelligencer*, 14 March 1780, 32.

2   See Eugene D. Genovese, *From Rebellion to Revolution* (New York, 1981).

3   Alex Haley, *Roots* (Garden City, 1976), 166–86.

4   See, for example, Kwesi Yankah, "Proverb Rhetoric and African Judicial Processes: The Untold Story," *Journal of American Folklore* 99, no. 393 (1986): 280–303; and John Messenger, "The Role of Proverbs in a Nigerian Judicial System," *Southwest Journal of Anthropology* 15 (1959): 64–73.

5   James Davenport to Eleazer Wheelock, 9 July 1740, as quoted in Jon Butler, "Enthusiasm Described and Decried: The Great Awakening as Interpretive Fiction," *Journal of American History* 69, no. 2 (1982): 319.

6   See William Dillon Piersen, "Afro-American Culture in Eighteenth Century New England" (Ph.D. diss., Indiana University, 1975), 218–19, 235.

Index

Aaron (slave of Morton family): belief of, in afterlife, 76; uses magic circle, 111

Abner (slave), purchases wife, 93

Adam (slave of John Saffin), reprimanded for dining with whites, 31

Adams, John Quincy, 42

Adams, Rev. Eliphant (slaveholder), 53

Africa, Moroca (slave of James MacSparran), punished for fornication, 88

Africanization of Yankee culture: variolation, 40; preaching style, 72–73, 150; divination, 85; gambling, 103; holiday style, 139–40

African slavery, 7–8, 144

African slave trade: from Gold Coast, 6, 7; from Goree, 6; from Guinea, 6; from Grain and Windward coasts, 6, 7; from Senegambia region, 6, 7; from Bights of Benin and Biafra, 7; from Central Africa, 7; from Sierra Leone, 7; sources of slaves, 7–8; conditions of, 8–9, 106, 144–45; from Fantee Coast, 11; from Anomabu, 58; from Popo, 103

Alabama: matrilocal plantation lifestyle, 92; black courts, 135

Albany, N.Y., 29

Alleyne, Abel: on slave polygyny in Barbados, 87; slave love of markets, 102–3

Anderson, John (black ruler in Hartford), appointed governor, 119

Andover, Mass.: settlement of free blacks in, 99; mentioned, 43

Antigua: slave trade from, 5; black royalty in, 127

Argentina, black royalty in, 127

Asher, Jeremiah, grandfather's capture in Africa, 106

Ashley, Rev. Jonathan (slaveholder): lectures to blacks, 56; mentioned, 75–76

assimilation: of young slaves, 5, 26–27, 28, 29; technological enticement, 10, 12; material enticements, 11–12; literacy as enticement, 12, 45; demographic factors, 22; limits to, 22, 38, 41, 45, 47, 50, 57, 60, 66–67, 68, 72, 94, 103, 143, 147, 148; and family slavery, 25, 28, 35–36; class in Africa as factor, 38–39; loneliness and, 39, 145; job skills and, 43; syncretism, 67, 85–86, 95, 102, 136; effects of shock on, 145

Bannock, Tuggie (daughter of Queen Abigail), as conjure woman, 82

Barbados: slaves from, 3, 4, 6, 7; African nobility in, 38; Afro-American culture in, 74; funerals in, 78; witchcraft in, 81, 83; polygyny in, 87; matrilineal survivals in, 92; markets in, 103; celebrations of black royalty in, 127

Barrington, R.I., 98

Bartow, John, on slave promiscuity, 89

Bassett, Eben D., 133

Belknap, Jeremy, 45, 47

Bentley, Rev. William (slaveholder): on black societies, 59; on black funerals, 77, 78; on blind Caesar's memory, 100; on Negro election day, 118, 124, 139

Berkeley, Dean, on black baptisms, 49

Beverly, Mass., 93

black militia, 136–38; satirized by whites, 139–40

Black Nim (deerhunter), 98

black rulers: grace by, 79; jurisdiction, 118; titles, 118; mode of election, 119–23; elsewhere in Americas, 124–28; lack of queens, 128; background of, 129–30; character, 131–34, 135; judicial functions, 134–35

Black, Mary (slave of Nathaniel Putnam), accused of witchcraft, 81

Bolton, Conn., 50

Bonny (West Africa), 9

Bosman, William, on God's gifts to races, 10

Boston (African-born ruler of Hartford, slave to Mr. Nichols), 129; described, 133

Boston, Mass.: sale of slaves in, 6, 7, 30, 40; black population of, 15; black sex ratio in, 20; black mortality rate in, 21; smallpox in, 21, 40, 53, 99; free blacks in, 22, 46–47; petitions for freedom by local blacks, 36, 60; loneliness of new slaves in, 39; black education in, 45; warnings out of town in, 46–47; almshouse population, 46–47; black clubs and societies in, 59; religious prejudice in, 72; slave funerals in, 78; Afro-American markets in, 102; election day holiday in, 103, 118, 123–24; mentioned, 93, 104

Bowdich, Thomas E., on God's gifts to races, 10

Bray, Dr., starts school for Negroes, 52

Brazil: slavery in, 35; black royalty in, 124–26, 127; black courts in, 135

Brewster, Nero (African-born king of Portsmouth): humorous anecdote about, 132; mentioned, 129, 134

Bridge, Ebenezer (slaveholder), mourns loss of slave, 32

Bridges, Rev. George Wilson, 67

Brightman, Mr. (slaveholder), 89

Brissot de Warville, Jacques Pierre, on mistreatment of blacks, 29, 46

Bristol (slave), stealing of, 71

Bristol County, Mass., black divination in, 84

Bristol County, R.I., percentage of black population, 15

Brockwell, H. A., on black religious enthusiasm, 71

Brookhaven, N.Y., Great Awakening in, 70

Brown, James (slave merchant), 4

Brown, Mrs. (slaveholder), 28

Brown, Obadiah (slave merchant), 4

Brown, William J.: on black-Indian marriages, 19–20; on freedom proverb, 34; on black education, 45

Browne, Rev. Isaac, on black religion, 70

Buckminster, Joseph (slaveholder), 33

Buckminster, Thomas (slaveholder), 33, 111

Bucknam, William (slaveholder), 104

Bull, Henry, describes operation of black court, 134

Burnham, Walter, describes white satire of black militia, 139

Byfield, Conn., 30

Caesar (slave): traps squirrels, 98; abilities in music and dance, 105

Caesar (slave boy), attempts to murder master, 83

Caesar (slave of Mr. Webster), preaching and attempted fornication of, 71

Caesar (slave of Parson Parker), outwits master, 108

Caesar (slave of Rev. Jonathan Todd and fiddler), 104

Cambridge (slave and music teacher), 104

Candy (slave), accused of witchcraft, 81

Canot, Theodore, on treatment of new slaves in Cuba, 10–11

Canterbury, N.H., 93

Canton, Mass., 30

Cape Verde Islands, 41
Carpenter, Boston, purchases wife, 91–92
Carpenter, Lillis, threatened by husband, 92
Carpenter, Willet (slaveholder), 81, 107
Casey (slave in Concord, Mass.), soul returns to Africa at night, 75
Casey, Abraham, hosts Newport African Union Society, 59
Cato (African-born slave), poor English of, 41
Cato (slave and fiddler), 104
Cato (slave of Parson Stephen Williams), suicide by drowning, 75
Cato (slave son of Jin Cole): belief of, in translation to Africa, 76; uses fingernail percussion, 105
Caulkins, Francis, describes black ruler, 132
Charlestown, Mass.: Great Awakening in, 68; witchcraft in, 81; poisoning in, 83
Charlestown, R.I., percentage of black population, 15
Chauncey, Rev. Nathaniel (slaveholder), 108, 110
Chauncy, Rev. Charles, on black religious enthusiasm, 71
Chester, John (slaveholder), 130
Clapperton, Hugh, describes African satire of whites, 138
Clarkson, Willie (black viceroy of Portsmouth, slave of Peirse Long), 134
Codman, John (slaveholder), slaves attempt to murder, 83
Coe, Truman, 28
Coffin, Rev. Paul, reports black diviner, 84
Coffin, William (slaveholder), 93
Coggeshall, Deacon, examines slave for religious belief, 58
Coit, Vance, 109
Colden, Cadwallader, 99
Cole, Jin (slave of Jonathan Ashley): royal heritage of, 39; belief of, in translation to Africa, 75–76, 94; inculcates values into son, 94; capture in Africa remembered, 106
Coleman, Rev. Elihu, on slave promiscuity, 26, 89–90

Collins, Zaccheus (slaveholder), 80
Colman, Rev. Benjamin (slaveholder), 9, 44
Colombia, black royalty in, 127
communication: by signs, 39; black English, 40–41, 44; bilingualism, 41–42
Concord, Mass., 75
Concord, N.H., 32, 93, 104
Connecticut: slave trade to, 3; black population of, 15–16; black sex ratio, 20; denies landholding to free blacks, 47; slave conversions in, 49; baptism of infant slaves in, 54; date of black elections in, 119; black rulers in, 127; black militia training in, 136
Cooper, James Fenimore, on New England Negroes, 112
Cranston, R.I., 54, 98
Cranston, Samuel (governor of R.I.), 4
Crèvecoeur, J. Hector St. John, on mixed race seating, 31
Cromwell, Conn., 53
Crow, Hugh: on dress of African coastal elite, 11; mentioned, 9
Cuba: treatment of new slaves in, 11–12; African customs in, 27; celebrations of black royalty in, 127; black courts in, 135
Cuff (black ruler in Hartford): abdicates office, 119; mentioned, 129
Cuff (slave), prays before stone god, 79
Cuff (slave of Isaac Fellows), sold as baby, 27
Cuff (slave of Mr. Torrey), humorous anecdote about, 110
Cuffe (slave of Slocum family), not permitted to take master's name, 35
Cuffee, Paul, 35
Cugoano, Ottabah, on dress of African coastal elite, 11
Cujo (slave), sold by trickery, 31

Daddy Caesar (Philadelphia slave), African dialect of, 42
Danforth, Charles (basket maker), 98
Danvers, Mass.: black election day celebration in, 118, 121; mentioned, 28
Davenport, James (revivalist), 68, 72, 151
Davies, Samuel, 66

Deerfield, Mass., 39, 56, 105
de Laussat, Pierre, 105
Derby, Conn.: black elections in, 118, 121; mentioned, 129, 131, 133
Devonshire (slave of Nathaniel Chauncey), wit of, 108, 110
Dewner, Andrew, purchases wife, 93
Dick (slave), speaks low Dutch, 41
Dinah (slave of Dr. Paine), African style of spinning, 97
Dinah (slave of Samuel Ham), African style of counting, 97
Dinah, James, matrilineal name of, 92
Dorchester, Mass., 96
Dow, Lorenzo (black missionary), 72
dress: African sense of style and color, 11, 101–2, 107; children's dress, 33; funeral dress, 77; female dress, 102; male dress, 102; election day, 120–21; Training Day, 137; discussed, 154–55
Dudley, Joseph (governor of Mass.), 4
Durham, Conn.: black elections in, 118; mentioned, 76, 108, 110, 129

Earle, Alice Morse, describes black conjuring, 82
East Guilford, Conn., 104
East Windsor, Conn., 109
education: in master's home, 28, 33, 44, 54, 55; miseducation, 29; limits on, 45; school, 45
Edwards, Bryan: on treatment for yaws, 99; on black metaphorical speech, 107–8
Edwards, Rev. Jonathan: on effect of Great Awakening on blacks, 68; mentioned, 67
Eldridge, George (black governor of Warwick Neck, R.I.), 174
election day holiday: dancing, 105; music, 105, 121, 122, 123; dates, 117, 118, 119; locations, 117, 118, 121; treating, 119, 120, 121; dress, 120–21; support for, by masters, 120, 122, 123, 130; parades, 121–22, 136, 159; inaugural dinner, 123; other activities, 124; African style, 139; white resistance, 159
Eliot, Charles, 79
Eliot, Jacob, on black religious enthusiasm, 71

Eliot, John, missionary work among blacks, 51
Eliot, Rev. Andrew, refuses gift of slave, 52
Ellery, William, purchases slaves, 4
Ellsworth, Captain (slaveholder), 137
emancipation, 33–34, 35, 47
Equiano, Olaudah: fears white cannibalism, 9; openness to new culture, 9, 12; amazed by white technology, 10; early loneliness, 39
Essex County, Mass., 15, 93
Ezer (slave of Cotton Mather), becomes church member, 53

Fairfield, Conn., percentage of black population, 16
Falconer, James, on language of slave immigrants, 41
Falmouth, Mass., 30
family life: separate residence, 19, 27, 36, 53, 93–94; insecurities, 27, 36, 91–94; parent/child relations, 28–29, 36, 94; purchase of mates, 58, 91–92, 93; African extended families, 87; matrilineal aspects, 92; attendance at dances, 105; problems discussed, 153–54
family slavery: closeness of, 3, 33, 34; precedents for, 25–26; paternalism of, 26, 29–30, 32, 35, 54; complexities of, 32–33; and size of slave holding, 35
Fanueil, Peter (slave owner), 5
Farmington, Conn., black elections in, 118
Fellows, Isaac (slaveholder), purchases slave baby, 27
Fells, Rev. Edward (slaveholder), baptizes slaves, 53
Fletcher, Simon (fiddler), 104
Flora (slave), drinking of, 71
Flora (slave to James Davenport), affected by Great Awakening, 72, 151
Fosdick, Elizabeth, 81
Fowle, Prime (slave), refuses during mistress's funeral to give place of honor to master, 32
Fowler, Priest (slaveholder), 34
Fowler, William: on black cooking, 101; on black humor, 96
Framingham, Mass., 33, 111

free blacks: conditions of, 22, 46–47; housing, 46, 99–100; obstacles facing, 46; association with old masters, 47; handicapped by slavery, 47

freedom petitions, 36, 60, 112

Freedom, Cuff, adopts new name during Revolution, 35

Freedom, Jube, adopts new name during Revolution, 35

Freeman, Chatham, on unhappiness with Euro-American marriage, 90

Freeman, Nancy: bound out, 27; marries son of black governor, 133; wife of black governor, 133

Freeman, Peter (black governor of Farmington), 174

Freeman, Quosh (African-born ruler of Derby, slave of Agar Tomlinson): strength of, 130–31; headman on master's farm, 131; bosses master, 133; mentioned, 129

Freeman, Roswell (Roswell Quash; black governor, slave of Agar Tomlinson): fox hunter, 98; son of black governor, 131; character described, 133

Frye, James (slaveholder), offers slave for sale, 41

Gambia, West Africa, wealth of, 107

Gardner, Newport (Occramer Marycoo): language skills of, 42, 46; musical talents of, 46, 104; opens singing school, 46, 104; religious leader, 59; supports return to Africa, 60, 104

Gardner, Polydore (fiddler), 104

Gay, Rev. Ebenezer (slaveholder), 80

General Ti (commander of black militia, slave of Capt. Ellsworth), 137

George (slave of John Winthrop), death mourned, 32

ghost beliefs, 85

Gill, Mr. (lieutenant governor of N.H.), anecdote of slave's wit, 111

Gilmanton, N.H., black divination in, 84

Ginney (slave of William Worthington), on heaven, 76

Gipson, Samuel (slave), business success of, 34

Gloucester, Mass., black religious society in, 59

Goodrich, Rev. Dr., 76

Grant, Anne, on instruction of northern Negroes, 33

Great Awakening: effect of, on blacks, 68–71; shaped by blacks, 72–73, 150–51

Greene, Christopher, 131

Greene, Lorenzo J.: scholarly work of, ix; on origins of new slaves, 6; on runaway notices, 143

Greenleaf, Justice Joseph, 110

Grimes, William: driven out of business by racism, 46; hosts black dances, 105

Guadeloupe, black royalty in, 127

Guiana, black royalty in, 127

Hagar (daughter of Hagar, slave of Peter Thatcher), baptized, 89

Hagar (slave of Peter Thatcher), confesses to fornication and enters church, 88–89

Haiti, black royalty in, 127

Hall, David (slaveholder), on death of slave, 32

Hall, Parson (slaveholder), whips slave, 52

Hall, Prince, founder of Negro Masonry, 59

Ham (slave), called witch, 80

Ham, Samuel (slaveholder), 97

Hamlet (slave): linguistic ability of, 41; drum maker, 104

Hammon, Jupiter, 66

Hampton (slave), speech of, 40

Harrison, W. P., on black ability to improve preaching, 73

Hartford, Conn.: sale of slaves in, 6, 43; black elections in, 118, 119, 121, 122, 123; black court system, 134; white election day parade, 139; mentioned, 51, 129, 130, 132, 133

Hazard, Thomas: writes about R.I. blacks, 30; cooking, 101; dance, 105; singing, 106; story telling, 107

Hebron, Conn., 102

Hector (slave), sold by master who feared him, 31

herbal medicine, 84

Herbert, Richard (slaveholder), 32–33

Holiday, king of Bonny, on superiority of white technology, 9
Hope Furnace, R.I., 98
Hopkins, Rev. Samuel: lectures to blacks, 55; mentioned, 59
Hughes, Griffith: on funeral practices in Barbados, 78; on witchcraft, 83
Humphreys, David (slaveholder), 130
Huntington, Sam (black governor of Norwich, slave of Samuel Huntington), 130
Huntington, Samuel (slaveholder), 130

Inall (minister), 58
Ingerson, John (slaveholder), 81
intermarriage (Black-Indian), 19–20
Irving, Washington, on slave trapping skills, 98

Jack (slave), anecdote of his request for freedom, 112
Jack (slave), linguistic ability of, 41
Jacklin, Robert, denied right to purchase land, 47
Jackson, Prince, accused of theft by black court, 134
Jamaica: slaves from, 6; religion in, 67; variolation in, 99; celebrations of black royalty in, 127; black courts in, 135; black satire of whites in, 138
Jimmie (son of Hagar, slave of Peter Thatcher), baptized, 89
Jo (slave of Richard Smith), difficulty in getting wife, 93
job skills, 43–44
John (black governor of South Kingston), 120, 174
Johnson, Rev. Samuel, on unbaptized Negroes, 49
Johnson, Thomas (black governor of New Haven), 174
Jonar (or Youngey), Prince (slave of Buckminster family), uses "pick the bone" proverb, 33, 111
Jones, Hugh, on class and assimilation, 39
Josselyn, Cuffee, capture in Africa remembered, 106
Jude (slave), tells fortunes, 84

Ka-Le (Amistad slave), notes American prejudice, 42
Kalm, Peter, describes witchcraft as poisoning, 82–83
Kemble, Fanny, on Afro-American cooking, 100–101
Kent, Titus (slave of Ebenezer Gay), carries fetish, 80
Kent County, R.I., percentage black population of, 15
Kimber, Edward, on training new slaves, 97
King Caesar (black ruler of Durham), 129
King Mumford (black ruler of Salem): described, 131; political influence of, 133–34
King Pompey (African-born ruler in Lynn, Mass.), honored for royal heritage, 117, 129
King Ring (black ruler of North Bridgewater), 131
Kings County, R.I., percentage of black population, 15
Kittery Point, Maine, 5
Knight, Sarah, on races eating together, 31
Koster, Henry: on small-scale slave holding in Brazil, 35; on Brazilian black royalty, 125–26

Labat, Père, on black satire in French West Indies, 138
Lander, Jack (Jack Southward), 35
Lander, W. (slaveholder), 35
Lanson, William (black king of New Haven), 174
Larcom, Juno: unmarried mother, 89; sale of children, 93
Leawitt (minister), dismissed for mistreatment of slave, 53
Lebanon, Conn., Great Awakening in, 70, 71
Lee, Jack (cattle keeper), 97–98; humorous saying of, 112
Leete, William (governor of Conn.): on slave trade, 3; on slave conversions, 49
Lewis, Mercy, accuses blacks of witchcraft, 80

Liberty, Cuff, adopts new surname during Revolution, 35

London (African-born governor of Wethersfield, slave of John Chester), 129, 130

London (slave), facial scars of, 40

Lovejoy, Mrs. (slaveholder), 28

Lucy (slave of William Coffin), 93

Lynde, Benjamin (slaveholder), treats slaves to holiday, 117

Lyndon, Josiah (slaveholder), 57–58

Lynn, Mass.: witchcraft in, 80; black royalty in, 117; black election day celebrations in, 118, 139; mentioned, 129

MacSparran, Rev. James (slaveholder), on slave promiscuity, 88

Malden, Mass., 27, 104

manners, 31–32

Mansfield, Thomas (slaveholder), 117

Manumit, Primus, wit of, 109

Mark (slave of John Codman), justifies attempt to murder master, 83

Marlboro, Mass., 93

marriage: bilateral descent, 87; family guidance, 87, 88; mixed, 87; polygyny, 87, 88–90; unilineal descent, 87; bridewealth, 88, 91, 93; premarital sex, 88–89; "Christian marriage," 89–90; "negro marriage," 89; divorce, 90, 92, 93; female rejection of, 90, 91, 92, 93; male rejection of, 90–91; serial monogamy, 90; spouse purchase, 91–92, 93

Mars, Jupiter, on lack of prejudice in children, 106

Martinique, celebration of black royalty in, 126, 127

Massachusetts: slave trade to, 4; import duties on new slaves, 5; black population of, 15; black sex ratio, 19, 20; date of black elections in, 118; black royalty in, 128

Mather, Rev. Cotton (slaveholder): on slaves as family members, 26; describes Afro-American speech, 40; learns smallpox treatment from African servant, 40, 99; on religious instruction of slaves, 42, 52, 53, 54, 55, 56, 79; on white prejudice,
50; on slave baptism, 53; on rules for black religious society, 55, 59, 88; on prayers of African slaves, 79

Maudlew, Quashey (Barbados slave), matrilineal name of, 92

Maverick, Samuel (slaveholder), forces marriage on slaves, 38–39

Medfield, Mass., 54

Melrose, Mass., 85

Meriden, Conn., 52, 104

Merriman, Hagar: childhood of, 28–29, 94; religious beliefs of, 76–77, 111

Mexico, black royalty in, 128

Miantonomo (chief of the Narragansett), ballad of, 106, 155

Middleboro, Mass.: Great Awakening in, 69; mentioned, 76, 111

Middletown, Conn.: black elections in, 118; mentioned, 41, 104

Milton, Mass., 88

mistreatment, 45, 53, 93

Monserrat, slaves from, 6

Moore, Archelaus (slaveholder), 93

Moorhead, John, on effect of Great Awakening on blacks, 68

Mose (African-born slave): singing of, 106; story telling of, 107

Moses (slave of Priest Fowler), pays college tuition for master's son, 34

music: fiddling, 31, 103, 104, 121, 122, 124; religious music, 66, 67; banjos, 103, 121, 122; flutes, 103, 104, 122; instrument making, 103–4; tambourines, 103, 121, 122; dance calling, 104–5; drums, 104, 120, 121, 122; musical instruction, 104; dancing, 105, 123, 124; election day, 105, 121, 122, 123; fingernail percussion, 105; singing, 105, 124; brass horns, 122; clarinets, 122; idiophones, 122

naming: classical cognomens, 7, 129; day names, 7, 129; father's surname, 35; freedom names, 35; master's surname, 35; matrilineal names, 92

Nancy (slave of Richard Herbert), childhood in white family, 33

Narragansett, R.I.: large plantations of,
43–44; conjure in, 82; black seer in, 84;
black story telling in, 107; black elections
in, 120, 121; mentioned, 14, 25, 100,
104, 129
national stereotypes, 6
Neau, Elias, 67
Negro Masonry, 59
Nero (slave), remembers master's children
in will, 34
Nevis, slaves from, 6
New Barbados Neck, N.Y., slave discov-
ers copper in, 98
New Bedford, Mass., 105
New England: refuse slave trade to, 4–5;
high mortality of seasoning in, 5; ethnic
make-up of, 14; black immigration into,
18
New Guinea district, Plymouth, Mass.,
101
New Hampshire: black population of, 15;
black sex ratio in, 19; black royalty in,
128
New Haven, Conn., black elections in, 118
New London, Conn.: percentage of black
population, 15–16; denies land owner-
ship by free blacks, 47
New Orleans: black royalty in, 128; Mardi
Gras, 159
New York: black religion in, 67, 79; slave
funerals in, 77; slave uprising in, 79, 136;
conjure in, 82–83; "negro marriages" in,
89; variolation in, 99; black royalty in,
128; black militia training in, 136–37;
mentioned, 66
Newfane, Vt., black divination in, 84
Newport (slave), language ability of, 40
Newport (slave of Ezra Stiles), wins church
membership, 53
Newport Colored Union Church, 104
Newport, N.H., 108, 109
Newport, R.I.: black population of, 15;
black sex ratio in, 20; black burial rates
in, 21; singing school in, 46, 104; slave
conversions in, 49; black education in,
52; black religious instruction in, 56;
black religious society in, 59; black elections in, 118, 119, 121; black judiciary in,

134; parade in, 139; mentioned, 5, 22,
29, 58, 83
Norfolk, Conn., 98
Norris, Isaac, comments on black musical
knowledge, 103
North Bridgewater, Mass., black ruler in,
118, 131
North Carolina, bridewealth gift in, 91
North Guilford, Conn., 34
North Kingston, R.I.: black elections in,
118; mentioned, 107
Norwich, Conn.: black elections in, 118;
mentioned, 129
Nott, Peleg (black governor of Hartford,
slave of Jeremiah Wadsworth): headman
on master's farm, 131; war experience of,
131; character, 132; humorous anecdote
about, 132; mentioned, 130

Oakley, Mary, loves black family servant,
106
Obidiah (slave of Cotton Mather), 52
Odiorne, Jack (African-born high sheriff of
Portsmouth), as official, 134
Old South Meeting House Church, Boston, black membership, 46
Oliver, Bridget, accused by slave of witchcraft, 81
oral traditions: proverbs, 33–34, 111, 147;
family history, 34, 106, 107; folk tales,
106–7; riddles, 107; metaphoric speech,
108; satiric commentary, 108–12; as edu-
cational device, 155
Osborn, Madam (slaveholder), 58
Oxford, Conn., black elections in, 118

Paine, Dr. (slaveholder), 97
Paine, Elizabeth, 81
Palmer, Rev. Samuel (slaveholder), bossed
by slave, 30
Panama, black royalty in, 128
Parker, Parson (slaveholder), outsmarted
by slave, 108
Parkman, Rev. Ebenezer (slaveholder):
mourns death of slave, 32; trains slave, 44
Parsons, Rev. Mose (slaveholder), treat-
ment of slaves, 30, 34
Paul, Thomas, black minister, 72

Pawtucket Falls, Mass., 108
Pepperell, William (slaveholder), 5
Pero (slave), sold by master who feared him, 31
Peru, black royalty in, 128
Peter (slave of Isaac Norris), makes fiddle, 103
Peter (slave of Mr. Powell of Newport), punished for witchcraft beliefs, 81–82
Peytraud, Lucien, 126
Pharaoh (slave of Zaccheus Collins), accused of witchcraft, 80
Philadelphia: black music in, 103; mentioned, 42
Phillippo, James, on black satire in Jamaica, 138
Phillis (African-born slave): henpecks master, 30; cooking of, 101
Phillis (African-born slave of Josiah Lyndon), religious history of, 57–58
Phillis (slave in Suffield, Conn.), fears thunderstorms, 79
Phillis, Doctress, herbal practitioner, 98
Phoebe (slave), entertains visiting husband in garret, 94
Piere, Quash (black governor of New Haven), walking stick of, 136
Platt, Orville H., in satire of black militia, 140
Plymouth County, Mass.: settlement of free blacks in, 99; mentioned, 15
Pomp (slave of William Bucknam, fiddler and dance caller), 104
population: mortality rates, 5, 20–22; foreign-born blacks, 7, 18; ethnic breakdown, 14; immigration, 18; children, 19, 20; sex ratios, 19–20; statistics, *see* by locations
Portsmouth, N.H.: black population of, 15; sex ratio, 20; black elections in, 118; black court in, 134; mentioned, 97, 129, 132
Potter, Aaron (black governor of South Kingston, slave to E. R. Potter), 174
Potter, Elisha R. (slaveholder), 120, 130
Potter (slaveholder of Concord), 26
Powell (slaveholder), beats slave, 81
Pratt, Caesar, memory skills of, 100

Prescot, Col. Richard, captured by Guy Watson, 131
Prime, Aunt Nancy, purchases husband, 93
Prince, Charles, 35
Prince, Lucy, explains slave manners, 31
Prince, Thomas, considers baptism of slave child, 53
Prince Robinson (African-born ruler of South Kingston), 82, 129
Prinn, Robin (fiddler), 104
Providence, R.I.: percentage of black population, 15; black religious society in, 59; mentioned, 4
Putnam, Ann, accuses black of witchcraft, 81
Putnam, Nathaniel (slaveholder), 81
Putnam, Stephen (slaveholder), 28
Pynchon, William, notes black holiday, 123

Quaco (slave), 94
Quamine, John (called Quamino): linguistic ability of, 42; conversion of, 58; plans mission to Africa, 58
Quamino, Tabitha, 35
Quaque, Philip, 58
Quash, Roswell. *See* Freeman, Roswell
Quassia (fictional slave woman), bosses her master, 30
Quaw (black governor of Hartford, slave of George Wyllys): described, 132; mentioned, 129, 130
Queen Abigail (slave of Rowland Robinson), 82

recreation: holidays, 45, 107; church attendance, 51, 55; associations, 59; markets, 102–3; election day, *see* election day holiday; music, *see* music
Red Bank, N.J., battle of, 131
Redwood, Abraham (slaveholder), largest Yankee slaveholder, 44
Reed, George (slaveholder), purchases young slaves, 26
Reed, William, 103
religion: baptism, 26, 53–54, 89; black missionaries, 42, 58, 72, 104; church mem-

bership, 49–50; conversion, 49, 53, 57, 58; white opposition to black Christians, 50–51, 55; segregation in church, 51; black perspective on, 52, 57, 149; religious instruction, 54–55; evening lectures, 55; passive Christianity preached to slaves, 55, 149; sermons preached to blacks, 56–57; black preachers, 57, 71, 72; preaching style, 72; concept of afterlife, 75–77, 151; concept of devil, 80, 82, 111. *See also* Great Awakening; music; suicide

religious societies: Negro Society of Boston, 55, 59, 88; white attempts at control, 56; Newport African Union, 59; African Society of Boston, 60; African Society of Providence, 60; mentioned, 59

remembrance of Africa, 106, 107

resistance: suicide, 25–26; requests for freedom, 26, 112; appeal to community, 31, 147; physical violence, 31, 143; talking back, 32, 71, 143; proverbial reasoning, 33–34, 147; cultural conservatism, 38, 74, 97, 146; of new slaves, 38–39; running away, 39, 40, 56, 71, 102, 104, 143; rejection of white reasoning, 50, 109–10; arson, 52, 143; disobedience, 56; drinking, 56, 71; lying, 56, 71, 143; religious beliefs, 56, 57, 66, 84, 110, 111–12, 149; theft, 56, 71, 143; black nationalism, 60, 149; conjure, 82–83; poisoning, 83; moral education of white children, 106, 155; satiric humor, 108–12, 138–39, 156–57; feigning illness, 143; ideology of abolition, 145; magic, 152; style, 155

retention of African culture: variolation, 9, 40, 99; manners, 32; choice of soil, 33; religious expression, 68, 69, 70; belief in rebirth, 75, 151; wandering souls, 75; burial site, 76; living dead, 76; money strings, 76; funeral rites, 77–78; fear of thunder, 79; oaths, 79; religious rites and images, 79; sacred circles, 79, 111; charms, 80; healing, 80, 84; conjuring, 81, 82; divination, 84–85; fear of spirits, 85; sexual mores, 89, 91; naming, 92; counting, 97–98; head carriage, 97; spin-ning, 97; use of hoes, 97; basket making, 98; herbalism, 98; herding, 98; hunting, 98; mining, 98; whistle making, 98; housing, 99–100; cooking, 100–101; memory skills, 100; ideal of beauty, 102; markets, 102–3; gambling, 103, 124; dance, 105; holiday style, 122; sports, 124; canes, 136; court of public opinion, 147; folklore, 155; election of rulers, 157. *See also* dress; music

Rhode Island: slave trade to, 4; black population of, 15, 20; percentage of free blacks in, 22; slave conversions in, 49; baptism of infant slaves in, 54; date of black elections in, 119, 123; black rulers in, 128

Robinson, Rowland (slaveholder), 82

Rockingham County, N.H., black population of, 15

Rosanna (Gambian-born slave), memory skills of, 100

Rose (slave of Stephen Putnam), childhood in slavery, 28

Rowe, Elizabeth, accuses black of witchcraft, 80

Rowley, Mass., 97, 112

Royall, William (slaveholder), 30

Rye, N.Y., black marriages in, 89

Saffin, John (slaveholder): complains of slaves' freedom, 31; on morality of enslaving heathens, 52

Saint Croix, black royalty in, 128

Saint Domingue, black royalty in, 128

Saint Kitts: slaves from, 6; African labor skills retained in, 97

Saint Lucia, black royalty in, 128

sale notices, 6, 30, 40, 43

Salem, Peter (basket maker), 98

Salem, Mass.: slave suicide in, 74–75; slave funeral in, 77; witchcraft in, 81; black seer in, 84; election day celebrations in, 118, 122, 123; mentioned, 35, 72, 97, 117, 131, 133

Saltar, Fanny, 42

Sambo (African-born slave of Peter Thatcher): fears white cannibalism, 39; Great Awakening and, 69

Sambo (son of Hagar and Sambo, slave of Peter Thatcher), baptized, 89

Samson (slave of Archelaus Moore): works to purchase wife, 93; fiddler, 104

Saugus River, site of black celebration, 117

Saybrook, Conn., 76

Scarlett, Humphrey (slaveholder), slaves attempt to poison, 83

Scip (slave of Benjamin Lynde), attends black celebration, 117

Scipio, purchases wife, 93

seasoning, 5, 21–22

Senegambia (African-born slave): riches of African father, 11, 107; riddles of, 107

Sewall, Samuel: argues against slave trade, 52; notes masters connivance in slave fornication, 88

Seymour, Conn., black elections in, 118

Shango, Yoruba god of thunder, 79

Sharpe, Rev. John: on slave funerals, 77; on "negro marriages," 89

Sharpener (slave), not given Sundays off, 54

Shelton, Jane de Forest, 105

Shepard, Thomas, 31

Sherburn, Jesse (bootblack), wit of, 108

Sidet, Bosum, victim of conjure, 82

Skene, Philip (slaveholder), 119

slave reproduction: mother's age at first birth, 19; opposition to, 19, 27; children in population, 20; forced mating, 39

slave trade: from West Indies, 3–4; refuse trade, 4–5; drawbacks on import duties, 5; ages of slaves, 6; morality of, 52; remembered by blacks, 106. *See also* African slave trade

slave women: dominate masters, 30; identify with master's family, 34; reject Christian marriage, 90, 91; as doctors, 98; as traders, 103

Slocum family (slaveholders), 35

smallpox: resistance to, 5, 21; variolation, 9, 40, 99; fear of, 53

Smith, Richard (slaveholder), 93

Snow, Susan, 92

Society for the Propagation of the Gospel in Foreign Parts, 49, 51, 71, 89

South Carolina: preaching style in, 73; fear of ghosts in, 85; black dance in, 105; satire of whites in, 138

South Congregational Church, Hartford, Conn., memorial service for black governor, 133

South Kingston, R.I.: percentage of black population, 15; black elections in, 118, 121; mentioned, 130

Southward, Jack (also Jack Lander), takes new surname at freedom, 35

South Woburn, Mass., 26

Spear, Chloe (slave): loneliness of, in first days in slavery, 39, 75; uses broken English, 41; denied education, 45; on church segregation, 51; on slave trade, 52; fear of death brings interest in religion, 53; metaphorical speech, 57, 108; religious beliefs, 57; belief in rebirth, 75, 90–91

Sprague, Phineas (slaveholder), pretends to be diviner, 85

Squire Neptune (black justice of the peace in Hartford), court decision of, 134

Stanton, Henry B., influenced by black nurse, 106, 155

Stedman, Captain John, on pride of royal slaves, 38

Stewart, James: on black appreciation of white technology, 9; on black treatment for yaws in Jamaica, 99; black plantation courts in Jamaica, 135

Stiles, Rev. Ezra: purchases African slave, 4; on Negro conversions, 49, 57–58; instructs and baptizes slaves, 53, 54, 56, 58; examines potential black missionary, 58; on slave singing, 66

Stonington, Conn., Great Awakening in, 68

Stoughton, Rev. John (slaveholder), 49

Stowe, Harriet Beecher: on Yankee slavery, 30; on instruction of black servants, 55; on spouse purchase, 93; on black trapping skills, 98; on dress of black women, 102; on black music and dance, 105; mentioned, 155

Stratford, Conn., 49

Strawberry Bank, N.H., witchcraft in, 80
Stuart, Isaac, describes black ruler, 133, 135
Suffield, Conn., 79, 80
Suffolk County, Mass.: black population of, 15; black sex ratio in, 20
suicide, as a religious act, 8–9, 74–75
Surinam, 38
Swift, Zephaniah, on slave funerals and beliefs, 74, 77

Tanner, Obour, 57, 91
Taunton, Mass., Great Awakening in, 70
Tennent, Rev. Gilbert, encourages black religious response, 68
Thatcher, Rev. Peter (slaveholder), 39, 69, 88–89
Thistle, Jethro, 89
Thoreau, Henry David, 75
Ticonderoga, N.Y., battle of, 131
Tituba (slave), accused of witchcraft, 81
Titus (slave of Samuel Palmer), bosses master, 30
Tobago, black royalty in, 128
Tobiah (black ruler from Derby, Conn.): grandson of African prince, 129; character of, 133
Tobias, Eben (black ruler of Derby, Conn.): dress during election day festivities, 121; great-grandson of African prince, 129; described, 131, 133; drills black militia, 138
Tocqueville, Alexis de, on mistreatment of free blacks, 46
Tom (slave of Parson Stephen Williams), suicide by drowning, 75
Tomlinson, Agar (slaveholder), 131, 133
Tony (slave), runaway advertisement noting dress, 102
Tory, Silvia (African-born slave), as diviner, 84
Tower, John (slaveholder), 106
Townsend, Solomon (slaveholder), 27
Training Day, 120, 136–38, 139
training of slaves: children, 5–6, 26–27; binding out, 27–28; new slaves, 42–43, 44; mentioned, 37

Travis, Joseph, on Afro-American religious possession, 70
Trinidad, black royalty in, 128
Trowtrow, Boston (black ruler of Norwich), 129
Tuft, Peter (slaveholder), says slave is bothered by witches, 81

Uruguay, black royalty in, 128
Usher, Rev. John, 55
Uxbridge, Mass., 53

Van Rensslaer, Jeremiah, on new Africans as poor slaves, 38
Varnod, Francis, on ghost beliefs in S.C., 85
Vassal, Henry (slaveholder), 34
Vassal, Tony: as part of master's family, 34; right of burial in Vassal family vault, 34
Venezuela, black royalty in, 128
Venus (slave of Ebenezer Bridge), her behavior and mistreatment, 32
Violet (slave of Mose Parsons), high place of, in master's family, 30
Violet, Dick, matrilineal name of, 92
Virginia: African nobility in, 39; loneliness of new slaves in, 39; acculturation of new slaves in, 42, 50; black singing in, 66; black religion in, 69

Wadsworth, Jeremiah (slaveholder), 130
Walker, Quok, legal case ends slavery in Massachusetts, 30
Wallingford, Conn.: black elections in, 118; mentioned, 90, 104
Walpole, N.H., 53
Warwick Neck, R.I., black elections in, 118
Waterbury, Conn., black elections in, 118
Watson, Guy (black governor of South Kingston), war experience of, 131
Watts, John, on northern market for slaves, 5
Webb, Rev. Nathan (slaveholder), mistreats old slaves, 53
West Hartford, Conn., 131

West Indies: slaves from, 3–5; seasoning in, 5; polygyny in, 89; variolation in, 99; black speech in, 107–8; satire in, 138; rebellion in, 143

Weston, Jubal (black governor of Seymour, slave of David Humphreys), 130

Weston, Nelson (black governor of Seymour, slave of David Humphreys), 130

Weston, William (black governor of Seymour, slave of David Humphreys), 130

West Simsbury, Conn., 41, 104

Wethersfield, Conn.: black elections in, 118; mentioned, 93, 129, 130

Wheatley, Phillis: memory of Africa, 27; early education and attainments, 28, 46; manners, 31–32; on black church membership, 57; eulogy for George Whitefield, 68–69; marriage of, 91

Wheelock, Rev. Eleazer, preaches to slaves, 70, 72, 151

White, Rev. John, 59

white cannibalism, slave belief in, 8–9, 39–40

white prejudice, 29, 42, 46–47, 50–51, 55

Whitefield, Rev. George: effect of Great Awakening on blacks, 68, 70; mentioned, 67, 69, 72

Wilcox, Caesar (slave): uses sign language, 39; broken English of, 41

Williams (minister), preaches to blacks, 70

Williams, Rev. Stephen (slaveholder), slaves commit suicide, 75

wills, 34

Windsor, Conn., black militia training in, 137

Winthrop, John (slaveholder), mourns death of slave, 32

witchcraft: blacks accused of, 80–81; fear of, 80; mentioned, 78

Wonn (slave of John Ingerson), makes accusation of witchcraft, 81

Woodbridge, Conn., black elections in, 118

Woods, Rev. Mr. (of Newport, N.H.), 108

Woodstock, Conn., 27

Worthington, Rev. William (slaveholder), 76

Wyllys, George (slaveholder), 130

Yale, Noah (slaveholder), 90

Yamma, Bristol, missionary wish, 42

Yaw (slave of Humphrey Scarlett), attempts to murder master, 83

Yoruba, satire of whites, 138

Zingo, leads wife and child to Christianity, 57–58